About the Author

Peter McQuade is a lawyer and businessman who has spent his career in the high-tech industry and lives in Brighton. His involvement with the Paris To Hayling Charity Cycle Ride has encouraged him to participate in and/or organise other rides in the UK and abroad in Portugal and Malawi. He has written and spoken extensively about his cycling experiences and about the positive contribution of such things not just to charitable causes but also to physical and mental health and to teamwork.

Raw Hides and Sore Heads

Peter McQuade

Raw Hides and Sore Heads

Olympia Publishers
London

www.olympiapublishers.com
OLYMPIA PAPERBACK EDITION

A CIP catalogue record for this title is
available from the British Library.

ISBN: 978-1-80074-259-8

This is a work of creative nonfiction. The events are portrayed to the
best of the author's memory. While all the stories in this book are
true, some names and identifying details have been changed to
protect the privacy of the people involved.

First Published in 2022

Olympia Publishers
Tallis House
2 Tallis Street
London
EC4Y 0AB

Printed in Great Britain

Acknowledgements

Mario Ferrari's illustrations are an ideal complement to this tale and I am grateful for his collaboration.

Thank you to all those who allowed me to interview them, to Lynne Harris for her proof reading of the final drafts and similarly to Connar Bingham for a review of earlier ones. The book has taken quite some time to write so the encouragement of many to push on with it was vital and in particular that of Jayne Ross. And, having done that, the constructive feedback from people given early drafts was most appreciated.

And also thank you to the thousands of people (cyclists and supporters) who have enriched this story by their own contribution over the years. Mike and Stella Burras' constant encouragement and help in many ways has been vital since the very first event. Finally, a huge debt of gratitude to my ex-wife Maryon and two children Chris and Alice. One evening, some years ago, when we were having a pre-ride dinner in Paris, Maryon first suggested that I had to write this book but it's a story that probably would never have been worth telling without the McQuade family's constant support and acceptance that each year summer would be disrupted by "The Bike Ride".

In 1986 Peter McQuade, a young lawyer working for IBM, agreed to do a cycle ride to raise funds for cot death research, following the sudden death of a friend's baby daughter. He couldn't imagine how it would change his life and that of so many others.

Prologue — A Strange Ride!

Rider 1: So, what is the Paris to Hayling like?

Rider 2: Well, you take hours getting out of Paris and miss taking an irretrievable turning onto an auto route by a mere spoke's width and then one of the so-called experienced committee members gets you lost, and you finish up at the top of a 1 in 2 hill. He then announces that we had gone the wrong way, and that we didn't need to be up there at all! And so, you go all the way back down, and then you get a puncture in your rear tyre. No sooner have you fixed that than you find you have one in your front tyre! By the time that is sorted out you are an hour late for lunch, and all that's left is a stale roll and a mouldy piece of Louis XVI cheese. "Le Patron" then cheerfully tells you that he is sorry that the red wine has gone, but your so-called mates had it all and they seemed to enjoy it! Then you get back on your bike, and just as you think things are moving smoothly, a spoke goes in your wheel, and then another, and you discover the sodding thing is buckled. Then for the first time today a support van turns up and then another and then another! Could it be a coincidence that you have broken down outside a bar? "What's the matter?" one of the Support Teams cheerfully asks. "Couldn't the bike take the strain?"

Then they loan you a 100-pound bone-shaker while they supposedly repair yours. Somebody obviously lent the Ride this antediluvian contraption hoping that it would never be returned. And then you get lost again! And then the back-pain kicks in. It's just murder, and can you find the Ibuprofen tablets? Not a hope! You must have dropped them back along the road! Much later, just as the sun is setting, you get into Rouen. There has been a cock-up with your hotel room, and your luggage got mixed up in Paris with that of a coach party of Japanese tourists, and it's probably on its way to Yokohama by now. Eventually the so-called organisation finds you a flea-pit of a hotel, and finally, about three in the morning, you get to sleep only to be woken by a drunken cyclist singing "Is This the Way to Amarillo?". He isn't meant to be sharing with you, or even staying in the same place, but he is so drunk that he can't even work out what planet he is on, let alone which hotel he is staying in.

And the following morning it all starts again. You ask the Support Team for your bike back, and they can't find it. Turns out they were repairing it outside a bar somewhere and nobody knows what happened to it next. Well, it does eventually turn up but then, just as you are leaving the car park, you have to swerve to miss a support vehicle and go arse over tit into a flower-bed. If that's not bad enough, you later get word that the Support Team have had to get a mechanic to break into your three-week-old car, which you generously offered to the Ride as a support vehicle. Apparently, this was because the driver had somehow locked the keys inside! By the afternoon you are well and truly fed up. Your knees are buggered, your arse is raw, your back is protesting something rotten, and your fuse is not so much short as totally shot away. Then one of the committee members tries to cheer you up. "Not long now!" he says. "Trust me, the end is just around the corner." How were you meant to know that the "end" was twenty-five miles away, with at least three nasty hills included? And then, of course, it starts pissing down. The wind in your face all day had been bad enough, but now you are soaked as well. So, that's why I told them that I would probably not be coming again.

Rider 1: When was that?

Rider 2:1993.

Rider 1: But you have kept doing it! Why on earth is that?

Rider 2: I would say that's bloody obvious! It's very well-organised and lots of fun!

I must confess that this narrative didn't happen exactly as written but it could have done. All, well, okay, *most* of the things mentioned did happen at some time and as far as the others are concerned, those who, like me, have had fun and laughter and occasionally tears (particularly up some of the hills) would argue that they could have done!

Chapter 1
From Sad Beginnings

The happy, if odd, story of The Paris to Hayling Cycle Ride started with a very sad event on a bleak, grey day in February 1986. Good friends Mike and Stella Burras had become the proud parents of twin girls in late 1985. Tragically, one of these, Louise, passed away as a result of a cot death. To attend any funeral is a sad affair, but to attend the funeral of a tiny baby is particularly dreadful. The sight of the small coffin being carried up the aisle and of grieving parents is a memory which stays with you forever. We were assembled in the United Reform church on Hayling Island. Hayling, for those who are unfamiliar with it, is a small island off the coast of Hampshire located between Portsmouth and Chichester.

After leaving the church some of my friends and I went to a Hayling pub, the Rose in June, for a nerve-steadying drink. The atmosphere was naturally sombre, and few words were initially spoken. As we were in our twenties, and even though two of the group had already lost a parent, our collective experience of death was relatively limited and even more so with regards to the death of a tiny baby. Then one of the group, suggested that we might spend some of the summer raising money for Cot Death Research. Everyone agreed, believing, I am sure, that apart from anything else, it would help the grieving parents. Afterwards, whenever I went back to that pub, I would think of that conversation and even look at where we were sat at the time. I could not have begun to imagine what was to follow. None of us gathered at that meeting had any great experience of fund raising. Yet, working together, we had raised over £5000 by August. We held a variety of events, including a sponsored pram push, a fun run, a superb fete, and one event which lasted into the next summer, and the next, and the next...

"Perhaps I could do a sponsored cycle ride? Maybe from Paris?" The assembled group seemed to think that this would be okay, presumably providing I did not ask them to join in, and possibly thinking that this reckless proposal would soon be withdrawn. However, any hope of that was soon scuppered when an article appeared in the local newspaper announcing my intentions. My fate was sealed; I was doing it! The only issue I had was... could it be done? I really had no clue. I was reasonably fit at the time and probably a better cyclist then than Bradley Wiggins, although he was only six years old. But I had never done anything like this. I couldn't ask anyone for advice because there was nobody to ask. There was no cycling tradition at that time. We had never won an Olympic Gold Medal nor produced a Tour de France winner and indeed had rarely produced any cyclists of real stature. Yes, people rode down to the shops on a basic three gear bike but the concept of the South Downs being crammed full of enthusiastic pedal pushers every weekend (both on and off road) would have made no sense at all.

There were not many sponsored cycle rides in the eighties, indeed, I think the only one of any note, was the London to Brighton. At that time, sponsored runs rather than cycle rides were the fashionable way to raise money through exertion.

Why is it that we Brits think we must do something strenuous to raise cash? It may not be entirely a British thing and some other counties such as the USA and Australia have the same habit, but I don't think it's a particularly universal concept. Indeed, I believe it only really caught on in the UK over the last thirty years or so. My father, who turned out to be a generous sponsor of the Ride every year until his death, couldn't initially get his head around it, asking "Why don't you just ask people to give money to Cot Death Research?" Well, I suppose the first answer to this is that sponsored activities grab people's attention, and therefore help you to raise more money than you might otherwise be able to. But is there also a deeper psychological explanation? Is it a hangover from former days when to be good you had to be seen to be suffering, doing penance, wearing a hair shirt and such like? And no doubt there can be some real pain in this sort of activity! Who knows! But it certainly seems to work for us Brits!

Before I went any further, I had to deal with a slight flaw with my grand gesture — namely, that I hadn't got a proper bike. So, one weekend in May 1986 I called into Gordon Davy Cycles close to Hayling Seafront. Cycling was the owner's life and he had also made it his business; he had a small but very well-stocked shop and an excellent reputation. This was an ideal place for a cycling ignoramus such as me to find out exactly which velocipede would make most sense for my French jaunt. I tried out several bikes from Raleigh, Claude Butler, and others. Interestingly, and reflecting on a by-gone age, all I believe were British made! Finally, I settled on a Dawse Tourer with ten gears. As was the norm in those days, the gear levers were on the bike frame which, initially at least, almost invited cyclists to wobble every time they went for a gear change!

The thought of a cycle jersey never entered my mind and, although lycra shorts were then available, they were hardly a common piece of apparel and it never occurred to me to buy any. Similarly, it would be some years before cycling helmets would be common. I bought a crude, analogue milometer for my bike, but it would be a while before I purchased sophisticated digital devices which also told me how fast I was going. And it would be many more years of course before a Garmin succeeded that and told me where I was or, indeed, on occasions, where I wasn't!

A week later, I tried to cycle to Chichester about fifteen miles away. I was soon knackered even before reaching Hayling Bridge, which was less than a third of the distance. For the first time, though certainly not the last, I was to learn the benefit of a pub stop! Having rested at The Ship at Langstone, the point where Hayling Island connects with the mainland, I struggled to Bosham, a mere ten flat miles to the east of Hayling, before heading back home. Chichester, just a few miles further, was, I decided, too far for my first attempt! Worse than being rather tired, I found that my backside was as red as a tomato and very sore! I had thus painfully learnt a valuable cycling lesson, namely that it can be quite literally a pain in the arse and that conditioning your rear is a vital element of one's training program! Of course, this was without lycra shorts but even wearing those it still applies! Over the years we have seen that it does not matter how generally fit you are, if you don't get out and give your bum some pre-ride training you are in trouble and you are going to need lashings of cream to survive the ordeal! And even experienced cyclists can still be afflicted in the rear. Apparently the three-times Tour de France cyclist, Louison Bobet, once needed one hundred and fifty stiches to repair his backside and even Eddie Merckx was known to drop out of a race due to posterior problems. Apparently in the early days of the Tour De France, in order to try and address this anatomical torture, before of course padded clothing had been developed, participants used to ride sitting on a piece of rump steak. Often, they would then eat it that evening!

In late May and June 1986, I practiced over and under the South Downs with as much concern for shaping up my posterior as for my leg muscles. However, I was never tempted to visit the butchers for some extra padding! The hilly terrain on the Hampshire/West Sussex border, as I came to realise more and more over the years, makes them ideal practice counties due to the sometimes-challenging topography, and of course, some great pubs. I collected sponsorship from friends, colleagues, neighbours and so forth, and in the process learnt a valuable trick, always make sure that the first name on your sponsorship form pledges a whole lot of cash as everyone will follow suit!

We managed to secure sponsorship for a number of companies including Sealink, a long-demised car ferry operator. Unfortunately, that meant using one of their routes, none of which were near to Portsmouth, so we planned for a Newhaven to Dieppe crossing. By the time I was ready to take French leave I could comfortably cycle thirty miles in one session, but of course I was going to have to do much more than that in one day. I planned to set out from Paris on Saturday 12th July, arriving back to Hayling on Monday afternoon for a July 14th French-style Celebration. George Wilson, a fellow local at another Hayling pub, The Royal Shades (pubs/cafés play a large part in this story as you may have already gathered!), offered to transport me across to Paris and act as my support vehicle. Just before my departure I was invited to the BBC Solent Studios in Southampton for an interview about my plans. With the myriad of rides, we hear about today, the idea of someone being interviewed about a solo Bike Ride from Paris might seem a little odd but this just emphasises how different the cycling environment was in those days and how unusual this was!

At that time, I worked as a legal counsel for IBM and, a few days before I was due to depart for France, I was asked if, when in Paris, I could drop in at IBM's European headquarters to assist with a business issue. I readily agreed, so now that it was a business trip all my transport costs would be met by Big Blue! This included my return journey; when signing off my expenses my boss said that I was probably the only IBM employee who ever put down cycling as their mode of transport on an international travel claim form! A few years later, when IBM went through its dramatic changes following the largest loss in corporate history, I wondered if anyone would pick up on this, and suggest that international business travel via bike might be a good thing to encourage! However, as far as I am aware, my pioneering work in the cost-cutting area went unheeded and indeed remains ignored to this day.

I duly did my business at IBM's headquarters in the concrete but rather splendid edifice of La Défense, and then George and I dined out at Brasserie de Lorraine. Now, as then, it's a fabulously elegant restaurant with fantastic cuisine and a splendid Art Nouveau interior. I think I was confident that I could charge this as a business expense, so I tucked into a gastronomic feast of "fruits de mer", washed down with liberal quantities of Muscadet. But as I sat there ensuring that I had enough fuel for the following day I was still very concerned about how things would unfold! I had gone and got all the sponsorship, been featured in the media and yet really, I still had no idea if I could do it!

Some hours later, on a splendid sunny morning, I set out from our hotel in the centre of Paris. With some nervousness, I passed through freshly hosed-down streets along the Boulevard Hausmann, into Avenue De Friedland and then offered up a prayer before risking my life going around the Arc de Triomphe! Circumnavigating this, either with car or bike, brings, as anyone who has done it will acknowledge, a whole new meaning to the word "anarchy." As I felt my way out towards Nanterre and beyond to the outer suburbs, I had mixed feelings, some excitement on the one hand, but still a major concern about whether I could finish. Why, oh why, had I opened my big mouth?

Twenty miles out of Paris my worst fears began to materialise; my right knee started to throb. Looking back on that first ride, and reflecting on the many changes since, I can see my aching knees as being one of the few constants during bike rides. At that time, however, I had no benefit of such philosophical hindsight, and really wondered whether I could continue. I began to imagine the embarrassment and indeed the shame that would result from my failure. All this build up, and a hangdog return to Hayling and reporting that I had miserably packed up just outside Paris! Fortunately, my knee did not get worse, and indeed, as I covered more miles, and warmed up my body, it seemed to improve. The miles passed by. As the day warmed up, I panted like a knackered spaniel on the uphills and freewheeled on the down-hills, gradually gaining in confidence as I realised my task was not impossible — just bloody hard!

Lunch was a quick baguette and a couple of beers. The afternoon passed acceptably, with the odd refreshment stop here and there to slake my thirst on what was now a truly hot July afternoon. Before I knew it, I was trundling into the picturesque spar town of Forge Les Eaux and had booked myself into the Hotel De La Gare. I was tired. In fact, tired hardly describes how I felt. Not even dead tired, indeed, possibly not even dead. As I ate my evening meal my hands were so numb, I could hardly hold my knife and fork, and I think I fell asleep twice, first in my fish soup, and then, having gamely survived the entrée, in my crème caramel. Twenty years later I would return to the town with one hundred and eighty fellow riders. Then I would realise what a delightful place it was, but that night I could have been in paradise, and it would still have failed to make an impression on me.

Although I had cycled seventy odd miles, I was fit, and I had done a reasonable amount of training. Moreover, this distance would be one that I would cover many times in the future. I could not understand why I was so tired. I can only put it down to nervous exhaustion, brought on by the fact that the whole challenge was such an unknown quantity and the fact that bikes in the 1980s were heavier and generally less cyclist friendly than some of those I would ride in later years.

The following day it was onward to the coast. The first twenty miles to Dieppe passed without incident, but then, about ten miles out, while rolling down a hill, I hit a pile of gravel. The bike went left, and I went right. Fortunately, I landed in a ditch. Even more fortunately, it was dry, and miraculously the bike was largely undamaged, as indeed was the rider. I ate a hearty dish of fruits de mer in Dieppe, and soon it was over the ferry for a night stop in Newhaven. The next morning was the worst part of the Ride. The hills between Newhaven and Brighton were nasty (indeed they still are) and the natural lumpiness of the terrain was made worse by the volume of traffic at this commuter hour. With this disagreeable stretch of road behind me, I negotiated Brighton and headed west along the coast (a flat route!) to Littlehampton, Chichester and then to Bosham, my lunchtime stop. Soon it was back to Hayling for a few hours of sleep prior to an "official welcome" in the evening. Everything had gone remarkably well, with no mishaps and, most importantly of all, £1100 was raised for the Cot Death charity. This was quite a sum in 1986 but it's always so much easier to gather sponsorship the first time. Firstly, because it's your first approach to the sponsors and secondly because they often think you will not make it! It was a one-off event. Or so I thought!

Chapter 2
Encore Une Fois

The following April, I was leaning against the bar of the Rose in June one Saturday night, a regular habit, when a friend of mine, Andy Page, asked if I was going to do the Ride again. My initial reaction was to say why? What silly sod would want to go through all that hassle once more? But I thought I would call his bluff.

"Yes, Andy, I will if you do it too "

"Okay, Pete, count me in!"

Another friend said he would do it too and then spontaneous commitments, fuelled by the odd pint or more of Gales HSB, a legendary local beer, rung round the bar. Drink talks, as we all know, and this was big talk, but the talk was surprisingly genuine since all kept to their word.

As in the previous year things had rather cycled ahead of me and, with the reconfirmation of the newly formed "Team Rose and June," I was committed yet again. After an article appeared in the local newspaper, The Hayling Islander, we signed up several more people, including six teenage students. George Wilson also added two more people to the Support Team; the final group, as I recall, consisted of eighteen cyclists and three Support Team members.

Of the group, Paul Fisher would go on to play a major part in the future, as would Guy Moss, who would support us for twelve years. Paul was a keen and talented racquets player and probably one of the fittest in our group. Although he had some serious cycling experience, he had no bike and had to borrow one to take part. Guy was very entertaining, very much a joker on early bike rides. But he also took his duties seriously displaying natural empathy for all his charges and not resting until the last one had extricated their aching rear from the saddle. Colourful local club and pub owner Barry Maloney was part of our team. Barry would cycle for the next four years and be a huge contributor to developing the event in its early years. He was a larger-than-life character, a successful local businessman whose overpowering bonhomie did much to set the Ride on the successful path it has taken over the last thirty years. If you rode with Barry you had to be prepared to stop for a beer, and many did! It created the tradition of a party atmosphere which has lasted to this day. With Barry, it was fun all the way; the miles slipped by almost effortlessly, rather like the Kronenbourg. The Bike Ride owes a huge debt to him and those he led astray in these early years.

Our ride was described afterwards, by The Hayling Islander, as an adventure and that is truly what it was. For one rider to cycle from Paris to Hayling, as I had done the previous year with no real planning, is one thing but for eighteen to try and do it in the same way is, in retrospect, asking for problems and we certainly got them! The first crisis, and, I should add, the first of many that we would experience over the next three decades, hit us even before we had left for France. We had borrowed a van to transport the bikes and provide support. On the evening before we left, as we loaded up, we came across a technical hitch — it didn't seem they were all going to fit in the van! Somehow, with some rearranging and the purloining of a bike rack we conquered this issue. We left on Saturday 11th July, a bright summer's morning, after a champagne breakfast at the Rose in June, but not before a detour to the Creek Road Bakery where one of our first sponsors wished to pack us off with some of his finest produce. Gerald Fuller, the proprietor of the establishment, would shortly achieve greater prominence when standing in the 1987 General Election, for the Creek Road Fresh Bread Party. Despite some interesting ideas (e.g., Defence Policy: Get a Guard Dog) I seem to recall that he lost his deposit, and never posed any real threat to the Thatcher regime. Of course, he knew all along he would lose his deposit, but felt that it was still cheap publicity and I guess it boosted the sale of bread rolls no end!

This year we had secured sponsorship from P&O Ferries and sailed from Portsmouth to Le Havre. The crossing to France was generally uneventful, but a couple of the younger riders, possibly overcome by the thought of being free of parental supervision for an extended period, got ever so slightly pissed (well actually totally rat-arsed). I do remember us having to make a couple of emergency stops en-route to Paris to address various facets of their inebriated condition. And then when we reached Paris it was quite a night! I just wish I could remember more of it! We stayed at the L'Ouest Hotel in Rue de Louvre close by the famous Boulevard Hausmann. How exactly three of us came to be on the ledge outside Barry Maloney's balcony in the early (late) hours of the morning I really don't remember. But we certainly caused no actual trouble or damage, with the incident being put down to English eccentricity. But I was a little nervous about returning to the hotel when some weeks later I came back to Paris with my new girlfriend Maryon (subsequently my wife!).

I didn't know Paris as well then as I do now and of course it would be some years before one could do any online search. So, I naturally thought of a hotel which I was familiar with, namely L'Ouest, thinking perhaps this would be suitable for a short stay. I parked the car outside and went in alone just to check something. "It's all right!" I called back to Maryon. "They don't remember me!"

The following morning, after precious little sleep (we had omitted to put that in the schedule), we took the vehicles to a quiet street just off the Seine, from where we planned to unload the bikes. Or at least, we thought it was a quiet street! I have never faced a firing squad and touch wood I will avoid doing so in the future, but for a second, I got an inkling of what it must be like when I turned around to see a group of gun-toting special police! Had we done something serious the previous night which we had forgotten? Did someone have a contract out on Barry Maloney? In fact, the reason for all the guns was that we had chosen to unload our bikes at the rear of the Iranian Embassy, where at that time a terrorist suspect had taken refuge! The police could not storm the embassy, so they were simply waiting outside. Obviously, a simple error which any cycle ride organiser could make! I am not sure who was more surprised to see who! However, after a brief check to ensure that we were not some sort of bicycling fifth column, and after an exchange of addresses with one or two of the girls (they wanted pen friends!) the police sent us on our way. For the second time in twenty-four hours, we had no doubt been dismissed as a bunch of English eccentrics.

I was to now learn the hard way that leading a group of cyclists out of Paris is not easy. We were of different cycling standards, and our senses of direction varied from the mediocre to the appalling. Moreover, our limited abilities in this regard were complicated by that fact that we were in various states of recovery from the previous night. But the biggest handicap of all, and this would remain the case throughout that year's cycling, was that we were taking our route straight out of a standard Michelin road map. We simply looked up the general direction that we wanted to go and tried to follow it, with no care as to likely traffic load or inclines. When I look at the detailed planning that we now get involved in, this seems to have been somewhat naïve!

We eased out by the Trocadero, which sounded like a night club that Barry Maloney owned, but in fact it is a rather large and impressive garden. We then ventured up to the Avenue George Cinq, turning left on to the Champs Elysees, and then onto the Avenue Grande Armée. I have never been quite sure whether the Grande Armée in question was the French or the German, and certainly never had the nerve to clarify the point with a native!

We negotiated the Arc De Triomphe satisfactorily but soon found ourselves trapped in the concrete jungle known as La Défense. Here like millions before and since we got totally confused. I quite like La Défense. I think it's a great compliment to Paris. When it opened in the early eighties it was an amazingly futuristic development and still is. But the road system, whether on bike or car, is very confusing. In the early days, taxi drivers sometimes refused to take you there! Here one or two of our group were only prevented from straying onto the motorway by vigilant gendarmes.

Somehow, we eventually made it out into the suburbs, and the countryside beckoned. But such was our state of disorganisation that by lunchtime we had reached the outskirts of Mantes, a rather drab commuter town a mere nineteen miles from Paris. We had taken a significant number of wrong turnings, and I was hoarse from having called Paul Fisher back, time and time again, from the brink of motorway travel. So, at 2:00 pm we calculated that we would have another sixty-five miles to cover. As far as I was aware, I was the only one that had ever done a major bike ride. I could just about convince myself that we could make Rouen by nightfall but unsure if I could convince anyone else. It was at that moment that Paul Fisher first contributed to Paris To Hayling history. I asked if there was anyone else in the group who had a done a long-distance Bike Ride before, and Paul said he had. I asked if he thought we could get to Rouen that evening and he quickly voiced a confident opinion in the affirmative, so off we set. A few miles later, when I asked when this long-distance Bike Ride had taken place, he told me that it was over twenty years before which filled me with no end of confidence! Had Paul said earlier "I haven't really got a clue if we can make it; I have done a long-distance cycle ride before, but I was a teenager at the time", then who knows what might have happened? We might well have packed up the bikes and got on a train. Had we done so, of course, my life over the next thirty years, and I liked to think that of many others, would have been much less fun, although I guess at times, I would have been a little less knackered!

The Hayling Islander was to later report, "They had only accomplished twenty miles by 2:00 pm, so Peter McQuade, Paul Fisher and Fiona Stevenson took the lead, and hotted up the pace." Naturally, I have framed this article since this is surely the only time that my cycling has been reported in such positive terms! We had soon left Mantes behind and followed the Seine along to the town of Vernon. Now we were enjoying the beautiful weather and equally fine countryside. Finally convinced that we were getting somewhere, I began to think we could relax. Then, just outside Gaillon, we saw it! There it was, stretching for a couple of miles in front of us, rising at our feet and finishing somewhere rather high up. This was the first real hill of the day. This was a true bastard, a hellish climb! To most "amateur" cyclists any hill is a nuisance perhaps partially compensated for by the fact that "what goes up must come down" (in theory at any rate), but this was taking a real liberty! What made it worse was that we had already been cycling a long time and it was hot. The sun was beating down on us and the sweat pouring off, and that was before we even started the ascent! As we struggled with an agonising climb in which the Marquis de Sade would have taken great delight, our efforts were cheered on by people basking in their gardens on this fine day. When I stopped for a breather, the legs were dead, the throat parched, and the lungs fit to burst. Boy was this fun!

I did not make it up that hill without walking, and nor did I in any other year. I have always felt that hills are very much a psychological thing and once you understand them, getting to know their good and bad parts, they became easier. And certainly, in time, I have normally climbed every difficult hill on the Ride even if I haven't cracked it the first year. But I could neither get my body or head around this one! Gaillon remained unconquerable!

We finally made Rouen, with the laggard Barry Maloney and one or two others being somewhat delayed by impromptu way-side social engagements in various cafés and not getting in until 9:30 pm. Such a late arrival had not been anticipated and so one of the support vehicles had to carefully guide these lamp-less cyclists into the city in the failing light! On arrival in Rouen, we made acquaintance with a couple of flea-pit hotels, which we would continue to use for the next three years. There was a little less revelry than the previous night in Paris. The charms of one of the quaintest city centres in France, if not indeed in Europe, were largely lost on our tired bodies. None of us had any energy left. So, it was after only a couple of beers at the Bar Agricole, with even Barry being only a mere shadow of his normal loquacious self, we were all ready for bed. Rather like Joan of Arc, martyred in this city several hundred years ago, we were toast!

But if we found it hard that day, maybe we should have spared a thought for those who had done the same route in 1869, the year of the first Paris-Rouen cycle race. It wasn't the Tour de France, or indeed the Paris to Hayling, but it was the first recorded long-distance road cycle race, and as such could be said to have been the ancestor of both events, and indeed the thousands of other cycle events that have come since. It took the winner, a Brit named Jamie Moore, ten hours twenty-five minutes, which is probably about the same amount of time as I took. However, when you consider the time of year (November), the state of the roads and the state of the bikes, the marvel was not that he went so slowly but that he went so fast! Mind you, unlike yours truly he probably had good directions and did not stop at so many bars! Maybe he also had the sense to skip the hill at Gaillon, and I doubt if he had any problems outside what would then have been the Persian Embassy. Moreover, I doubt that he had a Barry Maloney equivalent constantly suggesting that it was time for another Kronenbourg. It's perhaps also worth noting that some of the other 1869 riders were a bit slower than Mr Moore and didn't actually arrive until dawn the following day!

The next day, trusty Michelin road map at the ready, we ventured hesitantly out of Rouen. Having experienced a wonderful long descent into the city the night before, it was payback time, and we now expected a rather tough climb out of Rouen; we were not disappointed. A rather unfriendly hill welcomed us as we left the town, not quite as steep as Gaillon but certainly not one you would choose to cycle. It was made all the worse because it was jammed full of large lorries. There is only one thing worse than wobbling up a hill, and that's wobbling up a hill with a series of thirty-tonne trucks up your back side! However, within a few minutes of reaching the summit, we were going downhill again and cycling by the River Seine into the Parc de Brotonne, a picturesque nature reserve. This was beautiful and not for the first time I reflected on what a splendid country France was, while, also not for the first time, wondering what the French had done to deserve it!

We passed through the small town of Duclair and on to Caudebec. As we entered the latter I wondered if the strain of the last few days had finally caught up with me when I thought I saw a sea plane stuck nose-first, halfway up a cliff! But it really was there! It turned out that this was a memorial to the crew of a sea plane, a Latham 47 built here in Caudebec, which had been lost in 1928 on a rescue mission in the Arctic Ocean. Among the lost crew had been the famous Norwegian explorer Roald Amundsen who led the first expedition to reach the South Pole in 1911. Just after Caudebec we met another memorable climb, this one as twisting as Gaillon had been straight and even longer. Initially I thought it just as bad as Gaillon but looking back I don't think so because I managed to climb it, just! And certainly, unlike Gaillon, I found it easier in subsequent years as I got to know its twists, turns and bumps.

From the top of this hill, it was a twelve-mile windswept ride to Lillebonne. (Every subsequent year on this route we had the same awful breeze!) Lunch was cheese and ham at the supermarket and then we headed off on the final twenty-eight miles of the day's journey. If ever we take a vote on the most interesting stretch of any of the routes we have taken, this would not win it. You might just have gathered that I am not a great fan of hills, but equally, twenty-eight miles of unremitting flatness is almost as bad!

As we got close to Le Havre, we got confused by the road system; I was cycling just behind Paul Fisher. I followed him down what I thought was a cycle track only to find at the end that after two days of real hard effort but failure, Paul had finally succeeded in getting onto a motorway. We duly completed most of the remaining six or seven miles along this rather busy road which was a diversion I doubt either of us will forget, particularly since we spent a good part of it passing by some extremely pungent garlic fields. Somehow, we all reached our assembly point in Le Havre. All, that is, except one…

"So, you know Pete well. What is he likely to do if he's lost?"

"Panic, probably!"

With that reassuring interchange we set about looking for Pete. Pete was a local car salesman, who had joined up for the Ride with his friend, Brian, from whom he had become separated roughly twenty to thirty miles back. Our cars scoured every possible route, but there was no sign of him. Suddenly, we saw Pete pushing his bike along the street by a railway station, looking remarkably fresh. I never understood exactly what happened to him; however rightly or wrongly, there was a suspicion that the French Railways had assisted his efforts. We don't know for sure if Pete did indeed catch the train and he strongly denied it, and who would doubt the words of a car salesman? But if he was doing so, he was only emulating Maurice Garin who, having won the inaugural Tour de France in 1903, was disqualified the following year for... taking a train!

Sunning myself on a pavement café in the Cours de la République, I sensed that afternoon, as I would do again during the next umpteen summers, the huge glow of satisfaction of having achieved something just a little out of the ordinary. A very good night in the bars of Le Havre followed, though not a good night's sleep. The following morning, a Bike Ride tradition was started — namely, that of the mad scramble to make it to the return ferry. Ensuring that everyone was awake, semi-human and ready to go was the first challenge, but then we had another! One of our group had had the car keys of my virtually brand-new company BMW, (delivered one week before) and it was being used as our second support vehicle. But he couldn't find the keys anywhere. We rushed around the town, trying desperately to piece together our exact tracks from the night before. Most bars were of course closed now but at the last bar we had visited (at least the last we could remember) we were greeted by an amused cleaner who had just discovered them. We made it onto the boat with only a couple of seconds to spare! I am happy to say that despite several heart-stopping moments, including the temporary loss of support vehicles or their keys, and various riders getting lost for several hours, we have generally managed to return to the UK with the same number of people who left! The only exceptions have been a few casualties who have unfortunately been hospitalised and been detained there and one single cyclist of whom I will write more later.

As we approached the Needles, we faced yet another challenge! We wouldn't reach the Rose in June pub before closing time! Remember, pubs were not open all day then! The ferry docked at 1:30, and the Rose in June closed at 2:30. Somehow, we managed to persuade the captain to let us onto the bridge and a radio telephone message (the only method of communication in those pre—mobile phone days) was duly sent to the landlord of the Rose, Graham Perks. Pub regular and now intrepid cyclist Lindsey Gowers knew what to do. "When we get to the Island, I will need my medicine. Please can you make sure it's ready?" Fortunately, Graham understood, and when we arrived back at about 2:50, the requested medication (several pints thereof) was ready and waiting. A few hours later, I was presented with the first of many mementos that I would receive from the Ride. My fellow cyclists had clubbed together and bought me a condom. They had generously recognised my tired state from the combination of organising and riding, and as they explained, "You have been totally f****d the last few days, so we thought that this was the only possible present."

The Hayling Islander reported the Ride in a superbly evocative article under the headline "Adventure Bike Ride raises £3500". It further went on to report that "Tracey Hartles, whose longest cycle ride had previously been only four miles, stopped in a village for water at what she thought was a shop. But it turned out to be a private house and Tracey was plied with homemade wine by the French family. Nicely refreshed she found she had renewed vigour to complete the journey!" The Hayling Islander also wrote, "Andy Page and Lindsey Gowers were temporarily lost when they took a wrong turning, and Andy eventually collapsed in a bed of nettles by a railway track, adamant that his legs would not work any more." Neither Tracey, Andy or Lindsey were cyclists, but all were game for this adventure, and indeed took part in future years. Like Barry, they brought a huge sense of fun to the Ride for which all subsequent riders should be grateful.

It was much tougher cycling long distances in those early years, as bikes were heavier, and gears were more limited. If you had a set of ten, which seemed to be the most anyone had on a road bike then, the levers would typically be on the frame, making it difficult if you weren't so used to cycling. Entrants had often completed minimal practice and frequently borrowed bikes or perhaps used the only one they had, a basic shopper or sometimes a very heavy mountain bike. And as mentioned previously, ordinary cyclists didn't use any of the clothing or padding that is normal today. Time and again as I have researched for this book and talked to those who entered the initial Rides, I have reflected on stories of people who approached this ride in a way which, thirty years on, seems quite laughable. But this makes their achievements all the more impressive. This obviously applied very much to the "Class of 87" as it would to those that followed in the next few summers.

In October, we had a reunion party. I think it was taken as read that we were going to do the Ride again the following year, and most of us did! This was now no longer about one man's solo cycling efforts but rather about a community coming together to raise money in an ever so slightly eccentric but rather fun way!

Chapter 3
Bring on The Tandem Ladies

The following article was initially written by me for the 1989 Hayling Carnival Program, recalling the 1988 Paris to Hayling:

'After a Saturday night (and early Sunday morning) viewing the sights of Paris, and more than one empty bottle, the Paris to Hayling cyclists woke to a hot and sunny day ready for their long pedal to Rouen. There followed the now traditional panic to have everyone ready on time (no chance!) but eventually six support vehicles and a coach load of sore heads made for the outskirts of Paris to begin the Ride. Confusion reigned as we searched for the starting point and questions were asked — was I really Mark Thatcher's map reader?[1]

Eventually (before dark) the start point was reached, and we were off. Miraculously all took the same direction, albeit at somewhat different speeds. By 4:45 Peter Horsenell was leading the first riders into Rouen, while most were still struggling in 82 degrees of heat along a largely shade-less

---

[1] Mark Thatcher, the son of the then Prime Minister, got himself extremely lost during the Paris — Dakar car rally in the 1980s, disappearing for several days. This was obviously major news at the time. After he was safely located the story became a source of many jokes and quips.

road. However, all pushed on and kilometres and hours slowly slipped by. Super mechanic Chip Carpenter and our nurse Fran Osborne dispensed treatment to ailing bikes and bodies respectively, while the rest of the Support Team tried desperately to keep up with the cyclists' need for squash, as they fought off dehydration.

As the light failed and the last of the "survivors" rode their luck down the hill that runs into Rouen, riders swapped stories of aching limbs and sore derrières, undecided as to which was the lesser evil, sitting or standing. Next day, all were off again, pedalling out of Rouen along the D982 as it followed the valley of the Seine. All, that is, except Barry Maloney, who struck out where no cyclists had been before or at least, as the local Gendarmerie pointed out, where no cyclist was allowed to go, due to it being a motorway.

Duclair, Caudebec, the towns and kilometres passed as we rode along the valley. By lunchtime, the later riders decided it was party time and did not rush to reach Le Havre, preferring instead to sample the wares of the local hypermarket (drinks section) before making for the port. As we sat outside a café on the Cours de la République mutual congratulations followed, and all felt a glow of contentment in the fading sunlight.

A good night followed, although unfortunately we had another early rise as we headed for home on the 8:30 boat. Dudley Clarke-Jervoise continued on his exercise bike while the rest of us nodded off, dreaming of the Tour de France that we would never win.

After cycling from the Portsmouth Ferry to the Inn on the Beach, we were greeted by a reception of gastronomic magnificence. As quiches were munched and ale consumed, all riders forgot the blazing sun and ailments of the Sunday, seeking instead confirmation that there would be another Tour in 1989. They need have no fear; this event seems destined to ride on, and on, and on.'

During my life, like most of us, I have made my fair share of rash and often very wrong predictions, but I think I was fairly close to the mark regarding the future of our event. If 1987 was the first mass ride then 1988 was the year when we began to understand this was something that we could do every year. We were planning to take over forty riders, and with this increase we decided to take a coach over, and then after a night in Paris have the coach take cyclists to the outskirts of the city, from where we would start everybody riding. Well, that was the theory at least!

However, the start, as the article implies, really was quite a mess that year. After the en-route confusions of the 1987 event, we had also decided to plan the route in advance and to have route notes. To sort this out we organised the first of the Ride "recces" which henceforth took place at least once before every ride. Guy Moss, Paul Fisher, George Wilson, and I duly went out to France in February/March, and that's where the starting problems originated. One or two of the group rather overindulged themselves in Paris, and as a result, the route directions, recorded on a dictation machine the following day, were with hindsight not that comprehensible. This meant that when we came to write up the route notes, a few inaccuracies crept in! When we arrived back in Paris on Saturday afternoon in July, I sensed that there might be a problem, and did try and find the starting point for the following day's ride. When I couldn't, I warned George, who, having already tucked into a few beers, seemed unconcerned. He thought we could manage to sort it out the following morning which I guess we did — but not without a good deal of stress! The coach set off in search of the start as planned, followed by the support vehicles loaded with bikes. It soon became clear that I was right, and that we could not find the start. After probably an hour's total confusion, with the coach driving around in circles and riders wondering just what sort of an event they had joined, we found a lay—by, unloaded bikes and people, and sent everyone on their way!

It has been said many times that it has been the characters that have made the Paris to Hayling, and we had them in abundance that year. The stars of the show were probably Ann Sainty and Sheila Pearce. They entered on an ancient and heavy tandem with, as I recall, a very limited range of rather unpredictable gears. They loaded an already heavy bike with a shopping basket carrying an assortment of items, so nobody could say that they made it easy for themselves! However, during that year, and the year after, they not only proved to be competent riders, but also raised over £3000 for charity. Most of this was collected after they completed their practice rides, when they would ride around the local Warner's holiday camps relying on the generosity of the campers. I am not entirely certain what the secret of their success was, but I do seem to recall that during at least one of the summers, former British Heavyweight Champion Henry Cooper was doing some work with Warner's, and there was certainly one picture with Henry giving them some encouragement. I guess at that time, if you were collecting for charity, it was no bad thing to have a man who had floored Mohammed Ali close by so as to persuade "hesitant sponsors". Sheila and Ann's enthusiasm for what they were doing was infectious and I feel it is likely they that they encouraged others to join the Ride. In fact, in Sheila's case I am certain that was so, since apart from anything else, six other members of her family subsequently took part in the Ride including a son, a niece, a sister, two brothers and a sister-in-law.

1988 also saw the debut of then local landlord, Paul Mumford ("Mumfy"), who, in either a riding or support capacity, participated for many years. Paul was a real personality of whom more will be heard later. He was accompanied by his close friend Kevin Crocker ("Crocks") who would also play a major role in the Ride's success. Crocks cycled that year and in 1989 and 1990 before switching to the Support Team where he was a leading and virtually ever-present member for many years. Crocks, who always wore a very distinctive large straw hat, proved to be an unbelievably conscientious and able member of the Support Team. I can't believe that there are many people in the country who know more about supporting charity cycle rides than Crocks does. When asked to explain why he has done so many Bike Rides, Kevin simply said, "It gets in your blood."

Crocks and Mumfy had been persuaded to enter in 1988 by Barry Maloney. They had no real cycling experience, which was proving the standard qualification for entry, and they did it on borrowed and (of course) unsuitable mountain bikes. They had done no more than a few miles of practice (to the pub and back) and were totally unprepared. So, in many ways very typical new entrants! As Crocks recalls, "We had a few problems with the hotels that year. We turned up at one and they denied all knowledge of our booking, and another, the Hotel Amsterdam, turned out to be on the edge of the red-light district and most occupants were hiring rooms by the half hour rather than the night! And to make it worse our rooms had clearly been used very recently and were in a filthy condition! We went out on the town got in very late but even, so we weren't drunk enough to sleep in our beds, so we just lay on top of them for an hour until it was time to get up. So, we had almost no sleep and we had not long got on our bikes when Mumfy had to stop because he felt sick! I remember stopping at a bar in the afternoon; it was boiling hot, and we had those sorts of hangovers which you can't shift. We tried to get a lift from one of the Support Team, but they were not having any of it!" Crocks further recalls, "The hotel in Rouen was pretty bad as well, it looked like it hadn't changed since the Germans left it! It had bare floorboards, a loo behind a curtain and a horrible musty smell. Fortunately, we were found another room. The hotel we had in Le Havre was another brothel. Well, I think it was. Our room was not too bad this time, but downstairs blokes were looking at brochures with various women in it, pointing to one and then disappearing upstairs!" I am glad to say that as the event progressed our hotel booking process became more sophisticated, as did the hotels.

This was the year of the publicans. In addition to Barry Maloney and Paul Mumford we had in our party Graham Perks and his wife Sue, formerly of the Rose in June on Hayling but now running the Rose and Crown in Ventnor on The Isle of Wight. We were also joined by Pete Smith of the Inn on the Beach on Hayling. This was a pub/restaurant in which I would later invest. For some reason, the Ride has always attracted pub people, possibly because several of their customers have entered. Apart from four appearances by Barry and over ten by Paul, we would have many other publicans (male and female) entering from far and wide either as cyclists or as members of the Support Team. As far as I can recall only the legal profession can rival the licensee trade in terms of participation in the Bike Ride! Graham and Sue had generally encouraged me in my two previous endeavours for which I will always be grateful. They only joined the event once, but Graham went on to start his own charity cycling event based from the Isle of Wight but also involving cycling in France. Although much smaller in scale than the Paris to Hayling, it kept going for over twenty years. It could perhaps be said to be the first of several events which it could be claimed were inspired or spun out of The Paris to Hayling.

Barry Maloney recruited his brother Richard, along with his friend Alan Brown and a few others. Apart from his other business interests Barry was something of a trader, as was Alan, and sometimes they traded between themselves. One time I was on a skiing holiday with them, and I heard one reminding the other about a transaction involving a strange consignment of allegedly one-armed cricket sweaters which one had supposedly sold to the other! It sounded like something out of Only Fools and Horses! As indicated in my article Barry got arrested that year by the police for straying on a motorway. But he managed to extricate himself from it quite quickly and met up with all of us later. For some years, our poster would carry a cartoon of him being held up at gun point by a gendarme.

As mentioned in the newspaper article one cyclist Dudley Clarke-Jervoise rode an exercise bike on the Ferry. This took some organising. Back in the 1980s exercise bikes were all very "clunky" and indeed they aren't light even now! This had to be hauled up multiple sets of stairs, which was not easy. Dudley remains the only Paris to Hayling entrant to have truly cycled all the way! He was an executive with Warner Holidays (now part of Bourne Leisure), a company who gave us great support in the early days including hosting our finish on several occasions. Dudley's support in brokering this relationship was invaluable.

Ian "Chip" Carpenter also came for the first time, as did his then wife Cate. They were both to become regular Support Team members, as well as each cycling once. Over the years, Chip's practical approach got us out of a few crises and kept/restored many a bike to the road. As Chip recalls, not only were the bikes heavier and generally less easy to ride than modern ones, but also people often turned up without having given them even the most basic services meaning that problems were inevitable. Another notable debutant was Pete Horsnell. Pete first met fellow organiser George Wilson and me in the pub car park before the start, when we were having a serious altercation. Unfortunately, George had taken offence that I had put down the name of his girlfriend as his room share, which was accurate, but George was apparently concerned in case it got into the hands of her husband, who apparently was not aware of this arrangement! A remarkable thing about Pete is that he was quite easily the best rider in '88 even if the bar was quite low but, at forty-seven, also the oldest. More remarkable, however, is the fact that he completed eighteen further Rides but was never again the oldest rider. Pete was a stalwart of the event and in his own quiet way (well, quieter than Barry Maloney and Mumfy, at least) made a major contribution to making the Ride what it is today, recruiting additional cyclists and generally encouraging people in their pedalling endeavours.

At the time of the 1988 Ride, as I was working for IBM,

an article was published in its in-house newspaper, the UK News. This would pay great dividends. Pete Horsnell had signed up as a result of reading it and so did one or two others, triggering off a long succession of IBM riders, particularly from the Hursley (Winchester) Laboratory where Pete worked. In time this group also brought in other riders they knew in the Winchester area, making it virtually a secondary hub for the Paris to Hayling. Pete's addition to the Ride showed that this event could attract people from outside of Hayling and its neighbouring communities. This became even more apparent with the entry of Birmingham-based Pete Cheshire and Bob Streeter, both of whom also worked for IBM. Like Pete Horsnell they were very experienced riders. These three were the first such entrants and indeed even now such riders are in the minority! Pete Cheshire and Bob became great Bike Ride enthusiasts and came for several years with various friends. Pete was a special pioneer, being both the first rider to wear a crash helmet and, ironically, also during that same year the first to have a serious accident. Cycling onto the ferry in Le Havre, his front wheel got stuck in the ramp and he flew over the handlebars, landing on his nose, which, not being protected by his helmet, broke! Thus, his own departure from France was delayed by some twelve hours. "Broken Nose" did not however let this accident put him off. When he returned next year, he and his cycling mates had become Team Monnez (i.e., "Mon Nez" or "My Nose" in French) but also perhaps a subtle reference to Monet's gardens at Giverny, which we used to cycle past. Pete and Bob also came another six times with various friends and colleagues. Along with Tony Hart, who joined some years later, he proved himself to be possibly the most practical of all riders. One year he and two others came on a three-seater which they had built themselves, and after noticing some problems on the Paris to Rouen leg, he took the whole bike apart that night at his Rouen hotel before repairing it. Impressive stuff. For years I thought a three-seater bike was a tridem but it's not, it's a three-seater tandem since the word tandem refers to the arrangement of the seats rather than the number of cyclists.

"I haven't cycled in years, but I have a plan. I will do all my practice on an exercise bike and then borrow a bike for the event itself." This is not how we recommend you approach the Paris to Hayling; indeed, it's bonkers! But it is exactly what my future wife Maryon McQuade did in 1988. Given this and the extremely hot weather that year she not surprisingly struggled on the long day to Rouen. But aided by the bonhomie of Barry Maloney and associates, she made it! Due to pregnancies, some years looking after our young children and then some medical issues, Maryon never cycled again, but as a member of the Support Team, committee member and personal supporter of my work her contribution to the Paris to Hayling was incalculable.

After she rode, she came back intermittently over the next few years on the Support Team before becoming a permanent fixture in the latter '90s. Even in those years when Maryon was not formally part of the Bike Ride she often had a significant role to play. In the early days, of course, there were no mobile phones and although we introduced radios which helped Support Teams communicate with each other, there was still no way of getting hold of a cyclist who was lost or at least perceived to be lost. Therefore, in some years we had a "last resort" protocol whereby lost cyclists and a searching Support Team would phone Maryon in the UK and she would try and link them up.

Maryon was the first rider that moved on to support. Over the years many others followed this example. While it certainly isn't the case that you have to have ridden to provide the empathy which is a key ingredient of good support, it definitely helps. So, when Maryon and other ex-cyclists saw a huffing and puffing pedlar drag themselves up a vicious incline losing all energy and humour at roughly the same rate, they tended to understand how they felt.

We had a good finish or "Welcome Back" party at the Inn on the Beach pub on Hayling and the local newspaper carried the headline "Tour De France Nets £6500". However, afterwards, as Paul Fisher and I waited that evening for the delayed arrival of the injured Pete Cheshire, Paul told me he would not be doing the Bike Ride again. Exactly why I cannot remember; it may have been because of the champagne Barry Maloney charged to Paul's room or because someone had nicked his saddle, leaving him to cycle the last few miles rather uncomfortably. However, had he carried out his threat this event would have been deprived of a great servant. Whatever his then misgivings about becoming a serial Paris to Hayling cyclist, Paul Fisher was also the champion fund raiser that year with the in-house magazine of his employer Provident Capital describing him as "the most prodigiously sponsored rider to undergo the ordeal".

Good friends Rick and Cathy Hutchings came on support that year. Cathy came back in 1989 in support and was a cyclist in the future. Rick didn't think he was up to cycling at that time. "I was thirty-three and hadn't cycled since I was sixteen". But the following year he had a change of heart, presumably realising how mediocre most of the rest of us were and returned as a cyclist with an old and rather heavy bike which obviously fitted in very well! “While it was only a two-day ride in those days you had none of the stuff to make it easy for you and it hurt, especially my backside.” Rick was to go on to take part in over twenty Rides. Perhaps a little remarkable for one who rode with us so much, he confessed recently that he never really liked the cycling, although he continued by saying that he kept on doing it because of the social side! “It could be quite hard,” he recalls, “especially as you frequently woke up with a hangover“.” In later years Rick joined the Bike Ride committee, subsequently served as treasurer for nearly a decade and was key in us establishing the Ride on a sound financial footing.

While we had started to write route notes they were, by comparison with today’s ones, crude and rather brief. It was normal in our early days for support to spend some time foraging “off piste” for cyclists who were missing in action! Limited route notes were definitely a major reason for this. Over the years these have vastly improved and of course riders have also been helped by Garmin and by mobile phones which allow you to easily check if you have gone astray and fix the problem!

We have always made a big point about the Paris to Hayling not being seen as a race and it’s not. However, for many years there was one point where we did have a bit of a competition, this was on the way home. In 1986 of course I cycled from Newhaven and in 1987 I think we came back in the cars/minibus but from 1988 we used to cycle across Portsmouth with a police escort that would leave us as we reached the road leading to the Portsmouth to Hayling foot ferry. As we reached this road, riders would tense up as they readied themselves for the half-mile sprint to the ferry. The prize? To be among those on the first boat (it only had a capacity for forty cyclists) and therefore to have the luxury of waiting in the Ferry Boat pub on Hayling side as the others queued to cross.

Chapter 4
Bike Crash Radio and Some Special Bike Ride Characters

We now had three Rides under our belt and were attracting recruits from other parts of the country, while at the same time our reputation on Hayling was growing. Soon we were ready for the 1989 event. However, prior to departure there was a small accident. We had managed to borrow a tandem from Dawes Cycles which was duly delivered to my house the day before we left. About an hour later a local radio reporter turned up to interview myself and Paul Shaddick, one of the tandem riders. Despite not having yet actually been on a tandem he gave the impression that he was an experienced rider of said machine and duly took the unsuspecting reporter plus his bulky tape recorder on a spin down the road. Back in those days of course such a device would have been standard equipment for a reporter! It was literally only minutes before Paul failed to control the unfamiliar contraption and he and his "guest" careered into a neighbour's front garden. It was indeed fortunate that it was not a live broadcast.

The 1989 Bike Ride, like the 1988 one, was particularly hot. The Hayling Islander coverage was headlined:

"Paris riders bring back £20,000"

Reporter Pam Sylvester went on to write:

"With a conservative estimate of £20,000 sponsorship

money the hundred cyclists in the fourth Paris — Hayling Cycle Ride returned to a hero's welcome and buffet reception. The welcoming party at Mill Rythe included Stuart Wright, Renault Sales Manager who provided the back-up vehicles, members of the local Cancer Research Campaign and representatives of Hayling lifeboat station. Both charities will benefit from the Ride. The lifeboat station was presented with the key of a caravan. The caravan will be used to sell souvenirs at local events. The ride started on June 23 and was proceeded with a French party at Bay View Court. After spending Saturday in Paris all were up early on Sunday for the long haul to Rouen. Apart from Faye Pollard, 19, who fell off her bike just outside Rouen and had to go to hospital with lacerations, more bikes than riders needed attention. Jan and Dave Castle, on a tandem, broke down just outside Paris and had to change bikes. Prizes were presented by Miss Hayling Islander, Samantha Williamson to Gary Wooding and Paul Jones of Hayling who raised nearly £3000 with the help of Hayling Lions, Jan and Dave Castle for best efforts after their tandem broke down, and Kit Whiteoak, 55, the oldest competitor on his first ride, Sheila Pearce and Ann Sainty on a tandem who received the Caudebec Trophy for cycling up the hill without stopping and Crocks, technically the winner?"

The point about Kevin is correct as he was the first one off the Portsmouth to Hayling ferry. However, it is somewhat misleading since for most of the time in France he was somewhat to the rear of the event, often delayed by wayside watering holes. He remains to this day the only cyclist who has won a prize for being first home. He himself knew he couldn't top this impressive achievement and joined the Support Team for future Rides. A few miles into the Ride, Support Team member Chip Carpenter encountered an interesting problem when the three-man tandem fell apart. It turned out that it was two Post Office bikes welded together and, judging by the way it fell apart, not very well welded! This was clearly not an en-route repair job! Fortunately, the riders could continue on their way using spare single bikes. Two other notable debutants in 1989 were Normand Howison and Pam McLaughlin, who worked with Pete Horsenall at IBM's research facilities in Hursley. They were very strong cyclists who in future years would normally make their way to Paris by bike! At the time we thought this was very odd behaviour indeed but more of that later. It was also the first year that John and Brenda Wiltshire entered, bringing with them fellow members of the Gosport Running Club and as such this was probably our first team. John and Brenda were to cycle for twelve years on a tandem! Sadly, Brenda passed away from cancer and John then stopped entering. They were a delight to have on the Ride, recruiting various new cyclists over the years, and remain rather unsung heroes of those early years.

In 1989 we had clearly established most of the ingredients for a successful ride. We were getting a significant number of commercial sponsors which was helping to pay for the administrative expenses. These included Renault who had kindly started supplying us with vehicles in 1987 and were to continue to do so for more than a decade. P&O Ferries was a strong supporter for some years, and even after we had to move to a Brittany route to bring in some variety, they welcomed us back later at a favourable rate. And we also received sponsorship from Hayling-based companies such as Warner Holidays, Gable UK, a roofing company, CJ Driscoll, a local firm of accountants and Burras Engineering, Mike

Burras' own company. Burras, Gable and Driscoll would continue to support the event for many years.

In addition to the RNLI and Cancer Research, over thirty other good causes benefitted that year including a local boy with cerebral palsy who underwent treatment at the pioneering Peto Institute in Hungary. The mixture of fun and challenging cycling was proving to be an attractive recruitment message but so was the fact that you could raise money for the charity of your choice. As the Paris to Hayling developed and as other charity cycle rides became popular, we increasingly realised that this latter factor, as opposed to having to ride for one charity, the normal charity ride model, was a very attractive aspect of our event. Above all, we were gathering a truly eclectic bunch of characters who all made major contributions to the spirit of the event. Three newcomers in particular were to play a major part in the Bike Ride's development. Indeed, it's difficult to overstate their contribution. Rod Elliot' recalls how he got involved. "I only decided to do it after a meeting with Paul Fisher in the pub the weekend before. I guess I entered on the principle that anything you can do I can do better; I had probably had a few beers at the time." Rod, like so many first-time entrants, was not a serious cyclist. "I had never cycled further than the shops and in fact had to borrow my son's mountain bike complete with knobbly off-road tyres to do the Bike Ride." Rod soon realised the folly of his ways and no amount of Vaseline could hide the pain of mile after mile of sitting on a small piece of leather. "It was very hot, and I remember looking ahead at miles of undulating tarmac with lorries whizzing past me."

Rod was right in that in those early years we tended to focus almost solely on the quickest route to the next town, with little thought to picking the best cycling route. Despite the pain of 1989, Rod was to cycle again in our tenth anniversary year, though making sure that he had a better bike and also, mindful no doubt of his former problems, being suitably kitted out with padded lycra shorts. He also rode again in our fifteenth year, the five-year gaps being necessitated, I understand, by his need to restore his energy levels! But Rod's greatest contributions would be "out of the saddle". He was as a key member of the support team for many years and a valuable member of many "recce" teams. Rod also served as secretary for a couple of years and regularly sorted out our ferry bookings. Behind the scenes Rod was also an invaluable confidante and sounding board for me personally regarding various Paris to Hayling matters.

Fred Dyer became a more or less permanent fixture for many years after his debut in '89 and was also to play a major part in the Bike Ride's development. With Fred came his wife Judy who, for years, was the chief nurse on our Support Team except for one year when she cycled. Fred subsequently got all his family involved. In addition to Fred and Judy, both sons did the Ride and two of their daughters and a son-—in-law, while the remaining daughter has been in the Support Team. Fred eventually entered the Paris to Hayling more than twenty times and one of his sons, Tom, also took part in ten events with Tom's twin Chris also riding several times. Fred's fondness for beer and wine often got him into a few scrapes and there will be more of that later, but he brought much colour to the Bike Ride (largely with a red or rose tint) and, as one bar owner pointed out, he was a miracle worker in so far as he could turn wine into water at a prodigious rate! Fred's odd cycling style was, as we subsequently learnt, in large due to his hip which had been crumbling away over the years. When he had that replaced there was some concern as to how much cycling he would be able to do but his new artificial hip didn't seem to hinder him at all. For many years, Fred would take the lead in sorting out our routes as nobody could plot a route like Fred. He loved maps and seems to be able to read them far quicker than the average person. Today when we look at a new route, we normally start with using mapping software before then verifying with more traditional methods but in earlier years that was not an option and Fred's skill and passion in this area was invaluable.

Pete Alloway also entered in 1989. When he first started practising for the big event, he recalls that he was knackered after only seven miles! But he persevered and would cycle many more times, becoming a pretty decent cyclist. Like Rod and Fred, he became heavily involved in the Bike Ride's organisation and has been a major reason for the success of the event. He did have a rather bizarre hotel experience in Rouen that first year. "I checked into my hotel, knackered, was handed a key and went to sleep. The following morning, I got up and I had a good breakfast, although strangely there were no other cyclists eating. Only when I got on my bike and met up with other riders did I realise that I was in the wrong hotel!" Over the years Pete persuaded a lot of his mates to join us. They were generally rather colourful characters who greatly enriched the event. They were rarely quiet and never teetotal. A few of them will crop up in later chapters.

1989 was the first year that the Support Team vehicles were equipped with radios so when all of support began to turn up at the same time it was by design rather than accident. They made a huge difference to their efficiency and allowed them to work as a true team. Up to that point, if support vehicles wanted to co-ordinate, the best they could really do was to stop a cyclist and ask if they had seen so and so. Then if someone got lost, necessitating one or more vehicles leaving the route, the wheels really came off (pardon the pun). In this context, it's important to remember that this was before anyone had a mobile phone which would work abroad. But, as Rod Elliott has pointed out, there could be issues with the radios. "While they were useful, some people tended to use them like telephones and used them to communicate all sorts of trivial matters forgetting that when they are using them the airwaves are blocked to others who may have more vital information to pass on. I remember one year when Judy Dyer accidentally sat on her "on" button for two hours. None of the other Support Teams could find her to tell her what happened and for all that time we were listening to her and her companion chatting away!"

From that year the Paris to Hayling Cycle Ride would raise more money than any other single Hayling charity and indeed in some years it must have raised more than all others combined. The 1988 and 1989 Rides were organised by a team consisting of myself, George Wilson, the original support driver, Paul Fisher and Dudley Clark-Jervoise. There were thoughts that maybe the Paris to Hayling organisation could take on other things and therefore we formed ACE (Association of Charitable Endeavours). The number of other events that it took on was somewhat limited except that it was involved for some years with (no surprise here) a real ale festival, the Ayling Fest. But the name stuck and today the Bike Ride still banks under this name.

That year we began to change our approach to hotel

bookings. In previous years we had always stayed in "flea pit" establishments. They weren't all as bad as the one that Crocks recalled but none of them had been that good! Riders from those early years will remember the delights of La Vielle Tour and the Bordeaux in Rouen and such savoury Paris hotels as Hotel Wilson (no relation or at least I don't think so) as well, of course, as the dodgy Hotel Amsterdam where Crocks and Mumfy stayed. These dingier hotels also tended to be poor at administration and it was not unknown for us to turn up with totally wrong room allocations despite efforts to clarify all these things in advance. This was of course in pre-fax and pre-internet days when bookings were typically done over the phone followed by a confirmation letter and/or occasionally a telex. We were naïve, we did not realise that even with our then modest numbers we now had the clout to extract good rates from better hotels and thus move the whole show up market. A chance encounter with Island resident Dennis Pratt changed all this. Dennis had spent many years in the tourist industry, and he pointed out the error of our ways! We started booking in Ibis and Mercure Hotels wherever possible — both of these were part of the large French hotel chain, Groupe Accor. The good thing about using "chain hotels" is that when planning we would have some good idea of what they were like even before we visited, given the general uniformity of the designs. When Ibis and Mercure couldn't satisfy our requirements, we sometimes used other hotels owned by Groupe Accor or Kyriad and Campanile hotels owned by the rival Groupe Louvre.

Our move "up market" started with opting for an Ibis and Mercure hotel for the 1989 visit to Paris. We chose the Mercure and Ibis in Porte D'Orleans. For those planning to head west from Paris as we were, they were not in the ideal position as they were on the southern perimeter of the city, but I guess they must have offered a very good deal! From 1989 until we moved elsewhere in 1993, novice riders used to be coached across Paris whereas other riders would make their own way from the hotels. We got this down to a fine art eventually but in the early years there were one or two issues. I can clearly remember a very confident Paul Fisher leading the group out of Paris in '89 or '90 except that he wasn't! The sun seemed to be almost overhead, the heat was dripping off everybody and there we were lost in a large city with a lot of miles still to be cycled. As we circled the Eiffel Tour goodness knows how many times Paul was faced with a mutiny by a now less than merry band! Eventually the riders found their way out of Paris, generously deciding to take Paul with them! As successful and generally very busy hotels, we have often wondered how much they welcomed the business of a bunch of cyclists, particularly if we arrived oozing sweat. Furthermore, they have had to cater for our unusual storage requirements (a hundred to two hundred bikes). I am sure a nice bunch of compliant American tourists is a more attractive proposition in some ways. However, when it comes to bar takings, we have generally made it worth their while!

In 1989, as in past years, some riders barely got any sleep in Paris. The party atmosphere continued right until the end with Islander reporter Pam Sylvester getting caught up in the crossfire of our post-ride revelry. She was "wounded in action" when hit by a champagne cork. Alan Brown was the perpetrator of this, when he attempted to crack open a bottle of champagne he had won for having the sorest arse (not sure who judged this and how). This injury necessitated our brave reporter receiving some brief medical treatment.

At the end of 1989 we had a reunion at Warner's Mill Rythe Holiday Village. Roy Castle was appearing there at the time, and he joined us to present some cheques. Ironically, given the cause of his own death a few years later, the biggest cheque that he presented was to Cancer Research. Henceforth Cancer Research would be the major beneficiary of funds in virtually every year, receiving many hundreds of thousand pounds from our pedalling.

Chapter 5
Upsetting Norman and the Mystery of Barry's Shoes

As the 1980s ended, the Paris to Hayling Ride was becoming firmly established as a regular event, a prominent part of Hayling life. On Hayling you did not need to refer to the full name; if you said you were thinking of doing "The Bike Ride", people knew what you meant. A growing number of riders were finding the event habit forming and entered every year. We were regularly getting entries from London, Birmingham and soon even further afield with one couple travelling down annually from Glasgow to do our event. The number of charities and good causes that were benefiting continued to grow. We decided to buy a mini-bus for the local hospice; part of the deal was that we could also use it for our event. This arrangement worked successfully for many years.

In 1990, we received a letter from the Right Honourable Norman Tebbit MP (now Lord Tebbit). He was a senior Tory and former Cabinet Minister. Back in 1981 he was somewhat misquoted as saying that the unemployed should get on their bikes to look for work. Rightly or wrongly this alleged utterance had hung around Tebbit for some years when I wrote to him suggesting that he might like to send us a signed picture urging us to get on our bikes. I think I had the idea that at least we could auction the picture since he was very a well-known figure and a close aide of Maggie Thatcher'. What I had not expected was to receive a letter from Mr Tebbit in which he went to great lengths to explain that he had not told anyone to get on their bike but rather had simply referred to the fact that in the 1930s his father had chosen the option of getting on his bike to look for work rather than going out on to the street and starting a riot. He did however finish his letter wishing us all success for our fund-raising efforts.

That year we took a hundred and ten riders and ten support crew. Crocks recalls the pre-ride night in Paris.

"We had a good night in Paris that year. I remember we met up with some French people who had a couple of guitars and started promenading down some side street or other in the Pigalle area singing our heads off. The inhabitants of one of the houses overlooking the street were obviously not impressed and so they hurled buckets of water at us. This didn't put us off, though, and we just switched songs and gave our rendition of "Singing in the Rain"."

This year we also went to better hotels in Rouen and Le Havre. In Rouen, we chose the Mercure Champs de Mar, among others. In one or two years, we did stop using it due the fact that they could not take our large booking, but we were always happy to return. They sometimes displayed welcoming signs when we arrived and generally gave us great confidence that all would be as planned and agreed. The hotel was situated alongside the river, just as you enter the city, and it has been the point at which cyclist welcomed others even if they were in fact staying somewhere else. The biggest challenge we have had over the years is that there is a steep curb which people have sometimes ignored when getting of their bikes. The result is that in some years we have had more injuries as result of this curb than we have had following the whole day's cycling from Paris to Rouen.

We began to attract more teams, one of the most entertaining of these being The Hampton's team from the then large estate agents of that name. They rode, they drank, and they entertained. One of their number, Martin Collins, was an excellent guitarist who played for us on a number of alcohol-fuelled evenings. I also seem to recall he won a prize one year for an excellent fall!

In 1990 with a young family and a busy job involving a great deal of international travel I began to take a lesser role in the Bike Ride's organisation, although continuing to take part every year. That year, at the meal on the last night, riders presented me with a present for my efforts. I was very moved by this but to be honest what happened next was far more memorable. It was a warm, indeed balmy night as we left the restaurant to stroll back to the hotels. Most of the party passed through a square which was lined with several bars which overlooked a fountain. Many of us sat down for a last drink and inevitably one or two decided to go for a swim. I doubt if there were ever more than ten in the fountain, but someone had tipped off the police and first one, then another and then another and ultimately, I believe seven police vans arrived. For a few dreadful minutes I could see half the Bike Ride spending the night in the nick! But it didn't come to that. The few remaining swimmers were reprimanded but they let them go as they were not really misbehaving and not (particularly) drunk. We could never figure out why there had been such an overreaction but guess it may have been because sadly the English abroad did not have the best reputation at that time. We also never understood why the police confiscated Barry

Maloney's shoes.

1990 was sadly the last ride for Barry and his mate Alan Brown. Conscious of that fact they tended to linger in bars, they thought in this final year that they should bring their own support vehicle to alleviate the burden on the main team. So, some three hours before the ferry left Portsmouth, they persuaded (or possibly kidnapped) local man George Krause to join them driving Barry's jeep. In his new role as "chauffeur", George took them around Paris on our night in the capital which happened to be 14th July. They were stopped at a traffic light when a firework was thrown at them from a passing French car. Fortunately, they were lucky, as the firework went out upon landing in the vehicle. The passengers of the other car were less fortunate, however, and soon got the fright of their lives as one of Barry's crew reignited the firework from the cigarette lighter and threw it back on the bonnet of the other still stationary vehicle, resulting in a very large bang! In general, Barry and Co must have given their driver a hard time since when I met up with him fifteen years later for the first time since that ride, he still remembered his French excursion well.

Chapter 6
Mumfy Does Lunch

1991 would be the last Bike Ride that departed from Le Havre for some years. We were able to report that we had exceeded £80,000 in funds raised so far. Little did we dream that what had taken five years to raise, we would one day raise in one year and indeed, in some years more than that! Local solicitor John Frost joined us that year. I mention that because he was the first lawyer other than me to do the Ride, but many were to follow. Indeed, one year we had six on the event and outnumbered publicans as the most common rider occupation. I know that hardly makes it sound like a fun event, but I think it was! Lawyers have come in all shapes and sizes, solicitors, barristers, judges, lawyers in private practice, some in industry and others in academia! That year also marked the debut of the first of four Dyer children who were ultimately to take part. The Hayling Islander reported that, "The youngest entrant this year was Rebecca Dyer, aged sixteen, who unfortunately missed her pedal footing five miles out of Paris and ended up with a black eye. She bravely continued and finished the Ride."

Mumfy was "forced" to go on the Ride a few hours before departure by his wife Pauline who claimed she needed the break! He joined up despite having had no training. And what an eventful ride it was for him! With a growing number of riders, we had decided to separate cyclists at the start into a slow and fast group with the former going off first. Mumfy, who could never have been mistaken for Chris Froome, even in a very dark room, set off with the slowest but amazingly led the way and was technically first at lunch time. This shocked us all; it just didn't seem credible! It was as surprising as if Julian Clarey had just become World Heavyweight Boxing Champion. However, several hours later, by which time the quickies had caught up and all modest and healthy lunches had been consumed, Mumfy was still indulging in a gastronomic extravagance so that when he returned to the saddle, he was well and truly last and would remain so for the rest of the day! But he wasn't finished yet! The following day, according to the Hayling Islander, "The only person to go AWOL was Paul Mumford, Landlord of The Kittiwake, who was found a few miles from the finishing point at Le Havre where he had enjoyed a three-course meal and swapped three T-Shirts for a stuffed duck." I suspect that the Hayling Islander got it slightly wrong as, knowing Mumfy, it was probably a five-course meal.

New rider Kim Hopkinson was typical of the adventurous "have a go" spirit that featured so much in our early Rides. Kim had not long been living on Hayling and was talked into doing it and thought it would be a good way of meeting more people. "I purchased a bright pink, white and black British Eagle Mountain bike costing £150, having never owned a bike before, and I did loads of practice rides beforehand. I really enjoyed the Ride, but it was flipping hard!"

Chapter 7
Lorry Loads of Hassle

By 1992, after having experimented with various routes out of Paris towards Rouen, we were now settled on one which took us from Paris to Giverny, the home of Monet's Gardens, in the morning and then on to Rouen via Vernon and Les Andelys in the afternoon. While there would be some changes to this much of it would remain a core part of our route for many years. We discovered an agreeable watering hole a couple of kilometres short of Giverny, Auberge de St Eustace, where most riders stopped for lunch for a number of Rides until it closed down. Cleary the once-a-year revenue from our hungry and thirsty cyclists, while no doubt welcome, was not enough to fund the business for twelve months. Over the years a number of riders would also stop in Giverny at the famous gardens. Claude Monet, the founder, and arguably most notable member of the impressionist school of painters, lived in Giverny from 1883 to 1926 and his gardens, which featured in many of his paintings, are world famous. After Monet's Gardens this route passed through Vernon and then we reach the charmingly named village of Port Mort. The name always intrigued me because it could literally be translated as the rather sinister sounding Dead Port! This possible sobriquet was rather emphasised by the road that greeted us as we entered the village which was appropriately named "Route De

Le Cimetiere" ("Cemetry Street"). However, a little research suggested that the origins of the village's name are a little less sinister. It probably originated in the 4th century AD as Portus Maurus when the Romans housed a colony of Moor (North African) soldiers at this point on the Seine.

Having passed by Dead Port and after a nasty little incline, cyclists were presented with what, for some, was an even more worrying sign! George Bush once allegedly said that the French didn't have a word for entrepreneur. While of course he was ever so slightly wrong it is indeed true that in many cases they sometimes don't have a word equivalent to the one used in English, hence the abundance of Franglais such as weekend, crumble, and sandwich. Sometimes they borrow words or expressions which are then applied in a way that makes absolutely no sense at all in English. And here was a very interesting example, at the top of the hill was a sign saying "Danger — Ball Trap". Over the years this caused quite a lot of consternation to male riders until they found it meant "Danger Clay — Pigeon Shooting!" Phew! Having a few pellets whizzing around your head is one thing but possible damage down there is quite another! Within a few miles the route took us to Les Andelys. As we approached this ancient town on the chalk cliffs to our right, we could see the ruins of the famous Chateau Gaillard. This was built for Richard the Lion Heart/Richard, Duke of Normandy to protect the lower reaches of the Seine. This castle perched on a chalk cliff at the entrance to the town is rated as one of the finest castles of its time and most of it was built in less than two years — a remarkably short period for a construction of that size during that period but then, in those far off times, strikes by French workers were probably less frequent. The connecting road up to the castle is very steep so I don't think Richard had any cycling in mind when he commissioned this Norman residence but then who would if they had to wear all the sheet metal that seemed be "a la mode" at the time.

In 1992 we changed the second day route from Rouen to Le Havre to Rouen to Caen. This was a big step at the time, since it involved a last day of over ninety miles, a massive increase on the previous sixty. On the positive side, we no longer had to take the long climb on a busy road out of Rouen that had been our exit for the last five years. However, after crossing the Seine and before reaching the open countryside we did need to cycle through a very drab, chimney-stacked industrial suburb on the outskirts of Rouen. This was definitely not La Belle France. This really was a horrible part of France. One year, Crocks saw a pig apparently sniffing for truffles but, as he pointed out, how could any creature smell anything round there. It was criss-crossed by light railway tracks which, impressively, on more than one occasion, riders manage to get their wheels stuck in, launching themselves onto the adjacent tarmac!

Apart from the route change the 1992 ride will be remembered for the fact that we beat a lorry driver blockade before we even started cycling. French lorry drivers were protesting against something or other, a common occurrence of course. Consequently, taking the rather strident actions that our friends across the channel are noted for, they decided to block motorways and other main roads. However, the drivers of our convoy of two coaches, a minibus and assorted vans took to the country lanes in order to avoid the blockade. Morale remained high as it looks like we had got one over on the fiendish "camioneurs". There was talk of a Dunquerque spirit which struck me as kind of strange since, heroic as it was, that incident represented a retreat from France, whereas here we were more in line with another familiar facet of French history, an advance on Paris. At Rouen we were assured that the motorway was clear and so we re-joined it only to encounter a blockage of a hundred lorries; Sacre Bleu! However, after some protracted explanations and clarifications as to what we were doing, they agreed to let us through, and we made it to the French Capital. We were "helped" by Mumfy at this critical stage of that year's event. For some reason we had a pool cue from his pub with us. No doubt his brandishing of this and brave shouts of "The Tommys are going to get you!" from the safety of a secure vehicle terrified them into seeing reason. On our way back from Paris we had a bit of an incident in Rouen when the hotel we were using insisted on trying to charge us for evening meals we had never ordered and never wanted. It all got a bit nasty with certain gratuitous observations on the English character being served up by the hotel manageress. After all attempts at reasoning with them had failed we reverted to Plan B, hopped on our bikes and pedalled like hell until we were some way, away. We subsequently satisfactorily resolved this matter via mail on our return to the UK and no extradition warrants were needed.

After this, everything went smoothly until we were within a few miles of Caen. There, however, two things happened. First, we found our route blocked by tractors whose drivers were acting out of sympathy with the lorries and so we had to strike out across the French fields to once again teach the French who was boss. Secondly, cyclist Ann Borton was taken ill. Fred Dyer was driving a support van that year as he was injured. The first I knew of this was when Fred, responding to an emergency call, nearly knocked me off my bike and into a ditch as he was driving the other way along a narrow country lane. Ann was admitted to hospital, but her troubles had only just begun. The French Health service has a justifiably good reputation, but they struggled to diagnose Ann's problems. Accompanied by our chief nurse Judy Dyer, she was transferred from one hospital to another. Subsequently, Ann discharged herself and came back with the rest of the group under the supervision of the ferry's doctor. Then she was admitted to hospital in Portsmouth where she was operated on for appendicitis. Ann returned the following year but had an accident, after having got her bike wheel stuck in tram lines on the edge of Rouen. After a year off, presumably to summon up the courage and to save for the high cost of her travel insurance, she eventually completed the Ride in 1995 — Third Time Lucky. Since then, she has cycled again a couple of times and on one occasion was once again in the "sick bay" due to an asthma attack but has gone on to be a valuable member of the Support Team along with her husband Roger.

Chip Carpenter swapped a support van for a bike in 1992 and entered along with his friend and fellow Islander, Ian Pollicot. Ian was to cycle on several occasions and feature in several Support Teams. He was also in charge of "French Liaison" for some years which, as salacious as it sounds, was more focused on the Ride's opportunity to use his French bank account and therefore reduce our risk of currency movements rather than any physical contact with the French! His recollections included the following, "As a youth I was into cycling and once did a nine-hundred-mile ride from Derby down to Cornwall and back. My bike had been restored for my fortieth birthday and this seemed a good way to use it. In my early years on the Paris to Hayling I did a very wet ride and a very windy one. The wet one was particularly memorable. My shoes got absolutely soaked but of more note was the fact that many of the male cyclists rode with their heads turned around, on account of the weather the ladies put on a fantastic, if somewhat involuntary, wet T-Shirt competition that year. I also remember once being stopped by the roadside when a girl thrust her bike into my hands and rushed off into a field for a "natural break". She soon rushed out again, not understanding that the sign by the fields said (in French) "Danger Snakes". As I was coming into Rouen, I met up with a guy who was clearly struggling and offered to stay with him. I can't remember for certain, but his name may have been Brian. By the time we got into the town it was very late, but the word must have got around about my companion because everybody drinking outside the Hotel Mercure got up and cheered. To him it was like he had won The Tour De France. This is what this ride is all about."

Chapter 8
Advancing on Pegasus Bridge

In 1993 we made an important change in the last few miles of our route to Caen. The previous year had been along the busy N14, a major road, and with cars and lorries constantly passing it was not ideal for cyclists who were perhaps struggling on that part of a long day. This year we first headed for the coast before turning inland to the city. This involved a stop at the famous Café Gondrée at Pegasus Bridge next to the Caen Canal before we headed down the cycle path to Caen. In planning the D-Day invasions it was clear that the bridge at this point across the canal and the one across the nearby River Orne were of vital strategic importance. Without these bridges the Germans would have found it very difficult to bring troops and equipment from the east and south to attack the troops landing on the Normandy Beaches. Equally, the Allied forces would ultimately need these crossings to link the western and eastern flanks of the invasion forces. Therefore, on the night of 5th/6th June 1944, Major John Howard and men of the 2nd Battalion Oxfordshire and Buckinghamshire Light Infantry began the liberation of Europe with the specific objective of taking both bridges. After arriving in six gliders (with three of them crash landing!) in what has surely correctly been described as the most daring glider operation ever, they succeeded in taking these vital points (and keeping them) in ten minutes. In the process they arrived at Cafe Gondrée.

Today, Arlette Gondrée-Pritchard, who as a young girl lived in the house at the time it was liberated, still runs the café which has become a shrine for war veterans. Her parents, who had previously fed information about defences around Pegasus Bridge to the resistance, gave hospitality to the invading troops. This included the digging up of ninety-seven bottles of champagne which had been buried in order to hide them from the Germans. Visiting the café also known as Pegasus Bridge café was to become a firm highlight of the Ride for many years and still continues to feature. We sit outside the small but historic establishment clapping in the gallant finishers, drinking the rather strong beer, and then heading down the tow path towards into Caen.

Nobody kept us more amused in 1993 than Mike Saunders. Mike ran local hairdressers Yellow Strawberry and was clearly intent on having a good time. In addition to his standard bike, he brought along his unicycle. He kept us amused on the ferry with this, even more so when he juggled as well. He also kept us amused en-route and his cries "More Beer" and "Zip It You Muppets" were remembered long after his single appearance on the Ride.

Popular Hayling Islander Andy Lenaghan first came in 1993. Two sisters, a brother, a sister-in law, and a niece had already taken part, but it was Andy with his nine Rides who was to make the biggest impact. He served on the Bike Ride committee for a number of years and contributed to the Ride's evolution in several ways. Andy may well have stayed involved in the Bike Ride even longer, but his time became limited due to the fact that he was elected a local councillor, a role which he was to perform very successfully over a number of years. Some years ago, he summed up his enjoyment of the Bike Ride, "I will never forget the fun we had, plus the challenge of the ride and raising funds for the charities we supported as cyclists. The camaraderie between us all was unique, and I don't think it will ever be surpassed. Cycling through France sometimes with people you had never met before and remaining friends to this day is rather special."

Recently Andy recalled the time that he got lost on the Ride. Support was trying to locate him, so they phoned his mobile. However, to avoid any business calls during his cycling hours, he had had this diverted to his office. This meant that his colleagues were fully aware of his plight and the following week when he returned to work, he was greeted by a chorus of *Lost in France*!

That year we had a very stroppy entrant. I caught up with the riders in Paris, having been out there a couple of days before on business. I met them soon after they arrived in Paris at their hotels. This rider was giving all the organisers a hard time, complaining about everything, as, apparently, he had done non-stop since they left Hayling the night before. He was most unpleasant, but I had a cunning plan! I introduced myself and started to listen to his foul tirade of complaints. But as I did so I edged towards an adjacent cash machine and as we talked, I put my card in the hole in the wall and drew out some Francs. "Well," I said, "Sorry to hear you are not happy, but we aren't either and we are not Thomas Cook! "This voluntary team," I said, referring to those in the background, "have been working tirelessly for weeks to put your trip together so here is your money back. "We will get your luggage and then you can f**k off home." And in due course the rather speechless ex-entrant did. It's a long time ago but I am sure that somehow, we also sorted out his bike. We never saw or heard from him again! To my recollection this is the only time we have had to put our money-back guarantee into operation.

We changed the date in 1993, moving from June/July to September. Perhaps we were just a bit unlucky with the weather (cold, quite wet, and breezy) but it did not seem in retrospect to be a good move. We were to try it again the following year with no better weather and so reverted back and have kept it there ever since. Also, George Wilson suggested that we should rebrand the Ride as the Paris to Portsmouth, since a) nobody had ever heard of Hayling and b) it would please our sponsors, Portsmouth-based Brittany. This caused a lot of controversy and it subsequently turned out that, to Brittany, it did not matter anyway, so after a two-year "experiment" we reverted back to the former name.

Chapter 9
Lots of Dyers, Tony, Roy, Podge and Ernie

In 1994 we changed our Paris base, moving from Port D'Orleans to La Defence. In this area we have used several hotels but the key one has been the Mercure in rue Courbevoie, a huge hotel which in some years was to house an entire ride with more than two-hundred people, a feat which no other hotel has accomplished!

1994 saw the "debut" of three more Dyers. Twins Chris and Tom and their sister Ela. Tom went on to do ten Rides and to be a pretty good cyclist. Both Tom and Ella have also been in subsequent years. Ella went on to marry Steve Cook, who first came in 1993. With nurse Judy and Fred also on the Ride there were five members of the Dyer clan on that year's event!

However well-organized our Rides have been and however meticulous our route planning, most years we have encountered a set of roadworks, which weren't there when we did our recce as well as roads closed off for Bastille Day Celebrations. Inevitably these would be accompanied by a sign reading "Route Barree". Sometimes these used to throw the Ride into temporary mayhem, necessitating that the Support Team ad lib and create a few miles of new route before hopefully all riders could rejoin the planned one. However, on other occasions it was simply a case of getting off the bike and walking through the barricades for a short distance. In 1994 we met up with a Route Barree in Les Andelys which required us to get off and walk. This was the first time I got talking to entrant Tony Hart. Tony lived on Hayling and was aware of our event. He had been a keen cyclist since he was a young boy and was an active member of a local cycling club. Tony was tall and slim, an ideal build for a cyclist unlike some of us! He joined up that year with several work colleagues, all keen cyclists. I think it's fair to say that completing the Ride was well within their capabilities but as Tony recalls it was a long enough and varied enough ride that you could make it as challenging as you wanted.

From that year Tony would take part in virtually every event. Within a few years he would be a committee member and served on it for many years. "I wanted to put something back into a sport which I really loved"." Like many good cyclists Tony had, by necessity, become a very good bike mechanic and apart from pedalling himself he made a major contribution in helping others with various bike defects. More often than not diverted from his own preparations by these tasks, Tony would be the last to leave the hotel when riders set off for another day on the road. Tony would soon catch up other riders, but was rarely, if ever, in first since, as serious a cyclist as he was, he never took the cycling that seriously on this event and was a somewhat frequent visitor to the various cafés that we discovered en-route.

Roy Marshal was another newcomer in 1994, and, like Tony Hart, he would be around for a long time and make a significant impact both personally and via his business. Roy was an Island resident who owned a local jewellery shop. While he had known about the Bike Ride for some years before he joined up, he didn't actually know any of the riders when he entered. But it was the camaraderie which immediately struck him on the journey to Paris. As he put it, "If you are alone, you soon won't be alone." In time, both Roy's children would enter and he himself would help encourage a number of other junior riders, as will be covered in a later chapter.

This was also the year that Kevin "Podge" Stirzaker first joined us. Podge was a serious asthmatic and was told he had to give up smoking; he tried but without too much success. He decided that he needed some incentive to do so and thought that taking up cycling might help, so he took part in the London to Brighton ride. But then he felt he needed to continue. "I saw a picture of three rather attractive ladies preparing for the Paris to Hayling and I thought I would give that a go." Podge duly signed up, though apparently, he never saw the three ladies. "I assumed it was a plant for publicity purposes." Kevin loved the Ride and the sense of achievement and signed up for the following year's ride. He became a very keen cyclist and one year he cycled up from Italy to join the Bike Ride in Paris and he similarly joined in other years cycling from the South of France and Spain.

Another notable first-time rider was sixty-six-year-old Ernie Bateman. Ernie's first long distance ride had been as long ago as 1948 when he cycled from Portsmouth to Pontypridd. From then until 2003 he would be our oldest rider, often being a fitter cyclist than those years younger. I am not sure what his secret was but maybe the lager with which he filled one of his water bottles had something to do with it.

In 1994 Ernie won a cup for being the oldest rider. This was called the Montfort Cup, owing to the fact that it was given to us by the owner of bar in a little village called Montfort. We had had some sort of post-ride presentations every year since 1987 when I had been presented with a condom but initially the awards were purely informal for those who had made some special or at least notable contribution to the event. However, slowly we accumulated trophies, some serious and some funny. Several trophies were presented by bars possibly in appreciation of the time we lingered in them.

Dave Collins first joined the Support Team in 1994. "Somebody dropped out at the last minute, and Andy Lenaghan asked me if I could help. I wanted to do it, but it was very short notice, and I hadn't asked for any leave. However, unbeknown to my boss, I could access his diary; I therefore entered the necessary leave dates." Dave duly announced he was off on a short break. His subterfuge meant that, after his boss had initially expressed surprise and ignorance about his holiday, he was able to see it had already been entered in his diary, so the Bike Ride's support problem was solved!

Dave did a couple of years in a support van but for many years after he was a key member of the team on his motor bike. He wasn't the first motorcyclist on the Support Team, but he was certainly the most frequent. It was useful to have such a person with us as they could go quickly ahead of the ride and check for any en-route blockages and also locate lost cyclists and help get them back on the correct route. Dave brought his video camera with him, and we have a great film record of many years of our charity cycling.

The Committee had become increasingly frustrated with the fact that George kept them in the dark over many aspects of the Ride; he ran things with minimum consultation and operated at times in a bizarre way with which other organisers did not agree. Although I was at that time not taking an active part in committee meetings, I agreed to help sort this out. Various meetings and reviews were held, culminating with George's resignation. I spent a great deal of time working with others to put the administration of the Ride on a footing more suitable to an organisation which was raising far more money than we had ever envisaged when we started. We put into place a written constitution and a new committee more involved with the running of the Ride than hitherto. For a brief period, I was interim chairman but the reasons for my previous resignation still stood. Indeed, then I had been working in Luxembourg whereas now I was further away in Poland, Russia, and other parts of Eastern Europe. Paul Fisher was the obvious choice as the new Bike Ride chairman; he had done every Ride but the first one and had already been involved in the organisation in various ways. Under his chairmanship the Ride, while not losing its core values, progressed in many ways, raising much more money, and becoming more popular and far better organised. While many others contributed it wouldn't have happened without Paul. When money was paid in after the 1994 ride, we totalled £17,000, several thousand more than the previous year. From there the number of riders grew and fund raising took off exponentially so that soon we were regularly raising over £50,000 a year and attracting twice as many riders.

At the end of the year, we started a tradition which continues to this day. Back in 1994 Andy Lenaghan suggested a pre-Christmas cycle. A group duly headed out on the preceding Sunday for Gosport before returning to Hayling via the Portsmouth and Langstone harbour ferries. Andy recalls that he thought that dressing up in a Santa outfit would be in keeping with the season. Things just grew from there and when there was another ride in 1995 virtually everyone wore suitable festive clothing. Some years ago, we decided that the appropriate collective noun in this situation would be a "Merriment of Santas". The event has taken various different formats but in recent times it has involved a tour of hostelries on the Hants/West Sussex border. In some years it's been a rather damp event but more often than not it's taken place on a crispy sunny day with the countryside splendidly decked in a dazzling white frost. I once wrote an article about this popular event and I would like to think the following extract, recalling our stop at one of the en-route pubs, sums up the essence of the Santa Ride. "The fire crackled and so did the stories of last year's ride and indeed those of many summers past. Good cheer and good beer, stories I had never known, others that had come and gone as my mind struggled to cope with the countless anecdotes of our Gallic adventures. Hot and hazy July days by the Seine were so far away and yet so close! Happy faces, cheeks suitably Santa red after the morning's efforts. A rather implausible consequence of this unique cycling event."

Chapter 10
Our Tenth Anniversary Ride and Being in The Hot Seat

Paul soon made his mark in very positive way; his first ride, the tenth, was an outstanding success. Paul and fellow organisers could be justly proud of their achievements that year. Two of our regulars, Pam McLaughlin and Normand Howison, suggested taking about twenty-five riders from Hayling to Paris, making it a "two-way ride"." Apart from Pam and Normand, one or two small groups of riders had cycled the route both ways before on their own initiative, but this was the first year that we decided to officially support the concept. Paul and I both thought that the twenty-five who did this were a bit eccentric, if not plain daft, and, in any case, we found the perfect excuse not to take part in that we had to travel to Paris on the coaches with the main party to help organise "things". But in the following years an increasing number of cyclists chose to start their cycling on Hayling, including Paul and me. And indeed, soon the majority of riders would cycle both ways, some saying that cycling two ways was easier! While I hardly think that was true it certainly wasn't twice as hard, since you got into the groove and by the time you were on the last day it was relatively easy to churn out the miles. Also, you didn't have to cope with a coach journey from Hayling!

In 1995 Mike and Stella Burras entered the Ride. It was

the death of their baby that had of course led to the first ride. Since the beginning they had understandably been staunch supporters but now, as Stella said, "We had seen how much money it was raising and how enjoyable it was, so we thought we ought to do it ourselves." Stella got a bike for her birthday in April and quickly got into some serious practising. Mike, on the other hand, left it bit later. Mike recalls that not only hadn't he got a bike but also that he hadn't cycled since he was at school. "I went out and bought a £60 lump of iron from Macro, I hadn't got a clue. I didn't even know how to set the saddle up and so on the first ride out my knees were right up to my tummy; I must have looked a right prat!" He remembers his long ride from Hayling to Chichester. I got back as far as the Ship, and I had to stop; I ached all over and felt like I'd been working down the salt mines for three months. They enjoyed the Bike Ride so much that they came back again the following year with some friends. Indeed, Stella would do a number more Rides and both would return for part of the thirtieth Ride.

Sadly, that year's event was not blessed with memorable weather. I can even recall a soaked Mike Burras trying to cadge a lift in the van that he lent to the Support Team, but they weren't prepared to return the favour. The first morning was particularly wet and a very bedraggled group of cyclists reached the lunch stop at L'Auberge De St Eustace where usual hosts Stephane and Martine laid on a very agreeable and welcome buffet. However, this was nothing compared with the lunch that was to welcome us the following day.

Until that year the basic route strategy of the Ride had been to take the most direct point between A and B and if that meant some miles of nasty main "Route Nationale" roads then so be it. The "recce team" for the 1995 route were determined to seek out quality rural routes wherever possible. This was duly done and henceforth the emphasis would be on rural rides. It's the best way to cycle and to see France, since typically there are fewer fumes, better views, fewer lorries breathing down your neck and generally more time to soak up the ambience. Of course, country roads do have the downside that they are rougher and that can cause quite a lot of discomfort, particularly with respect to the back side! Also, quieter roads are often unmarked and there is more chance of going off down some irrelevant country lane and (worse) sometimes a painfully long gap between bars.

As a result of our rural plotting for the 1995 ride we selected the tiny town of Cormeilles for our second-day stop. This was a delightful settlement, the "capital" of a distinctly rural canton of the same name. Here, unbeknown to any ride member except Paul Fisher, Michel, the owner of the Bar Restaurant Le Commerce, had arranged to close off the road in the middle of town, erect a big blue marquee complete with floor boarding, tables and chairs and hire a keyboard player. To cap it all we had all the food that we could eat for forty francs (four pounds). I recall my words were "How the **** did you organise this, Fisher?". He was soon to follow this with other spectacular stops where typically for a fixed price you could eat as much as you liked and had a generous quantity of wine thrown in. We had had the odd lunch stop before and indeed the stop at L'Auberge De St Eustace had become a feature, but it was not anything like as well organised.

After Cormeilles we set out across some new picturesque and quiet route through the Pays d'Auge, a noted area of natural beauty. Its famous for its stud farms, cheeses, and apple trees, and, as result of the latter, part of the area is splendidly named the "Route du Cidre" (Cider Route). The locals here are very proud of their cider and it is generally regarded as the best in France. Indeed, like good French wines, the local apple juice has an AOC classification system. Each year we did this route we had an afternoon stop at the tiny village of Beuvron En Auge. This has regularly been voted one of the prettiest villages in France. Sitting outside the strangely named Bar De Coiffeur (hairdressers bar!), sipping a cool cider (what else?), and looking at the quaint village square with its immaculately kept half-timbered house it was not difficult to see why.

We had a last night party in Caen to celebrate the ten years. Entertainment was provided by Noddy, a performer of sorts then living on Hayling who had also taken part in the Ride. Noddy's speciality was a hot chairs routine whereby he could apparently hypnotise people to think that the ordinary chairs that they were sitting on were boiling hot! Apart from the fact that the participants were not hypnotised but rather briefed beforehand the magic was faultless! Noddy surprisingly never quite made the big time with his act.

Sadly, we returned with quite a few "wounded soldiers" that year; two of them had caught their wheels in the same railway track as Ann Borton had done. We had used several venues for our Hayling finish but in our tenth year we were lucky enough to be able to return to our spiritual home the Rose and June. The eighteenth-century barn adjacent to the main building had been refurbished and we were able to use this. We decorated the barn in a suitable way and organised prominent displays for our sponsors. A band entertained us, and a good time was had by all. Would we make it to twenty years? I don't remember the question being asked but I am sure we all saw this as a long way off.

John Adcock officially joined the Support Team in 1995 although he had been assisting the Bike Ride for some time, often helping to prepare things for the finish on Hayling while we were still in France. In some capacity he was probably involved in all the next twenty years. While there were many people who worked behind the scenes to help ensure that the event ran smoothly and could overcome various challenges John made an exceptional contribution in this respect. He was regularly supported by his late wife Vanessa. John had spent most of his career as a manager in the finance and administration departments of IBM and he certainly deployed this experience on occasions to the Bike Ride's benefit.

Chapter 11
Burt, P-Rick the Fat Fishmonger and Cherries

Obviously, we approached 1996 with some trepidation. How do you better the fun and general success of the Tenth Anniversary Ride? In fact, we successfully built on the achievements of the previous year, and I look back on 1996 as being a truly memorable year in our history. Interest remained strong, rider numbers increased, and we raised more money, £40,000 as opposed to £30,000 in the previous year.

The "experimental" two way ride of 1995 became a mainstream alternative and indeed I signed up for it myself. The route for this and some years after consisted of Caen to Evreux, Evreux to Paris (where the "one way ride would join"), Paris to Rouen and then Rouen to Caen. Day one from Caen to Evreux was pretty tough not only because it was a ninety-mile cycle ride which followed after a few hours' sleep on the ferry at best but also because it involved two rather nasty hills around mid-morning. Day two from Evreux to Paris was somewhat easier and featured some great route but the next two days were also ninety-mile-plus days, so this was quite a tough little tour! After 1996 we would stop in Evreux many times over the years. It was a nice Cathedral city to the southwest of Rouen and just over sixty miles west of Paris.

In our eleventh year we also decided to visit Jumieges on our route from Rouen to Caen. This village is situated between Duclair and Caudebec on the south side of the Seine. It is home to a famous abbey which once owned Hayling Island. There has been an abbey in Jumieges since 634 but it was rebuilt in 1067 when it was consecrated in the presence of William the Conqueror. It was once one of the most famous in Europe with many of its abbots occupying senior positions in the Catholic Church. It has fallen into decline since the French Revolution but even with its faded glory it is still a major tourist attraction. The connection with Hayling can still be seen to this day in that they share the same coat of arms. Outside the abbey we were welcomed by the mayor and townsfolk of the tiny riverside community, before signing the "Livre D'Or" (visitors' book) and receiving a bag of rather nice cherries. In return we presented Jumieges with a historical map of Hayling before crossing the Seine and continuing on our way. We had not fully thought out this part of the event, however, since the capacity of the ferry was pretty small, and it therefore took an age to get all the bikes across. And then we still had to get the vehicles over to join what, for some miles, had now become a virtually support-less ride. While we did have the odd rider or two who got lost that year it was difficult to understand how anyone could not follow the route that day, since all you had to do was follow the trail of cherry stones between Jumieges and Caen.

Those years saw the Bike Ride debut of Mark Pfaff and Rick Pearson. Mark Pfaff and I had known each other at school in Weston-Super-Mare. We had kept in touch vaguely after leaving. Mark, called Burt by some cyclists due to his resemblance to Burt Reynolds, was a rather colourful character who lived part of the year in Africa. He was rumoured to be a mercenary or even a gun runner, but the reality was a little more humdrum. He had made some good money out of one or two business deals including running and subsequently selling a very successful jeans shop in Oxford Street, as a result of this he was able to retire very early indeed.

Sometime in the early '90s Mark had taken part in a charity ride in Russia for local children. I had heard about this and got him interested in our ride. He had met Rick, who lived on the Isle of Wight, on his Russian trip and persuaded him to sign up too. Mark and Rick went on to do many Rides. Both were quite fit but whereas Rick would be nearer the front, Mark tended to trundle along at the back on a rather old and heavy mountain bike. However, that didn't stop Mark winning a prize in his first year as the most impressive newcomer. He got this less for his cycling than for the fact that when his bike broke down in an out-of-the-way place, he ran several miles (with bike!) to find ride support rather than waiting for them to find him! Rick, who had recently finished a successful army career, was a keen hasher about which more will be written later (see Chapter 20). As a hasher he had to have a hash name, and this was P-Rick and henceforth I will refer to him by this name and as far as I know more or less everyone does! P-Rick thoroughly enjoyed his cycling, I asked him a few years back what his greatest memories of the Ride were. I got an interesting reply which is set out verbatim, "2001: Me sleeping in the corridors of hotels to get away from Barry's snoring. 2005: Me and Bilbo skinny dipping at Le Havre. 2004: Me and Kev Knight being late on parade at Le Havre. 2003: Me and Dave having to be picked up by the bike catcher van in Cherbourg. Also 2003: A delightful blonde by the name of? Oh well! And the chap that ran off with the French bridesmaid rather than return to England. 2005: Me singing Hey Jude with the band at our twentieth-year celebrations." To most readers (and indeed to the author!) not all of this might make sense, but I think it conveys a sense of fun which P-Rick like many other riders have experienced on our jaunts!

1996 was not only the first year of Burt and P-Rick but also that of a memorable Hayling character, Alan Rae. Alan perhaps looked like the archetypal butcher, a stout man with ruddy cheeks. He had taken a keen interest in the Bike Ride from its early days and finally decided in 1996 to take the plunge and put his not inconsiderable frame onto a bike. Going out on practice rides with him was an interesting experience with a very high ratio of pubs to miles. Several of his customers expressed concern as to the safety of the "Burley Butcher" as some of us used to call him. I must have been talking about him to the taxi driver who regularly took me to the airport when I went away on business because one day the said driver picked up a colleague of mine from Heathrow for a meeting, I was holding on Hayling and soon he knew all about him. Something, however, got lost in translation because this colleague said to me, "I have been hearing about your bike ride and especially the fat fishmonger!"

Alan completed two Rides very competently. Indeed, the first year he won the Proof That You Can Award, given to a rider who has "performed" beyond expectations and shown that you don't have to be a really good cyclist to cycle a really long way! That's not to say that he didn't have his problems! Ian Polllicot recalls that they were following route notes which said go over the brow of the hill and then turn immediately left. Alan, however, just kept on going down the hill.

Eventually he was "rescued" by our motorbike support rider Dave Collins who informed him of the error of his pedalling. Unfortunately, to get back on the route Allan had a long climb back up the hill. Not long after he was frantically looking for a skip in which to throw his bike as he had decided that he didn't need it any more!

Alan's main cycling companion that year was Steve Munt. Steve, like Alan, and I guess so many of the Bike Ride's participants, was a "one off". He was known to some as "Munty of the Yard", the yard in question being Portsmouth Dockyard where for some years he had been a policeman. He had been involved in the Bike Ride for some years as a member of the support team before he decided to support his mate Alan by getting on a bike. On the second day out of Paris, Steve was feeling rather proud of himself as he climbed up the nasty hill on the edge of Rouen. "I am not sure why I am so good on the hills," he was heard to say. "Maybe it's the fact that I am part Cherokee Indian"." His fellow cyclists were, to say the least, a little mystified, totally failing to understand the connection between an Indian tribe from the south-eastern part of North America and the ability to cycle uphill on a steep and busy French road! Moreover, his friends were also somewhat surprised by the genealogical revelation since they were sure Steve originated from Isle of Wight stock. I don't know about you, but I have never seen any films with bicycling Indians and the concept seems a little incongruous. Can you imagine John Wayne taking aim at a peloton of "red faced savages"? Any further thoughts of the cycling expertise of an original American were soon dismissed by the fact that a couple of hundred yards down the road Steve was in serious discomfort and felt a need to get off and push. He then proceeded to flag down a support van and request that one of the medicine women bandage him up. It seemed he had lost his own Battle of Wounded Knee and at this juncture the uncomfortable Steve looked more of a Pale Face than an Indian.

Another debutant in 1996 was Hayling Islander Leigh Hunter. He had done some cycling before but nothing as extensive as the Paris to Hayling. He was to go on to do many subsequent Rides, serve on our committee and in general be a great contributor to the event. In subsequent years he was to enter with his daughter and son Shona and Josh and treasures those years as being particularly special. Leigh was a good cyclist but, I think it is fair to say, not exceptional, so I think I was not alone in being surprised when he joined up for the Race Across America in 2007. This is a rather brutal event involving three thousand and fifty-three miles from San Diego to Atlantic City which makes the Paris to Hayling look like jolly pedal down to the pub! Some people have been known to do this solo but Leigh, although containing the necessary degree of madness to do our event, was not quite that daft. Instead, like most participants, he was part of a team of four, joining up with some Portsmouth firefighters to raise a chunk of money for the local hospice.

1996 was also the year we came across a rather unusual hotel in Evreux. If ever a hotel could be said to have character it was La Biche, though there was some fierce dispute among Bike Ride regulars about whether it was good or bad character. The description on its own website later stated that it was "full of history" and, bearing in mind that it originated in the sixteenth century as a hunting lodge of Francis the First, this seemed a fair comment. The name "Biche" emphasised that, given that it is French for doe. It is also interesting to note, of course, that the establishment had had such a long tradition of catering for people in the saddle! In the nineteenth century it was a favourite stopping point for the embryonic Automobile Club De France and before the Second World War it was supposedly the best restaurant in Normandy with an impressive wine cellar. Among its famous guests was the Duchess of Windsor. In the middle of the hotel was a splendid courtyard covered with a glass roof and surrounded by a gallery off which there were bedrooms. By the décor one wondered if it might also have been a brothel at one time! On the one hand it was incredibly French, with a welcoming front bar where you expected to see Rene or Yvette from "Allo, Allo" and a very good classical French restaurant with splendidly Gallic dishes such as cassoulet and fruits de mers to fill you after a hard day in the saddle. On the other hand, it had some English aspects; the bar had a pool table and various English beer mats and cloths (courtesy of a passing bike ride). Moreover, there was a certain Fawlty Towers aspect to the place. One time one of our Support Team members was given a key to a room and having searched for some time, became convinced that was no bedroom of this number. He brought the key back to the reception and an animated discussion followed with the one of the staff insisting that there was a room with this number. It never became clear what was going on but finally another key was given out with a different room number, but it got him in the room. Also, on at least two occasions they were in such chaos at our time of departure that when we came to pay an outstanding balance, they said they would send the bill. But on both occasion some months later we had to chase them for it. But the owner was not Basil Fawlty. Alcino Alves Pires originally from Coimbra in

Portugal supported us strongly and always gave us a big welcome. One year he even rode out to our lunch time stop to cycle in with us. Alcino was also notable in another sense. In a country which is notoriously, and some might say justifiably, chauvinistic about its cuisine he was surprisingly a top official in the national association of restaurateurs despite being Portuguese. Maybe the fact that he also had a black belt in Karate had something to do with it. I liked La Biche; it was not everyone's cup of tea but nevertheless a number insisted on staying there each year, preferring it to the vapid plastic of some modern hotels.

The Sussex Brewery Team has been perhaps the Paris to Hayling's most prominent team. It originated back in 1996 when a group of friends from the Sussex Brewery pub in Emsworth decided to give the Bike Ride a go on, as was so often the case at that time, their mountain bikes. Gradually they gathered more riders, began to adopt a very smart team outfit, migrated to road bikes, and got better at cycling. They effectively formed their own cycling club and rode regularly at weekends. And in addition to joining in our escapades they staged their own annual multi-day ride which initially would focus on the Isle of Wight but then began to involve other places including France, the Channel Islands and more recently the Isle of Man.

As you would expect from a cycling team that originated in a pub, they very much enjoyed the social side of the Bike Ride and while they no longer do our main ride every year, they are still involved with the spin-offs such as the C2C, of which more will be said shortly. When I met with them a few months ago in the Sussex Brewery pub in Emsworth, Mick Ward, one of the original 1996 riders, described the Paris to

Hayling as one the biggest adventures of his life although Malcom Emery, another rider from that first year, added that I needed to remember that Mick had had a very sheltered life. Mick continued, "How else would you run through such a range of emotions in just few days, elation, laughter, frustration, fatigue, and even on occasion, intoxication." Malcom interjected, "Don't forget the foot rot." And yes, cyclists did indeed get very wet on occasions, with this, as I understand it, being a prerequisite for foot rot and, although only rarely, cold too, as the Sussex Brewery team remembered very well. But more often they and other cyclists got very hot, and I am not sure that many other Paris to Hayling participants actually got the same painful condition as Malcom which is generally found in sheep rather than people! As the team evolved and grew, they became noted for their smart team outfits courtesy of Marianne Forster, who sometimes cycled with them and was a talented dress maker. While not the only group of cyclists to do so they were quite fond of breaking out into song. So, for example, one evening while standing with their bikes waiting to get on the ferry at Portsmouth, which has almost always been a lengthy and tedious process, they suddenly broke into *Please Release Me*. And on another occasion in France when one rider mentioned to another that the corn was higher than the same time last year, they naturally delved into their Oklahoma collection and their dulcet tones singing *Oh What A Beautiful Mor*ning could be heard for some distance across Normandy in the still air of an early July morning. Given their longevity and indeed their togetherness as a team they have some great recollections of their ride experiences which will crop up from time to time in further chapters.

It was about this time that Mumfy started doing a little less cycling. Initially this meant that he would cycle a bit and then, horror upon horror, cheat by getting a lift from his mate Crocks. One time he was in the back with his bike when Crocks caught up with Paul Fisher, who also decided he would like a lift but obviously wanted it done discreetly. Mumfy hid under some covers and so Paul never knew he was there. Paul was duly dropped off a few miles down the road and was most mystified when meeting up with him soon after, that Mumfy seemed to know verbatim the conversation that he had earlier with Kevin. That year we were accompanied for our last few miles by a jazz band on the back of a lorry. This was a great way to finish, and we repeated this for several subsequent years.

We had always had a reunion party in the autumn giving riders a chance to meet up with other riders, to pay in their money and to hear of plans for the following year. And for some years we had had an annual charities evening where we would present cheques to various charities, and which gave us a chance to explain the background of how we raised funds for these worthy causes. Also, in some cases we were able to persuade their representatives to recruits riders to cycle under "their banner". But now we started including other cycling events in our regular calendar. We started a Reunion Ride which still takes place at the end of August or early September, and we were also now holding a regular Santa Ride about which I will explain more later.

Chapter 12
The Strange Case of Andy "O", Finding Muids and a Very Stressed Rod.

The Alan Rae Challenge was a bit of an odd event but fun; it took place for the first time in 1997. The initial idea came out of a conversation in The Rose and June with Alan Rae challenging Paul Fisher to see who would be the first to reach Hayling after cycling from London and pledging £100 to charity if he lost. Fred Dyer set out the route and around thirty other riders joined in the fun. The result was a foregone collusion as Paul was significantly nippier on a bike than the Burly Butcher, but Alan wanted the worthy event to continue and so put up £100 for the next year as well. Discounting the Santa and Reunion rides, which only involved short distances, this was the first additional ride organised under the Paris to Hayling umbrella, there would be others soon!

The 1997 Paris to Hayling had more than its fair share of incidents. The first item of note was the curious matter of new rider Andy "O". Andy turned up in Paris somewhat later than the rest of the group. On the overnight ferry Andy had rather overindulged at the bar, somewhat of an occupational hazard for departing Paris to Hayling riders. Eventually he had gone to bed in his cabin but then got up, partially clothed, and, according to his later narrative, he went out for a breather on deck. He came back down looking for his cabin but couldn't find it, found an empty one and overslept. By this time, the coach with the rest of the cyclists had left for Paris, his absence having somehow been overlooked. A little later Andy turned up at the ship's information desk dressed in very little plus a blanket and explained his predicament. Having fortunately been reunited with his clothes and overnight bag, which had been found in his original cabin, he got on a train to Paris and located the hotel through some guesswork! This was no mean matter when all you knew was that the hotel was a Mercure and when you dared not phone home to check the details as your partner was likely to ask you how you became separated from the rest of the group!

Not so amusing was the series of incidents that befell us on the Friday we left Paris, which would henceforth be known by the Bike Ride organisers as "Black Friday". Firstly, we awoke to discover that one of the support vans had been broken into and two bikes had been stolen. These included Paul Fisher's spare machine which had the most fiendish saddle ever invented. Obviously, I don't know who finished up with the bike, but I would not be surprised, assuming the thief to be male, if they didn't finish up singing castrati. The "knock on" effect of the break-in was that that year's Support Team leader, Rod Elliott, needed to spend four hours at the local police station in order to ensure we were covered on insurance. As Rod puts it, "There was this tiny room and four of us in it, a French copper typing with two fingers on a battered old typewriter, me, the hotel manager and some other bloke — God knows why he was there. It was ninety degrees, there was no air conditioning, no room to swing a cat and we were all smoking!" "This was clearly no way to start the day. However, no sooner were we clear of this incident than we discovered that one of the support vans was overheating. Soon after a support crew member got an urgent call to return to the UK as his daughter was seriously ill, but, fortunately, she made a full recovery.

Another incident soon followed, Rod Elliott managed to separate himself from the keys of my BMW which was being used by him as a support car. He had changed into his shorts and left them in his other trousers which had been placed in the car which had then automatically locked. Some hours later, following telephone calls to BMW's Munich headquarters, mechanics arrived with hammers and chisels and drilled into the boot of the car. That day it was the Paris to Hayling's Rodney who was a true plonker, as he would be the first to admit! Our problems were not over yet since, when we got into Rouen, we had more than our usual share of room issues and poor old Rod was working until past midnight to resolve these.

That day, alongside the issues referred to above, we also had a very memorable afternoon stop! Muids (pronounced in French as moo-eed) is a small settlement about twenty-four miles from Rouen wedged between the Seine and the Plain of St Andelys. I believe it has gathered neither fame nor infamy (well, not until we arrived) during its indeterminate period of existence. It's only feature of note is an ancient water mill which was the subject a nineteenth century painting by the then well-known American/French artist Aston Knight, but for Bike Ride regulars it was to acquire special significance. On the final twenty miles or so to Rouen from Paris, riders had in the early years left the Seine at Les Andelys and taken a straight cross-country route, only re-joining the river on reaching the city rather than following the meandering river. Although a shorter route, this involved crossing a dreary plain where the wind always seemed to be in the wrong direction and there was little shade or indeed anything of interest unless you were heavily into corn fields. However, in 1996 some riders went "off piste" and discovered Muids. They realised that riding a little further along the Seine beyond Les Andelys and turning inland at this village would be a way of avoiding much of the downside of the former route without adding the huge extra miles that would have come with sticking to the river all the way.

So, in 1997 we changed the route to incorporate a visit to Muids. Although a small village it was made to look a little larger by that fact that it's very thin and strung out for what seems like miles along the banks of the River Seine. A key attraction of this village lay right at the far end, La Chaumiere, a small bar. That first year as we planned our stop, we had duly warned the proprietor of our arrival. But he seemed to assume that as "serious" cyclists we would drink very little of his limited alcohol supplies. No doubt he thought that we would fly through the village with barely time for a small glass of water! Of course, at that time he had not seen our pedallers, only a handful of whom cycled at a speed which could be equated even remotely (and of course metaphorically) as "flying" and he certainly hadn't grasped that for most a mid-afternoon beer break was essential! The bar was an instant hit and virtually all riders stopped there with some even taking the opportunity of bathing in the Seine from "La Plage", a small section of riverbank, complete with a diving pontoon that lay across the road from the bar.

On that sunny July afternoon when we first descended on

Muids a strange collective delusion came over the Ride. We were still some miles from Rouen and yet we began to party as if we were at the end! Even those who had plotted the route seem to be caught by this mass hysteria, overlooking the reality of the remaining miles. We emptied La Chaumiere's admittedly limited beer stocks, and the proprietor agreed that he would be better prepared for the next year! In fact, inspired by our visit and following our suggestion, he installed draft beer for the first time. This must rank as the greatest cultural contribution made by The Paris to Hayling Cycle Ride — indeed, probably the only one! Henceforth we would pass through Muids every year that we cycled to Rouen.

Soon after we left Muids we had a rude awakening! We had to climb out of the Seine valley onto the exposed plain to the east of Rouen, before descending again into the city. Well, there it was! The route notes clearly stated, "A gentle climb through the trees", but this was no gentle climb, it was a bloody hill! Bad enough at any time of day but worst of all late in the afternoon after a full day in the saddle and some time at the bar. Paul Fisher always had a good command of the English language but his flowery use of same would have been more at home in *The Oxford Book Of English Verse* than in a set of route notes being used by riders, who by now had the single objective of reaching Rouen ASAP to rest their sore buttocks and get out of their sweaty cycling kit. The air was full of curses concerning Paul's parentage and worse; anyone would have thought that he actually put the hill there. In any event Paul was never allowed to write the route notes again! However, he can claim to be the author of the only piece of route note prose that anyone can remember! Even today the phrase "a gentle climb through the trees" will be instantly and amusingly recognised by many Paris to Hayling veterans.

The following day we had another tremendous lunch at Cormeilles and our traditional finish at Pegasus Bridge. This year several of our cyclists were so overcome with emotion that they decided to jump in the canal. This was not a good idea and indeed, judging by its dodgy appearance, I suspect that the last people to immerse themselves in these waters might have been the paratroopers back in 1944. Laurie Warner came off worst, as Laurie remembers, "Paul Fisher said that whatever you do, don't jump in the canal, so of course people did." As he was getting out Laurie cut himself and when back in the UK was admitted to hospital with a tetanus infection. He was on a drip to try and clear his system but as he delicately related, "It wasn't working, my arm was blown up with a huge amount of pus!" Fortunately, other measures were taken, and Laurie was sorted but clearly that could have turned out very badly indeed! The return from Pegasus Bridge to the hotels was not without incident either as Fred Dyer managed to collide with a local French cyclist. Fred recalls it as follows, "There were nine of us cycling in formation, eight in pairs with myself at the back. The oncoming cyclist was on a heavy tradesman's bike and headed straight at the group expecting them to part, which indeed they initially did, but I couldn't very well split myself in two! By the time I saw him it was too late, and we collided." I arrived on the scene soon afterwards to see a stunned Fred sitting on the canal bank with a distinctly bent wheel in his hands. Eventually, with some reluctance, chief nurse and wife, Judy Dyer and Steve Munt came out to attend to Fred, Steve having now switched from his role as Cherokee cyclist to that of wagon train driver. Fortunately, Fred was really none the worse for wear, although his bike certainly was. Judy was superficially very stern with him as he was still in her bad books from having overindulged somewhat the previous day. He and battered bike were bundled in the back of the support van with few words exchanged. Fred remembers, "Judy appeared to be very pissed off but when she got back in the front of the van with Steve, and thinking I couldn't hear, she started to giggle."

All the strain of the last few days was beginning to take its toll on our now hyper-stressed Rod Elliot. I remember him frantically trying to call people out of the canal. The following day he was nearly tipped over the edge by an incident on the return ferry. There was a misunderstanding over our group's breakfast arrangements which we were trying to resolve with a French purser who, to put it mildly, did not seem to be a confirmed anglophile and was oblivious to the large group of hungry cyclists looking desperately for a good solid breakfast. At that point, a rider who had given us no end of grief over the last two days grabbed Rod's arm. I can recall her whining words as if it was yesterday, "Rod, I want my breakfast!" The timing was not good, and she got a full two barrels' worth as Rod tried simultaneously to deal with her and Monsieur Jobsworth.

The stress of this year's ride wasn't over yet. We arrived back on Hayling and made our traditional muster at the Ferry Boat Inn with the support vehicles driving round from Portsmouth to meet us. It was a hot Sunday and there were a lot of customers at the pub and lots of people launching boats and jet skis on the slipway. As a result, we were soon approached by a harbour official, who, remonstrating with us in terms which I can only describe as unsympathetic, told us to move on. The problem was that the crowds and noise were such that only part of our group got news of this, so a good, few cyclists were already down the road before others, realising what was happening, hopped on their bikes to catch up. The result of this was that the air was blue with accusations and counter accusations concerning our sudden and rather undignified departure. While all this was going on, we came across local photographer (and past rider) Malcolm Harris perched at the top of a lamp post or something similar. He then proceeded to take a fantastic photo of the Paris to Hayling cyclists and indeed it is my favourite Bike Ride picture. Everything looks as calm as a group of cyclists proceed majestically along the Ferry Road! In reality it was total chaos! We had one of the best finishes that year courtesy of the Maypole pub with over six hundred people welcoming us home on a glorious Sunday afternoon. It was not only great for us but also for the capable landlord and landlady Jeff and Lin Parsons who I understood put the takings towards a holiday in Mexico. Lin had done the Ride herself and would become a regular rider for some years. Reflecting on Jeff and Lin's success that year it's nice to think that as a bi-product of our charitable efforts we have helped local businesses. Indeed, primarily through bikes equipment, travel, and booze (probably in the reverse order), we reckon we have put several million pounds into the Hampshire economy.

We initiated a new trophy that year, The McQuade Cup given by my father in memory of my mother. This replaced The Bavent Trophy and was awarded to the most impressive newcomer. The Bavent Trophy had unfortunately been seized by bailiffs in a pub in Weston-Super-Mare, following the bankruptcy of the landlord. The trophy was on display at the pub on behalf of Mark Pfaff, the 1996 winner who had gathered a lot of his sponsorship there.

Just as I had encouraged people from IBM to join when I worked there, now I was at Oracle and did likewise; some rode and some joined the Support Team. Vincent De Lattre, a Swiss national living in Portugal but working for me in Africa (yes, confusing, isn't it!), and Brandon McDonald from Zimbabwe made a great coupling in this respect. Brandon did an impressive job a couple of times in impromptu traffic controlling. He then revealed that he had honed these skills in earlier years as a traffic cop in Zimbabwe. A couple of years later Brandon was able to do me a little favour. At our annual charities evening we had arranged with some local notable to present the cheques, but they had had to cancel. Brandon was visiting the UK on business, and I had invited him to attend. We managed to convince people that Brandon was the Zimbabwean cultural attaché and we had him present the cheques in this capacity. Several people were very impressed with my good diplomatic connections. Mind you, this was in the mid '90s when there was nothing sinister about the relatively successful African country of Zimbabwe. Today, sadly, anyone who tried to pass themselves as anything to do with the dreadful government of the most beautiful country that I have ever visited would, I guess, run the risk of being lynched. I am pleased to say that Brandon got out of Zimbabwe successfully and is happily settled with his family in the picturesque South African town of George.

John O, an American who worked for me, also rode in 1997. He couldn't handle the lack of air conditioning in some of the hotels, the shortage of iced water in the support vans and the fact that few of the wayside cafés took American Express! He was a lovely guy but a gift to those looking for a Star-

Spangled Caricature, someone who despite some years of living in Europe was truly an "innocent abroad". He once had a fierce argument with a couple of his colleagues claiming that Vietnam was a moral victory for the US — interesting! I would love to know his take on George Bush or Donald Trump.

Jon Tawse joined in 1997. "I took it very seriously that first year and was one of the first to finish. But then I realized that those behind me were coming in with smiling faces and generally in a pretty happy state, so I knew I was missing out on something." He changed tactics when he came back the next time and fully embraced the bar stops and would continue to do so. John would do many more Rides and serve on the committee for a number of years and have two spells as chairman.

It transpired that that year we had raised £50,000, which was the first time any of our Rides had achieved that milestone. Local businessman Robin Sutherland had raised £2,500. This was very impressive, particularly since he had also raised a huge amount the previous year, but incredibly another rider, Roz Webb, smashed the fundraising record by collecting £3,854 for the Lisa Thaxter Memorial Trust, a charity which helped children and adolescents with cancer. It was to be some years before this record was broken. Poor Rod, he had worked his socks off on the Ride and in the weeks preceding. A few weeks later, to fully address his shattered nerves, Rod decided to walk part of the South Downs Way. He recalls it as bliss! There was not a single demanding Paris to Hayling cyclist in sight!

Chapter 13
Wind, Rain, Punctures, An Apple Tree and The Finish That Went Wrong

1998 was the year that Mumfy abandoned all ambitions to be a cyclist, retired his bike and became an official Support Team member, joining his mate Crocks to make a popular combination. But anyone who thought that was the start of a more responsible episode in his "Bike Ride Career" would be mistaken. Initially he used to carry a few masks, and this was the beginning of a fancy-dress tradition, that's now perpetrated by various cyclists and Support Team members, particularly on the last day. But nobody did it like Mumfy. Sometime in the late 1990s he started to bring his 1930s police uniform. This was not a case of the long arm of the law but rather, as some Bike Ride wit put it, the short arse of the law given Mumfy's limited height.

One time he was standing by the side of the road merrily waving traffic on when, to his surprise, more or less all of it was returning a few minutes later. The bewildered drivers were asking him questions he did not understand before they then drove off in the other direction before returning yet again! This continued for some time before he realised the problem. He was standing by a T-Junction directly in front of sign to a wedding which all these confused travellers were desperately trying to find! Another time when a French youth appeared round the corner of the road doing a wheelie, Mumfy did what any safety minded copper should do and stepped out in the middle of the road to tell him off. Then people emerged from the two cars following and they became very agitated; apparently, they were the youth's support cars as he was trying to break some record for a long-distance wheelie. Sadly, thanks to PC Mumford of Her Majesty's Constabulary (Normandy Division), these plans were scuppered. On another occasion he asked motorists for their documents informing them that this part of France had been taken over by the British. When Mumfy disappeared to France for an extended break some years back it was assumed that the French authorities had caught up with Paul and put him where he belongs, perhaps even shipping him out to Devil's Island. The reality was that he was down in the Cote d'Azure enjoying retirement. Despite the fact that he was annually on the verge of causing a major diplomatic incident, he remained a free man!

The 1998 Ride was described at the time as a great ride for those who liked wind rain and punctures. I couldn't argue with that! Doing the two-way, four-day event, I had a gentle laid-back ride from Caen to Evreux in the company of Paul Fisher and others. However, when I had just reached the outskirts of Evreux something seemed to "go" in my knee. I just about made it to my hotel but when our nurse Judy Dyer came to strap my knee her advice was firm — don't ride tomorrow. Imagining how little sympathy I would get if I even tried to ignore her, I made plans to join the Support Team for at least a day. The following morning as I peered out from behind the curtains, I saw that angry clouds were spread all over Normandy tipping out rain with a real intensity. I must confess to feeling a trifle relieved! The route that day would take the Ride through some minor and very gritty roads. In this weather we were sure to have problems as the grit sticks to tyres and causes punctures. Sure enough, from my cosy position in Mumfy's support vehicle, I witnessed "cycle carnage" as the riders had a succession of punctures. Indeed, in one particularly wretched part of the route we turned the corner to see the road totally blocked by drenched cyclists attending to burst tubes. From then on, this stretch of route was referred to in Bike Ride circles as "Puncture Valley". The worst of the rain was over at the end of that day but the after effect was felt throughout the next day as collected grit worked its way into the tyres. It was estimated that in total we had a hundred punctures that year, easily a record.

We were joined in Paris by the "one way" riders who had their bikes transported by van while they arrived by coach. Arriving in Caen on the same ferry was Tony Hart and his friend Bill Wyvill. They achieved a Bike Ride first in that they had declined to travel to Paris by coach but had rather opted for the more athletic alternative of cycling all the way from the English Channel in one day. No mean feat at the best of times but much tougher in the prevailing wet weather. We toasted their arrival in Paris with Champagne but then matters were complicated by the fact that Bill hadn't had an alcoholic drink for weeks before this effort as part of his training and therefore was soon rather overwhelmed by the celebrations. The predictable consequence was that he fell asleep in the restaurant before yours truly and a couple of others hauled his frame over the Pont De Neuilly and back to the hotel where a very understanding Jim Walton, local Hayling GP and Paris to Hayling cyclist, checked him out. Joining us in Paris via Eurostar was local MP David Willetts, straight from Parliamentary business. He had expressed a desire to do the Bike Ride for some years but until now he had not managed to fit it in his schedule.

The following day there was some confusion as we left Paris. The ride was split in three with leaders for each section. Pete Alloway was chosen to lead the first group out. While his immense contribution to the Bike Ride could never be doubted it was in hindsight a strange choice to place the sometimes directionally challenged Pete in such a role. In any event, as I was riding out with the second group, we spotted Pete and his party on a fly over above us merrily cycling in the wrong direction back towards the centre of Paris!

Our reputation in Muids had obviously spread as our visit there got press coverage that year, which was arranged by Serge Hiard, the owner of our bar stop. The article in the local paper was entitled “Une Chaumiere and Des Coeurs”. It tells the brief story of the Bike Ride finishing with an expression of hope that we would return in future years. The following day on the Rouen to Caen route we had an interesting meeting in Cormeilles. We were greeted by cyclists from Hayling’s twin town of Gorron, sixty kilometres to the south. This then led to a three-way civic ceremony involving David Willets, our local MP, the mayor of Cormeilles, M. Jean Drummer and the mayor of Gorron M Jean-Marc Allain. Various gifts were exchanged, and a cider apple tree was presented to us by a Calvados distillery together with complimentary bottles of Calvados. David Willets proved himself to be a competent cyclist; indeed, cycling between Paris and Caen he was making good enough time to take in Monet's gardens at Giverny. However, that did cause a minor panic since for a time nobody realised that he had deliberately gone "off route". Given this fact there was a concern that we might have lost a senior politician! But all was sorted before support felt the need to contact the UK embassy. I had wondered whether this might be the start of a flood of Parliamentarians. Dennis Skinner, for example, then listed cycling as a hobby (though I could not really have seen him and David as roommates!). Possibly Boris Johnson, a new but already high-profile MP, might have been a more likely candidate. But sadly, neither he nor any others came forward and David remains our sole Westminster representative.

This was probably the year that there was some serious refreshment competition among the support vans. Maryon McQuade recalls it like this, "I was sharing a support vehicle with my friend Georgie, and we decided to get some sweets for ourselves. When some of the cyclists saw them and asked if they could have one, they soon went. I guess it was the sugar that they were craving." So, they got some more sweets and made themselves very popular. Until that time the Support Team had carried water, squash, bananas and generally energy powder and glucose tablets but that was the limit of their vittles. Other support vehicles cottoned and started supplying their own, and soon as well as sweets there were flapjacks and also peanuts and crisps for the salt. And within a couple of years, it was standard for us to stock all the support vehicles with such items. In subsequent years it went even further with these things being set out on tables by the side of the road accompanied by bunting and signs in the style of a pop-up café.

Jeff Lane first made an appearance in 1998; in an event

which has been blest with colourful characters, Jeff was one of the most notable! Today he is a successful psychotherapist and part time comedian. Back then he was working in a Portsmouth market as a demonstrator. "It was my job to talk about household goods that needed to be talked about." I suggested to him that made him a sort of Pompey Dell Boy and then added, "Oh, sorry, Jeff, I wasn't suggesting you did any fly pitching."

"Well," he responded, "I did do a bit of that, and I have certainly been called a lot worse." It was a friend of his at the market, Mike Jones, who suggested that he do the Ride. "It was the year I turned forty, and my friends thought I would celebrate with a party and a massive piss up! But I thought it was time for a bit of a stock take on life and decided to do something different. I had heard about the Paris to Hayling, and Mike suggested that I give it a go. I wasn't immediately convinced, particularly since I had a lifelong hatred of all things sporty. This seemed a potential fiasco with nearly two hundred miles of cycling over two days, but Mike said that it was straight forward — you started in Paris and headed for the coast which meant that it was all downhill. My geography isn't that good, but I felt that there was some logic in this. The idea of cycling from the height of Paris down to the sea began to feel a little more appealing."

"Jeff did a couple of practice rides and they worked out okay. He figured that if he could cycle thirty or so miles of these rides then when in France all he needed to do was to string a few of these together with breaks and he would have no problem. So, he signed up for the Paris to Hayling Ride."

"But oh boy, was I in for a rude awakening. It was tough; I got within a few miles of Pegasus Bridge and had to stop. I bought a huge peach from the roadside, and I eventually managed to get back on the bike. As I crossed the bridge and stopped at the café, I was tempted to throw my bike in the canal." Jeff never wanted to ride again! "But after some of the magic liquid that they sell at that café I was feeling quite a lot better. I was aching somewhat, but I was beginning to think that I would perhaps give it another go. However, as I thought about this more the following morning on the ferry back, I thought that if I were to do it again, I should take the training more seriously and then call it a day."

Jeff did return in 1999 and indeed for more summers more before he finally called it a day. Jeff reappears later in my tale!

There was bit of an incident on the last morning in Caen as several of our number had spent the whole of the last night in the bar. In fact, as Pete Alloway recalls, they were in the bar so long that when one keen and particularly prompt riser came down for breakfast, he complimented them on the fact they were up so early! Well, several of the late-night cyclists needed to get their bags out of one of the rooms but they had lost the only key they were given. The hotel receptionist said that there was no pass key, and the only other key was with the manager who was not on the premises. We explained that the boat sailed in fifteen minutes and that we had to be on it. The "Gallic Shrug" of the receptionist showed that she was in no mood to help. Rod Elliott recalls it as follows, "While I was still arguing with the receptionist, one of the riders said that he thought he could get into the room. He disappeared and then there was an almighty thud. He and the girls soon reappeared with the bags which had been grabbed after the door had been evidently forced. We all made a hasty exit from the hotel!" The rider in question was a Metropolitan Police Officer and he clearly knew something about breaking and entering.

No matter how well things are prepared, they can of course still go wrong. We felt this acutely at the finish that year. We had carefully warned the newly arrived landlord of the Maypole about the size of the event on more than one occasion but there were nowhere near enough staff and people were queuing for twenty minutes to get a drink. And then, amid the chaos, even worse news; we couldn't present the various ride trophies because prior to departure we had given them to the landlord who had then stored them in a cabinet to which the key had gone missing. We eventually sorted this out but not before the committee's stress levels has risen sky high. The gentleman in question has long since departed from The Maypole so it's in no way a reflection on the current management of this well run and popular Island pub.

Sue Wilson came for the first time in 1998. "I had been egged on by my sister Carol Bailey and her husband Bill." Carol had already completed the Ride, as had her husband Bill on several occasions. Carol was now a member of the Support Team as she would be for many years. Sue thought it was a mad thing to do and couldn't see that it could possibly be fun, thinking it would be far more sensible just to give money to a charity. However, matters were rather taken out of her hands when in March her daughter Esther paid her deposit for the event as a birthday present. So, Sue duly came along with Esther. When I asked Sue what she remembered about that first year she was reasonably clear. "I was terrified! And it was two long days!" She told me that the last twenty miles to the official finish at Pegasus Bridge were the hardest. I expressed my surprise given that apart from a short sharp sod of a hill that appeared out of nowhere there were no hills on that part of the route. "It didn't matter," Sue replied. "By that time, every molehill was like a real hill, and it was only the encouragement of Rick Hutchings that got me through it. Mind you, it didn't help that I didn't know much about cycling at that time. I borrowed my sister's Peugeot bike which had gears on the frame, and I didn't really know what to do with them. I only had spoons for tire leavers, and it wasn't until Day Two when someone asked if I had my helmet on back to front, that I realised I had been cycling like that since March when I bought it." After that year Sue had got a tremendous sense of achievement and, as for the pain, "It's a bit like childbirth really, you forget the pain and only remember the good bits!" And so, Sue came back the following year and indeed every year since, either as rider or as a member of the Support Team.

Apart from myself nobody else has been involved in all these events. Sue was part of an interesting chain reaction. Bill Bailey was the first to take part and then got Carol involved. Carol got Sue and Esther signed up. Esther roped her husband Andrew Lennard in. Andrew persuaded his brother Will Lennard. In time Will got his wife to do it and then all three of their sons! Quite a family event! But the special part of Sue's involvement comes when she meets a bloke! And there will be more about that in a later chapter! We hadn't expected members of the Support Team to raise money for charity. It was enough that they were giving their time voluntarily and even paying for their trip, which is probably unique among charity rides of this sort. However, that year Phil "The Bill" Baker for himself sponsored to the tune of £375 for the benefit of a young Portsmouth child with multiple handicaps. Phil first became connected with the Ride as the Police motorcycle rider (hence the nickname) who would escort us on our trip across

Portsmouth before joining us for several Paris to Hayling Rides. Indeed, he also joined us for one memorable recce when one evening he fell over in a flower bed, presumably due to drinking too much of the local water, and was, as Rod Elliot recalls, very difficult to dislodge.

Chapter 14
Jeff Gets Hooked

The millennium drew to a close with the fourteenth Bike Ride. In recent years we had been a little annoyed by the scarce coverage that we had received from The News, the local Portsmouth evening paper. Despite the interesting story behind its evolution, and notwithstanding the fact that we were now arguably southeast Hampshire's major fund-raising organisation, we rarely got a mention. I called the editor about this and to his and The News' great credit he more than redressed the balance. He assigned experienced reporter Simon Toft to ride with us. Simon wrote a series of articles before the Ride and then joined, recording his thoughts for posterity in The News. In all we had seven articles in The News that summer. Simon's diary made good reading, accurately conveying the experience of a first-time cyclist, the fears, trepidation, and the discovery of some beautiful countryside and the euphoria of completing a tough but achievable challenge.

One of the articles that Simon wrote was about Reg Beacher. Reg had a bike shop in Fishbourne, a small village on the outskirts of Chichester. The locality is famous for its Roman ruins and by the looks of some of the bikes in the yard attached to the shop, they could have been there long enough to have been used by centurions. There were old contraptions of every shape and size plus a parrot. Reg was a bit of an eccentric but as far as I can remember there was nothing whacky about the parrot; he didn't cycle he just perched and occasionally swore at customers. This bike shop was no Halfords or Evans, it was a Beacher stamped with the whimsical style of Reg and his wife Paula. They both knew their stuff and, whilst the said yard looked like a cross between the location for The Antiques Road Show and Bargain Hunt, within the shop there was a range of great bikes and accessories. I was pleased to buy several bikes there and so did many other riders.

Reg was a real bike enthusiast and although an erudite bloke with a broad general knowledge, cycling was clearly a passion about which he could talk for hours, and it wasn't just the bikes but also the accessories. I recall one Paris to Hayling regular telling me of the time that he called in to buy a seat post. Although quite an experienced cyclist, he thought a seat post was indeed just a seat post, just a metal tube that you fixed a seat on. Reg, however, gave him quite an education on the pros and cons of the variety that he had for sale. "Blimey, I was only planning to stop for five minutes, but I was there for a lot longer than that." From now on he saw seat posts in a completely new light!

Reg had first entered the Bike Ride in 1997 and was to do several other events but in 1999 he entered on an antique three-wheeler. His Higgins trike dated back to the 1940s and he had restored it to its former glory, but it didn't have the comforts of a modern racing bike. The leather saddle was far from user friendly and with three wheels there were more vibrations when he hit the potholes. It was a bit slow and tricky round corners and indeed on one occasion the bike managed a corner, but Reg didn't, finishing up in an adjacent hedge. Consequently, for a time thereafter he was known in some circles as Reg the Hedge rather than Reg Beacher. He would serve on the Bike Ride committee for a number of years and do a number of our other rides. He regularly supplied the Bike Ride with sale or return bike parts and has generously given riders the benefit of his vast knowledge. Moreover, while we have had two- and three-people-tandems and recumbents as well as a variety of more conventional road and mountain bikes, Reg remains the only person to have entered on a trike.

We had struggled to find anywhere big enough to take our group at lunchtime for the two-way rides on the first day from Caen to Evreux but that year we came across Le Joyeux Normand. Le Patron, as I recall, rarely smiled and he wasn't from Normandy, so the name was a bit confusing although his wife was a bit jollier, and I believe a local. But what was important was that they had a splendid bar and restaurant which could fit a very large number of cyclists, they were to host us for a number of years. For a modest sum they would serve up a splendid and unlimited buffet with wine. Perhaps the one drawback was that it was over sixty miles into the route, so we were generally pretty hungry by the time we reached it. But having less miles to do in the afternoon was probably best given the gastronomic experience we went through there. It was in the middle of nowhere, surrounded by acres of cornfields with an undertaker's next door. Of course, that was pure chance but given the exhausted state of many of our riders when they arrived it could have proved useful and, in any case, might well have enhanced our reputation for detailed planning.

Lynne Harris was pedalling away in an adventurous ride

in India when a fellow cyclist Rosemary Crane suggested she should join her on the Paris to Hayling which she had already done previously. "I lived in Farnham at the time and had never heard of it." She persuaded her twin sister Pauline to join her. While Lynne had the India cycling experience behind her Pauline was more of a novice. "My sister dragged me into it. When I looked at the details I said, '"I can't do this. The first day is a hundred miles!' I did really struggle and the second day I suggested to Lynne that she carry on with Rosemary as there were plenty of other people around. On the last day I went seriously wrong and went up a hill that I then realised I didn't need to climb! As I sat on the side of the road I cried and swore I would never do this again. When I came down the hill, I met another cyclist who invited me to ride along with him. He suffered from Crohn's disease but was determined to complete the Ride and was an inspiration. I thought, what on earth am I complaining about, and sorted myself out and pressed on to the finish. When at the end I crossed the finishing line the roars and cheers changed everything, and I knew I wanted to do it again the following year." Pauline would indeed cycle many more times, as would Lynne, who also served on the committee and became involved in our event in various other ways. A few years later when she joined in one of our "recces", Lynne recalls, "Like most cyclists probably, I hadn't really thought much about what goes on behind the scenes. To be honest, seeing the people who went on these, none of whom were exactly teetotallers, I thought it was a bit of a "piss up!" To be fair to Lynne and her initial assumption, there have been occasions which support this position, such as the confusion over the beginning of the route in 1988, Phil the Bill tumbling into a flower bed and a couple stories yet to be told. But in general, as Lynne found out, things were a bit different. “I was amazed at how hard people worked, the focus on details and the challenges of linking routes, lunch stops and hotels.” She was astonished with the attention the route planners, principally Fred, put into recording the route in detail to minimise the chances of a cyclist getting lost. Mike Jones, who had persuaded Jeff Lane to do the Ride the previous year, likewise persuaded Simon West to enter in 1999. “For a long time, it will probably be the best thing I have ever done. My knees were gone, I thought I was going to need replacements, I was drinking like a fish — well, I am still drinking like a fish — but starting cycling somehow got my knees working again and I met all these great people“.” Simon had recently suffered some personal tragedies but reflecting on the Paris to Hayling, he said, “It changed my life! I was completely adrift, and the Ride gave me direction.” Simon would go on to do a number of our Rides. His affirmation of how he values the experience is shared by many and underlines how this really is more than a standard charity cycle ride.

Jeff Lane came back, as he vowed he would, and took the training more seriously, putting in one thousand five hundred miles of practice rather than the hundred and fifty of the previous year. “As a result, I was in a different league.” Jeff would indeed go on to be quite a proficient cyclist. As he crossed the English Channel to return home he and Simon chatted. They agreed that something special had happened on that ride and that they were both into this event long term. As Jeff recalls, “It was the first time I felt I was part of something other than work, business, or that sort of thing. I was part of a group of people with whom I would otherwise have had no connection, with whom, in other circumstances, I may have had nothing in common or indeed I might not even have liked. But we were all now part of this collection. It was the nearest

I had come to being a member of a very large family. It was not about us all getting on, it was not about thinking how wonderful we all were and not even about sharing values. It was all about being in this together and being prepared to help each other through this regardless of what it took. And that was what made it so special for me. It was the bonding thing, just like large families were supposed to be."

Jeff would go on to do a further eleven Rides. He looks back on the Bike Ride as one of the most significant things he has done and one of the better decisions he has made in his life. "This is partly because, of my immediate circle of close friends, the majority are either people I met on the Bike Ride or people I met through them. And also doing the Bike Ride has made me realize that I could do things I didn't think were possible. When it hurts you just dig a bit deeper and there is always something else there. No matter how tired and pissed you are feeling you can always go on. When I first started to do the Ride, I used to wonder what happened when it rained, well now I know. If it rains you get all wet and then you get all dry, nobody dies, so in other words no matter how bad things are they will normally get better. "That clearly is something which has value way beyond a bike ride." I wasn't surprised to hear that Jeff wrote the essay required for his psychotherapist accreditation on the Bike Ride and what he had learned from it.

We had more riders (one hundred and eight-six) and raised more money than ever before. It was a hot year, especially the day from Paris to Rouen. Indeed, we had one case of sun stroke, though bizarrely it was a rider from Zimbabwe, a mate of Brandon's. The ride was generally free of incidents until the last day in France. I think this may have somewhat disappointed Simon Toft, but he needn't have worried because he became the incident of that year's ride! Just before lunch on the last day in France he crashed when the peloton in which he was cycling came to a sudden halt. Although not a small guy, he was tossed like a rag doll into the sky before hitting the ground. Fortunately, he was wearing a helmet and, although suffering damage to his wrist, was able to continue. If he was still feeling worse for wear maybe he took comfort in the fact that he won the Cute Butt of the Ride award the following day.

Following on from John O in 1997, we had another entrant from the USA in 1999. Dave Collins was involved with the twinning between Portsmouth and Lakewood, a suburb of Denver, and as a result of this he persuaded a keen cyclist from that community to fly over and do our ride, namely Matt Armbruster who rode a recumbent bike. This, as far as I can recall, is the only time we have had such a machine on our ride. Matt came back again a few years later with some friends on a conventional bike. But Matt clearly had a passion for alternative cycling since he quit his job as a rocket scientist and set up High Roller USA, a Denver based company which makes adult versions of children's trikes, with the pedals attached to the front wheel! So far, he hasn't asked to enter on one of these! Maybe he thinks we are too mature to let someone enter on such a childish contraption — think again, Matt!

Pete Alloway brought a group of cyclists up from Spain to join us in Evreux. "Pedro's Pedalers" were to prove to be the first of several groups who started their ride in the south of France/Spain/Italy before joining us later. The Pedalers had cycled a thousand miles through blistering heat and over some steep terrain. I would've love to have joined them but could not spare the extra time, so I bade them farewell as they left Hayling. Pete was gaining a reputation for sometimes getting lost so as a precaution I gave him a map of Portugal explaining that it was in case they accidentally turned right instead of left when they arrived in Santander. They didn't do that, fortunately, but they did have quite a few challenges and adventures. The first problem was almost immediate; they were planning to book hotels a day at a time depending on the mileage likely to be covered and to that end, in these pre Booking.com times, had a Michelin hotel guide with them, but this was for France only! It didn't help them on the first night which was in Spain! But in any event, they had some great adventures, understandably got lost a couple of times and indeed so much that on one very hot day they had to cycle seventy miles after 4:00 pm!

We have had some good finishes and some not so good as in 1998. The 1999 one, however, was superb and certainly made up for the cock up the previous year. Nick May, the landlord of the Lifeboat Pub, had organised things superbly. Here a crowd estimated at over a thousand awaited our arrival following a procession through the Island, led by a jazz band on a lorry. At the pub there was a pig-roast and the supporters and riders continued to be entertained by the jazz band.

We had had autumn reunion rides before but in 1999 we planned a particularly successful one to the Royal Oak at Hooks Way, near Chilgrove, north of Chichester. This was a delightful spot nestling in the South Downs at the bottom of a very steep descent. The landlord of the pub used to work at the pubs on Hayling so knew all about the Ride and was delighted to welcome dozens of thirsty cyclists. Suitably refreshed, the riders left the pub to cycle up the hill and back to Hayling, a round trip of about thirty-eight miles. We kept this particular venue in place for some years.

Chapter 15
Back to School on The Millennium Ride

As Millennium Fever gripped the nation, and indeed the world, it was taken as read that we would do something special for 2000. And in what was surely our most ambitious event to date, we took a record group of two hundred and fifteen in that year. We planned no less than three rides. This was done with the best of intentions but as we set about planning this triple assault on Normandy, I don't think I was alone in getting just a bit confused with the inherent complications that it entailed. I suggest you read the following carefully!

There was to be a one way "two-day" and two way "four-day" event as in previous years but also a "five-day" ride which would involve an excursion to Gorron, Hayling's twin town. Lying seventy miles south-west of Caen, Gorron wasn't exactly en-route to Paris, and therefore there was some debate about the practicality of this visit. However, Paul Fisher, an active twinning association member, very much wanted to do this and the rest of the committee were eventually happy to fall into line. Further it was strongly supported by former rider and committee member Ian Pollicot who, with his wife Averil, had done a fantastic job in establishing the twinning association as part of Hayling life. As I recall it, about forty of the total two thousand riding group opted for the "five-day" via Gorron.

Unfortunately, it will not go down as the most comfortable days in our history. The biggest factor in this was the weather. It was atrocious! Cycling from Caen to Gorron through the distinctly hilly Suisse Normande region would have been tough enough without the excessive precipitation and wind. But this was made worse by the fact that the plans for accommodating the cyclists in Gorron went awry at the last minute. The group was booked in a local hotel which then informed us that it was double booked. Unfortunately, the improvised Plan B which involved accommodation in a local school was not that good!

Jean Simpson of The Sussex Brewery Team wrote notes after the Ride, and I think her recollections reflected the experience felt by most. "Torrential rain and wind made cycling difficult and, especially when we started to lose body heat, feet and hands suffered, not to mention my mascara and nail varnish." Jean also notes, "Arrived in Gorron to a reception in the main square and a few drinks in the Bar Des Sports. Nicely relaxed and warm only to be told that we had another five miles to cycle to a school in nearby Levare which was to be our accommodation for the night. It was very windy by this stage and uphill all the way. A bad time for me. The school (more like an institution) was a nightmare with mattresses on the floor and few showers. We had to queue for blankets and there were no sheets. A serious sense of humour failure here. However, the promises of food back in Gorron spurred us on. At 8pm the bus was due to arrive to take into town. At 8:30 it turned up. At 9:30 we were still waiting for food in the only restaurant interested in serving. Much wine was consumed then and back in the bus to the institution. Slept fully clothed (it was freezing) — sheer exhaustion!"

The following day this rather dispirited group had a hundred- and eight-mile ride to Verneuil — sur-Avre. As Jean recalls, “We had been warned that would be the most gruelling day and they weren’t wrong!” This was indeed the longest day ever in the history of our ride and the nasty climb at forty-eight miles was probably the toughest that had ever featured! The following morning Jean made several notes about her cycle team members. One came into the breakfast room looking like death and another announced that he had been ill during the night, so ill indeed that he would be riding with a spare pair of shorts and a toilet roll. Fortunately, Imodium was swiftly dispensed and as far as I am aware there were no adverse outcomes! Additionally, another of the Sussex Brewery Team indulged in a piece of accidental vandalism in the hotel. The lights at breakfast kept on fusing and eventually it became clear that this was coinciding with each time that Malcom Emery (he of the foot rot) turned on the gas boiler. This was then taken away and eggs were off the menu! Later that day the Gorron group met up with the “four-day riders” and all pressed on to Paris, meeting up with the two-day riders as they arrived in the French Capital by coach.

Liz Marsden had first done the Ride in 1994 with her husband Dave. In 1998 she had entered again with some friends. They didn’t do that much practice but were surprised how comfortable they found it so decided that they would do it again, though not until 2000. Carolyn Wager had also entered for the first time in 1998, although she had found it hard and had struggled on those last few miles to Pegasus Bridge. Carolyn joined them in 2000, as did other ladies so they were quite a large team. I don’t think they had a name for themselves but by the end of that year’s ride they would have one (see below!). The group met Sylvie Hemmings just before leaving for France. Sylvie, who was at that time living in Reading, had been encouraged to take part in the Ride by a friend of hers who had done it themselves. Unfortunately, the friend dropped out and poor Sylvie turned up at the start not knowing anyone. But thanks to Liz and team that all changed and pedalling through France together resulted in her forming some firm friendships. Indeed, within a couple of years Sylvie had decided to move to Hayling, closer to her new cycling companions.

I remember Liz saying once that she thought that the Paris to Hayling was the greatest social club in the world. I would like to think she was right, although I do recall that her comment might have been fuelled by some not inconsiderable festive lubrication. But if she was correct then what she might not have grasped was that she and her friends had demonstrated this fact in the simplest but most practical way. For Sylvie, the Ride was indeed life changing but the impact of that first ride didn't stop there. She, like her new friends, would do many more Paris to Hayling's but, most important of all, later on she would meet her new husband Martin Field, a member of the Sussex Brewery Team.

In 2000 Pascal Pichon joined us. Pascal was a colleague of Podge at Vodafone. He wasn't the first Frenchman on the Ride, but he was certainly the first to make a real impact. Podge had been walking around Vodafone offices trying to collect sponsorship. Pascal said jokingly that he thought this would be easy. Podge then challenged him to join and so he did! I know he won't mind me saying that he is quite large for a cyclist! But his heart and commitment to our event diminished his physical size and he brought so much to the event over many years. He was a committee member for a long time and was invaluable both as a web master and in liaising with various people in France when Paul Fisher's or my' reasonable but far from fluent French was not enough. Whenever there was as a serious issue en-route which required serious French expertise he would selflessly take over and rescue things. He was a qualified pilot and on one occasion flew Paul Fisher out to France on a bike recce and, in another year when for some reason he couldn't take part, he flew over the returning peloton to take photographs. Unfortunately, the latter jape brought him a reprimand for low flying!

Like most first-time riders Pascal found that first ride a challenge. He had cycled in his younger days but not seriously. Again, like so many new entrants, it was the back side that gave him the biggest problem. Pascal recalls that he was regularly meeting up with Liz Marsden's group of lady cyclists. He would typically be cycling a little quicker than they were and then stopping to sort out his posterior discomfort. They would overtake him and the same would happen again and again. A few miles from the end he commented on their neat cycling formation, which reminded him of a procession of the Seven Dwarfs. In response they said that if they were the Seven Dwarfs then he must be Snow White. The name stuck and so Liz and her team had a name and over the years they were to cycle a lot with Snow White.

Cycling into Paris, John Kinchen had a real tumble as he entered Baines. John a Hayling resident and his friend and neighbour Andy Hickman had first joined us in 1997. They did 11 Bike Rides but generally their participation was low key without any dramatic events. But John had the tumble of the year in 2000. Passing through the town Beynes on the way to Paris he had a disagreement with some traffic calmers and was soon scraping the tarmac and painting it red. Fortunately, he was wearing a helmet and although he was certainly damaged this saved him from serious injury. John recalls, "I was impressed by how everyone pulled together in the crisis. You were talking to the ambulance man in French. Maryon took me to the hotel, and someone fixed my bike and delivered it back to me the following morning. Also, a lovely physio whose name I forgot massaged my stiff shoulder. He also recalled that during the following days Claire Hancock (a nurse and support team member) did running repairs on his plasters.

In Paris we had been joined by a Meridian TV team consisting of reporter Richard Jones and his cameraman/sound recordist Adrian Broome, who filmed us the following day as we cycled the eight-two miles to Rouen. It was very windy and probably the toughest ride we had ever had on this route which led Richard to conclude that we were all mad! On the last day Richard cycled fifty miles himself, which was quite remarkable since he'd had no practice. Meridian did two features on the Ride which gives an indication of the recognition that this event was now getting. They were at one time struggling to get any decent film of the cyclists and then had the bright idea of putting a camera on Tony Hart's helmet and having him cycle towards advancing cyclists but moving off route just in time to avoid a collision. It did work but only just!

At the time we had a lot of organised stops. These were welcomed by cyclists since they saved time in hunting for somewhere to eat. However, this was always difficult on 14th July when many bars and restaurants were closed so it was typically a case of "sort yourself out", which somehow or other all seemed to!

Malcom Emery recalls how they dealt with the challenge that year en-route from Paris to Rouen. “We were getting rather desperate but then, as were cycling through the tiny village of Pressagny-l’Orgueilleux, we spotted an open bar. We trooped in, ordered beers, and asked if there was any food. Unfortunately, they said they had nothing available as they were saving it all for a big booking that evening.” The team were obviously disappointed but at least they could take comfort and indeed some sustenance from the beers! But then the wife of the barman came out and said she could do some chips. This lifted their spirits, and twelve portions were ordered. But then as Malcom recalls, she came back out and asked if we would like some slices of ham with our chips! As Malcom remembers, “Things were looking up and the beer was delicious too! And then came the piece de resistance when she asked if we would also like some eggs. So, in a few minutes, despair had turned to elation, and we were about to have a veritable feast washed down with great beer! The hostess laid the table outside, which was on a small lawn the other side of a busy road. The location meant that the owners risked danger every time they came to serve food or drink. This was made worse by the fact that there was a bend in the road at the point of crossing.” Following on from a serendipitous encounter the Sussex Brewery team re-booked the following year and indeed this became their traditional lunch stop until we changed routes some years later.

Although she would return many times again Pauline Gibbs had to pull out of the 2000 ride for an unusual reason which could have proved tragic. That year, as in most of the years around that time, we had a very extensive and successful series of weekly practice rides with sometimes as many as sixty turning up for a Sunday pedal with the rides getting progressively tougher as we approached the big event! The last of the 2000 season was a fifty-mile round trip to Fernhurst in Surrey. It was an exceptionally hot day in late June. Pauline takes up the story, “I had drunk a lot of water but, as the lunch stop was very busy, I didn’t have much food and hadn’t had any salt that day. I got back as far as Rowlands Castle and was just a few miles from Langstone but then I sat down under a tree feeling very tired. I said I didn’t think I could cycle any more. I was given a lift home. Then I don’t remember anything. Apparently, I was soon on the way to hospital and placed on life support! I had Hyponatremia.” This is a potentially fatal condition when the balance of electrolytes in your body is disturbed due to excessive water intake. Fortunately, Pauline did make a complete recovery but was advised not to ride for a while! She was not the first or last Paris to Hayling rider to be incapacitated by a surfeit of liquid, but I think she is the only one where this has happened with water.

Chapter 16
What? Not Another Ride?

After many successful years of the Paris to Hayling, I began thinking about a second ride. I lived in Weston-Super-Mare for seven years in the late '60s and '70s. I had always maintained contact with the town via old friends and due to the fact that my parents-in — law still lived there. I still use to visit fairly frequently, even on a few occasions when the tide was in! Therefore, I thought, why not a ride to or from Weston from the Bristol Channel to the English Channel, making it the Channel to Channel or C2C!

We kicked around the concept for a few years and at one time even thought about doing it in one day! But as it would be a hundred and twenty miles minimum, we felt that such a ride, while doable (and some subsequently did), would have limited appeal. A two-day event looked more practical. One sweltering day in August 1999 Fred Dyer set out from Weston to plot a basic route. I was staying in the town with my in-laws at the time and I accompanied him as far as Cheddar Gorge! Another ride regular who had travelled from Hampshire to Warminster by train met Fred there and joined him in his route-plotting exercise and by the end of the day they had established a provisional route which, with a bit of refinement, we did for the following six years every May. The idea was to make it a super-practice ride or, for those who, for whatever reason, chose not to do our main ride, a convenient alternative. As it was in England within a relatively short distance of Hayling we could also afford to make it a reasonably relaxed and informal event in contrast to the Paris to Hayling which has had to become rather regimented.

I always felt that there was a real risk that the C2C wouldn't work simply on the basis that you can have too much of a good thing. Yet the C2C was a hit from the start. We were careful not to try and make it a copy of the Paris to Hayling but rather an event. As it's always been held in mid-May we have mixed weather ranging from the bitterly cold and wet to, on a few rare days, sweltering premature summer heat. In these initial events the big feature of the first day was cycling up the five-mile-long and distinctly vertical Cheddar Gorge. The overnight stop was at Salisbury where we discovered a gem of a hotel, namely the Red Lion, a place of real character which has a well-reasoned claim to be the longest operating hotel in the country. Later, as this ride expanded, we also used the White Hart, which likewise has a real historic pedigree.

The first ride was in 2000, but a couple of the Sussex Brewery team, who had planned to take part, were injured in early May when out practicing one Friday night and had to drop out. They were approaching the Richmond Arms, a pub in West Ashling a few miles from their Emsworth base, when Pete Whatley, one of the original members of the Brewery team, decided to go flying over his handlebars. He broke his collar bone but was content to secure a lift home (which he did) with the intention of going to A and E the following morning. After refreshing themselves at the Richmond Arms the other riders continued their way but did not get far before another rider went over his handlebars. This time it was not his collar bone that was damaged but his wedding tackle. Possibly assisted by the anaesthetic from the Richmond Arms, the said rider somehow managed to cycle back to the Sussex Brewery pub in Emsworth where his wife had arranged to meet him. She realised that he would have to get to hospital as soon as possible and it made sense to also pick up the injured Pete on the way! So, what had been planned as a gentle Friday night ride turned out a bit different! Both cyclists were successfully patched up in due course by the A and E team who were surprised to be dealing with two separate accidents from the same small bike ride.

The second C2C in 2001 was one of the best. The following is an adaptation of an article that I wrote at the time.

The Second Channel to Channel (C2C) Cycle Ride took place over the weekend of 12th and 13th May, blessed, particularly on 12th, by superb weather. This Ride was treated by some as a super practice ride for "the Big Event" ("Paris to Hayling") while for some who could not make the French Trip it offered an alternative chance to raise money for charity.

Most riders travelled to the start point at Weston-Super-Mare by coach on Friday afternoon. Inevitably the departure was delayed by one or two late arrivals but the temptation to punish Paul Fisher's tardiness by leaving without him was marginally resisted.

If the pasta meal served at our hotel in Weston proved the perfect pre-ride food, a trip round several of Weston's countless pubs was perhaps not such good preparation. One new rider in particular appeared in sore need of a speech therapist and a Zimmer frame by mid- night. Paul Fisher and I visited a pub nearby the hotel, the Raglan, sadly now closed. The pints of Thatcher's Cider went down nicely and in no time at all Paul and I found ourselves involved in deep conversation with the only other occupant of the bar, a chap called Des whom I had known for many years. Des used to play in a band called Fumble. This band is probably unknown to or forgotten by most readers, but they won accolades for their appearance at the Reading Festival in the early '70s, starred in a West End Musical, toured the world with some of the greatest names in rock, were a favourite of Bowie and Pink Floyd's Dave Gilmour among others, and were recently described as having been criminally underrated! For some reason Des and the two of us were discussing Romansch, Switzerland's obscure fourth official language about which we knew little or nothing more than that it was indeed Switzerland's obscure fourth official language. Then Pete, a former member of '70s boy band Racey, walked in. Paul was clearly confused as to why the only other occupants of this bar should be two ageing rock stars, but the rumours that this caused Paul Fisher to break into a spontaneous bar top rendition of Racey's "Some Girls Do, Some Girls Don't" are to be discounted due to the disappointing fact that it was totally untrue.

The following morning all thoughts of rubbing shoulders with Weston's answer to the Bay City Rollers were forgotten as we headed off on our sixty-eight-mile track. The first few miles were very easy, but then finding a beardless Imam would be easier than finding a hill on Weston Sea Front! That all changed when we climbed Bleadon Hill. Readers, please note that this is the name of this undulation and in no way intended as a commentary on the rather sharp incline (though it could be!). But then came the big one, Somerset's answer to Mount Everest, though with decidedly better cider, Cheddar Gorge, five and a half miles of slope, a right old vertical challenge!

Once on the Mendips the cycling was much easier until a rather nasty hill before lunch. We found this as we approached Horningsham, a small village lying on the southern edge of the Longleat estate. As I climbed that hill my sense of humour, like my energy level, hit rock bottom. Only the good humour and encouragement of Pascal Pichon allowed me to crack this. Pascal showed that morning that Eric Cantona was not the only contemporary French Philosopher.[2] *"The sooner you cycle it the sooner it's behind you," he had earlier wisely remarked and later as we hauled our tired bodies up the hill to Horningsham, he sagely commented, "Gravity is the problem." No mention of trawlers or seagulls but impressive stuff none the less. Who says David Willets is the only intellectual to have entered one of our Rides!*

After lunchtime, the hills were fewer and gentler as we hit the Wylye Valley and some delightful pub stops. Here, and I should emphasis prior to any hostelry halt, Hayling headmistress Jan Randall had a very nasty accident. She came off her bike and, landing on her head, totally obliterated her helmet. Anyone who saw this crushed eggshell of a head piece would need no convincing as to the importance of wearing a cycle helmet. I know she took it to school with her the following Monday and I hope her pupils took notice.

In the tiny village of Stockton, the Carriers beckoned us with its TV set especially for us to watch the Cup Final. We sat there, sunburnt, and knackered, as Michael Owen tore Arsenal

---

[2] For those unfamiliar with the great footballer of the 1990s, Eric Cantona became almost as well known for the way he saw things off the pitch as for the way he saw then on it, as in, "When the seagulls follow the trawler, it is because they think sardines will be thrown into the sea."

apart in a few minutes of second half genius. And so on to Salisbury, sadly bereft of 33% off our Support Team as my wife and her friend Georgie Hesketh had been seized by a sudden attack of "retailitis" which only the factory outlets in the nearby town of Wilton could alleviate.

That evening some of us ate a pleasant meal at a "café style" restaurant in Salisbury. We quickly convinced the staff that we were totally mad (not a great deal of effort needed on that score) and then also rapidly convinced the American owner to do the main Paris to Hayling Ride later that year. James duly entered and seemed to enjoy the Ride as much as we enjoyed his delightful restaurant.

If the Saturday morning was dominated by hills, Sunday morning was full of valleys as we kept close to the Test, the Itchen, and the Meon rivers. We had marvelled for over sixteen years at La Belle France (the Bhopal-like complex outside Rouen excepted) but this was "vraiment La Belle Angleterre!". We spent much of the morning passing burbling rivers resplendent in rich green foliage, but it was a shame that the landscape had to be cluttered by a bunch of scruffy and generally ageing cyclists.

On the Bike Ride we have had our fair share of lunatics and indeed starting it would arguably be an accreditation in that area, but just before lunch we had a particularly masterful demonstration of this condition. P Rick's bike seized up so what does he do? Well, naturally, complete with bike, he decides to run the last mile to lunch. However, one problem, he has been misinformed as it's actually three and a half miles, some of it being extremely uphill!

Lunch, sadly, was one of those frustrating cock-ups which occasionally hit organised rides when, despite all appropriate preparation, things still go wrong because people don't keep their promises. Our chosen pub was not ready for us and had clearly not taken heed of our advice on numbers and so forth. I suggested to the management that they move to Torquay and run a small hotel since I once saw a television series which indicated that rudeness and a complete lack of consideration for customers were key ingredients for such an operation in that part of the world!

Despite the frustration of the spoilt lunchtime people clearly enjoyed the event. The informality and friendliness seemed to be key attractions as, of course was the route which was almost totally lacking in major roads.

In 2003 we decided that we would take some younger riders on the Channel to Channel. These included my thirteen-year-old son Chris. He overcame being chased by goats in Cheddar Gorge and sickness and bike problems on Sunday to become the youngest person ever to ride solo in a Paris to Hayling or Channel to Channel event. It should also be stressed that it was his idea to enter rather than his dad pushing him into it! Chris would soon take part in the Paris to Hayling itself and create his own piece of Bike Ride history.

After six successful years we decided to switch routes, starting at Weymouth but maintaining Salisbury for the overnight stop. Weymouth was and is a pleasant Dorset town with a certain Georgian grandeur, particularly along its esplanade. We found a nice hotel and each year we were there a ride down to the town from Hayling was organised as well. Leaving Weymouth, we cycled through some beautiful, if at times rather challenging, countryside on our way to Salisbury. One notable place was the picturesque and historic village of Milton Abbas. This a beautiful 'chocolate box' village, with its main street lined by thirty-six identical thatched cottages. It was arguably the first 'planned village' in England but what they didn't plan was the cycling as the main street is straight up, rather steeply so! The second year that we opted for Weymouth, I cycled part of the way to our starting point. This proved to be possibly the windiest few hours cycling that I have ever experienced. Indeed, as I was cycling along the Dorset coast a few miles before Weymouth, the ferocity of the wind coming in from the English Channel was so fierce that I was blown off my bike!

We enjoyed Weymouth but we decided that the cycling in Dorset was just a little too brutal and therefore opted in 2008 to return to Weston. We took up residence again in the Royal Grosvenor hotel where we had stayed for several years previously. But, fancying a flattish ride for a change, we opted to take a route that crossed the Somerset levels via Glastonbury, rather than ascending to the Mendips via Cheddar Gorge.

One of the original thoughts behind the C2C was that people who could not get away until Saturday lunchtime could cycle out from Hayling to Salisbury and meet us before joining in on the second day. However, that rationale got rather dented when the departure time had to revert to mid-morning on account of the time spent in en-route pubs. One year, even though it has the tallest cathedral spire in the country, this group managed to miss Salisbury completely. Indeed, one of the disorientated "peloton" was hoisted on top of a bus shelter to survey the surrounding countryside to establish the location of Salisbury.

It's never specifically been planned that way but, in more years than not, the Saturday of the Channel to Channel has coincided with the FA Cup Final. And until recently when the kick-off was moved to the evening, that would take place in the middle of our afternoon riding. Rather than putting people off coming it seems that generally it's been a positive thing with riders often enjoying a stop in a pub to watch the match. Needless to say, that Fred Dyer has normally been in the thick of this essential feature of the afternoon's proceedings. And so, it was in 2006 when he found a pub with a television that served a particularly interesting and then relatively unknown Cornish Ale called Doom Bar. We savoured this with alacrity as we watched a match which, as in 2001, was shaped by a few minutes of genius from a Liverpool player, though in this case it was Steven Gerard rather than Michael Owen.

The Channel to Channel continues to this day. We stopped going to Weston after a couple of years and organised the Ride as a round trip to Salisbury. And then we opted for Bristol where we have had successful rides every year since 2012, cycling via Bath. I have enjoyed cycling from Bristol. It's a great city; in my view the best large provincial city in the country. There are some fantastic pubs and personally I have found that King Street, a sixteenth century street in the heart of the old city centre, to be an ideal place for some pre-ride relaxation, often visiting the Old Duke, one of the country's leading jazz venues. For many years, a visit to the Llandoger Trow also featured. Even though it was part of the Brewer's Fayre chain it still had something of the special and individual ambience you would associate with a pub which has been reported as being both the inspiration for the Admiral Benbow in Treasure Island and the place where Daniel Defoe met the real Robinson Crusoe, Alexander Selkirk. Sadly, this establishment is now a block of flats! But above all I have always enjoyed a trip to Apple, the converted Dutch barge at the end of King Street which serves a positive cornucopia of fermented apple juice! Since moving the event to Bristol we have been able to use the Bristol to Bath cycle path, probably the best one in the UK and a great credit to Sustrans, the Bristol-based cycling charity. And from 2013 we were able to use the Two Tunnels Cycle Way, another Sustrans project. This splendid development takes cyclists from the centre of the city right out on to the Mendips via a cycle path using disused railway tunnels.

Chapter 17
Some Sad Goodbyes but Some Special Hellos

It has often been said that it's the people that have made the Bike Ride, and we would meet some very special people in 2001 who would go on to make extraordinary contributions to our event, but we also lost some people who had already made a significant impact.

As we planned for the 2001 Ride, the community of Hayling and the Bike Ride was hit by a double tragedy; in May Steve Munt died suddenly and within a few weeks his mate Alan Rae was also dead. They were not only great Bike Ride supporters, but they were also personal friends of several of the organisers and participants. By a bizarre co-incidence, I received the news of Steve's death via a telephone message from my wife Maryon as I was about to go through security at Frankfurt airport and then a few weeks later received news of Alan's' death in the same way as I was passing through the security at Munich airport.

We'd been finishing the Ride in Caen for over ten years and reckoned it was time for a change and decided to return to Le Havre. We decided to keep with the format of three rides which we had started in 2000. Fred, despite Judy being very ill, had managed to help a great deal with the planning and subsequently he came to see us off at the port. I recall a memorable exchange when Fred warned his son-in-law Steve Cooke to go steady on the beer, as Steve pointed out that was rather like Hannibal Lecter telling someone to lay off the liver and Chianti!

The "Five" Dayers" headed overnight to Cherbourg and rode south down the Cherbourg peninsula on a hot sunny day along the Normandy beaches, stopping for lunch just past Carentan. There was a strong wind, but it was warm and, on our backs, so we positively flew along in the best conditions possible. Many of the group stopped at the war memorials by Utah beach and it was certainly moving to reflect on the brave actions of the allied forces all those years ago. In the afternoon, possibly because we were away from the coast, the wind disappeared as we cycled slowly through the muggiest conditions possible and, with little shade, I can only describe it as like cycling through treacle. The heat was now making things difficult, however a stop in Bayeux was well received with some even finding time to see the famous tapestry before the last twenty-odd miles into Caen.

Podge Stirzaker used to cycle a bit faster than Pascal Pichon, but not on this day; he was suffering from excessive cross-channel indulgence or, to put it in more basic medical terms, he got pissed the night before. This meant that when we hit the first hill of the day he was off his bike and walking almost immediately. His morning ride was interrupted by a few emergency, roadside stops, and by the afternoon he was in real trouble, although he did make it to the end. But as we neared this point Pascal gave us a real fright a mile short of Caen, which was approached by cycling through a rather pleasant forest, we lost him! A support van passed me going in the other direction and I said he was just behind me. A little further on they began to worry that they had not yet caught up with him. He seemed to have just disappeared and that was no mean feat for someone of Pascal's dimensions! Soon after they fortunately found him, alive but totally horizontal in some long grass by the roadside. He was simply so exhausted by the afternoon's exertion that even though he could see the outskirts of Caen a few hundred yards in the distance he could cycle no more!

But to be fair to Pascal it really should be emphasised that it was a scorcher. After I struggled into my hotel, I talked to several of our most competent riders, and they too were knackered! A hundred-mile ride in the heat of course is bad enough, but to have done so after an overnight ferry crossing where sleep is at best minimal is rather challenging! I am not sure whether he was motivated by compassion or intrigue, but I received a phone call later from my then boss. He was in Paris that day and so not far away and was aware of the heat. I think he just wanted to check whether there would need to be a claim on our corporate life insurance policy.

The following day was mercifully cooler. The "Four Day Ride" had crossed the channel overnight and we met up with them at lunchtime before overnighting once again in Evreux. The next day we headed for the first time to the elegant town of Versailles, just on the outskirts of Paris, where we met those on the "Two Day Ride" who had by this time arrived by coach. Its famed palace is surely by any measurement a place of significant splendour and just as much so, its grounds. It's quite easy to see why the impoverished French peasants got so upset by it but it was, however, a truly delightful spot to be on a very pleasant summer's day.

After our overnight stop in Versailles, we headed out of

the town via the Marly Forest before meeting up with our regular Paris to Rouen route at Meulan at the side of the Seine. After another wonderful stay in Rouen, we embarked on a completely new route heading northwest out of the city passing through Yvetot and then, having hit the coast at Etretat, we turned left for Le Havre. The riding was great, but the weather was awful, a complete contrast to the first day. Indeed, it was so bad in fact that when we got to Le Havre and tried to follow the directions for our finish at a beach bar we struggled. The route notes read "head for the lighthouse and turn left" but navigation was complicated by the fact that we struggled to find the lighthouse!

But the atrocious weather was forgotten by the evening when we had a great party in Le Havre with a band that we had invited over specially. They were called the Quiet Men but were quite noisy in a very agreeable sort of way! They kept us entertained with their raucous Rock and Roll until the early hours. Some of our group disappeared into the gypsy wedding next door. Support Team Member "Phil the Bill" was spotted dancing stripped to the waist, Paul Fisher lost his wallet and one rider who was last seen dancing with a bridesmaid failed to show the following morning, making him the only rider never to "officially" make it back. Neither he nor Paul's wallet were ever seen again. We had the rather difficult task of explaining the said rider's non-arrival to his girlfriend. He didn't live locally but not hearing anything further. we assume that he made it back okay and that he patched things up with his girlfriend! Alternatively, of course, he could now be living with his new gypsy love in a caravan in the Carmague and/or offering to patch up French people's drives!

Barrie Dawson had planned to join in the 2000 ride, but

he could not do so due to being diagnosed with throat cancer. Despite being given a fatal prognosis he pulled through and entered in 2001. During the course of thirteen Rides, he would go on to raise over £67,000 for a throat cancer charity. In his first year alone, he raised more than £3000. He was one of many who wrote into the organizers to express their appreciation. "I would personally like to thank you and your team for doing such an excellent job with the organization of this event. The attention to detail was 200% and, as I have a conference and incentive company, I truly understand what this entails." But Barrie didn't only contribute a lot of money, he also added to the fun of the Ride. He gathered a team around him (Team "C"), all of whom could cycle, but generally only chose to do so in brief interludes. None of them believed in rushing things particularly if they could find a good "en route" pit stop. Indeed, when I pointed out to Barrie that he was the Bike Ride record sponsorship collector he said he thought he and his team probably held another record, having once arrived at their hotel at 1:00 a.m. Quite rightly, he felt that was likely the latest of any arrival on any of our Rides.

Another member of the Team C who joined that year was Paul Whayman. Paul hadn't cycled in years but was motivated to do so to raise funds for various charities and organisations associated with his daughter's condition. She was tragically suffering from Battens disease, a childhood ailment for which there is no cure and from which she sadly died. Paul recalls signing up with his long-time friend Tony Roberts who would also be a Team C member, "We trained for months, and this became a means of focus away from the reality we were facing as a family. We first met up with Barrie on the second day of our ride; as was to become the norm, Barrie was lost! We chatted and cycled for the remainder of the day and of course shared a passion for the refreshment stops. Back home we lived only a few miles apart; at the end of the Ride, we agreed we would keep in contact and perhaps train for the following year's ride. It wasn't long before this training turned into a weekly, Saturday afternoon meet up where we cycled for two or three hours and spent a similar amount of time in the local pub." Paul and Tony would continue for another twelve Rides and their linking up with Barrie powerfully illustrated the strong bond of friendship forged between so many of our riders.

Meryl Brown and Jenny Daley would make a big and lasting impression on our ride following on from their first appearance in 2001. They were soon at the heart of the organisation and their presence would generate many laughs, some glorious cycling, and some fantastic sociable times. Meryl got involved in the Ride when one of our then committee members, Trina Finney, had recruited her at a New Year's Eve Party in 2000. Meryl had suffered the loss of her husband in very tragic circumstances a few years before and had become rather reclusive. Trina thought that involvement in the Paris to Hayling would help her to get out more. Subsequently I was to learn from her family that indeed getting involved with the Ride became a huge part of her life.

She brought along her close friend Jenny Daley. Meryl was new to cycling and although Jenny had cycled a few miles she had never taken on any challenge like this. They were soon to become proficient cyclists but initially, as Meryl recalled some years ago, they really had no idea. Apparently on their first practice ride, being worried about the impact of sweat, they had a full makeup kit but were not really equipped to fix a puncture! In the first year they struggled but completed the Bike Ride successfully and so enjoyed it that they decided to join the committee. This was very good news for the Paris to Hayling as they were to help to revitalise the event in so many ways. Meryl would in due course become deputy chair and Jenny, social secretary. Jenny recalls, "Getting involved was life changing, it was one of the best things I have ever done! It opened up the whole world of cycling, gave me a great interest and improved my self-confidence and as a result of the Ride I made many new friends"." And they did indeed make many new friends as well as introducing some existing ones to the Bike Ride. There is a close-knit group of "Paris to Hayling ladies" who still regularly socialise and cycle together to this day, even though few of them still take part in the annual ride.

For some years Jenny and her husband Mike, by then a cycling convert and a Paris to Hayling participant, went to live in Turkey. While they both took their road and mountain bikes with them, they initially thought that the terrain was far too tough for any serious cycling. However, they gave it a go and persevered, although seeing other cyclists was a rarity, but then one or two other expats said they would like to join and then some more and they formed a cycling group "Blazing Saddles". And it soon grew; before long there were several mountain bike groups, divided according to cycling standards, and one for road biking as well. Jenny says that there are now nine cycling groups around Feithye whereas previously there were none! A nice if somewhat unexpected knock-on effect of the Paris to Hayling.

Wendy Rolfe was another newcomer that year. A typical story. "Friends who had already done the Ride persuaded me to do it. I had no real experience of cycling. I vividly remember my first practice ride. It was a short one along the Hayling Billy Trail on a cold day in early Spring. I had all the wrong clothes on, including an anorak that bellowed out like a spinnaker." However, surprise, surprise! Wendy got the bug, and the right clothes, and went on to do many Paris to Haylings. And with the friends she met through these she went on to cycle in Majorca for many years and elsewhere. And along the way Wendy has become a very good cyclist! She is a successful physio, and I am sure the fact that so many of the Paris to Hayling regulars were pushing their ageing bodies to the limit and beyond must have brought her a few extra clients.

Fully rehydrated Pauline Gibbs was back in 2001 and was joined by her daughter Kerry, who would do many more Rides and serve on the committee. Kerry partied on the ferry over, but her mother was concerned that she couldn't do this and cycle nearly a hundred miles the following day. However, while she recalls it as being hard, Kerry managed it fine, coping well with the hills and the long day, not to mention a significant hangover! But she did nearly throw in the towel even before she started! She had recently been living in East Anglia, which is of course rather flat! So earlier in the summer Jeff Lane, who was out cycling with Kerry and her mum, thought he ought to give "Suffolk Girl" some hill practice. This meant that Kerry was immediately educated in what Jeff refers to as the eight hills of doom. This involved climbing Portsdown Hill, a nasty slope on the edge of Portsmouth from no less than eight different directions. This would test the stamina and humour of an experienced cyclist acquainted with undulations let alone one who had just arrived from the pancake flat land in the East! By her own admission she was not amused but she still made it to our July event.

Over the years, while we have many riders who return year after year, there have been some who have only ridden once but still made a big impact. Mike Saunders, mentioned earlier for his antics back in 1993, was clearly one of those, as was Phil Button in 2001. Phil won the award that year for being the most impressive newcomer on his one and only Paris to Hayling Ride. Petersfield-based Phil had decided on the spur of the moment to cycle down to Hayling a couple of Sundays before the Ride and, stopping off for a pint or two in a local pub, he got talking to Support Team regular Kev Saunders. Kev suggested that if he liked a drink and a cycle ride then there was only one place to be in two weeks' time. One thing led to another, and Phil grabbed one of the last remaining places and joined us. Though ill prepared, he managed with ease and duly deserved his award.

2001 was undoubtedly a successful year but having earlier been marred by the deaths of Steve Munt and Alan Rae, a further shadow was cast when Judy Dyer died on Christmas Day. One of the privileges of being involved in the Hayling Charity Cycle Ride has been the fact that you meet so many great people. No one illustrated this better than Judy Dyer. For countless summers Judy was a key part of the Bike Ride as chief nurse, Support Team member, cyclist and of course as "matriarch" of the Dyer clan, who collectively have taken part in far more Bike Rides than any other family. Everyone who met Judy on the Ride liked her immensely and all will remember her with great affection. But this was just one of the many activities in which Judy was involved and it was clear from the massive turnout at her funeral on the Island that everyone else in her busy life felt the same way about her as the Paris to Hayling participants. The committee also decided to name the 2002 Ride “A Ride for Judy”. Fred was determined to raise a record amount for Cancer Research. We encouraged others to do this and commissioned special water bottles which would be sold to raise further cash for this cause.

A young Pete practising before the first event in 1986

Barry Maloney: The party atmosphere which he engendered in the Bike Ride's early years set the tone for the fun

Mike and Stella Burras (1998): They and their family have been great supporters (and participants) in the Bike Ride since the beginning

The first mass Paris to Hayling in 1987. I had ridden route in 1986 but that was on my own

Pete Alloway (1995). I have worked closely with him since the early days of the Bike Ride. His contribution has been invaluable

The Santa Ride has been a popular event since 1994

The Sussex Brewery one of the most entertaining and certainly the longest lasting Paris to Hayling Team

The original "Team Ditcham" in 2005. Ditcham Park would go on to play a major part in the Bike Ride and cycling would become the school's major sport

Cyclists coming across the bridge to Hayling in 2010. In some years riders would cover the bridge from one end to the other

Paul Fisher (left). Despite the sad ending to his involvement in the Bike Ride his contribution was immense

"PC" Paul Mumford on duty at Pegasus Bridge

Team C – "Lost of The Summer Wine Meets Tour de France" - Left to right Paul Whayman, Barrie Dawson. Paul Clutterbuck, Tony Roberts and Paul Brennan

Tired Cyclists: Either the cycling or partying (or both) had taken its toll as cyclists travel from France after Ride No 30

Can Can Dancers - 2005 End Of Ride Party

Pete Now

Chapter 18
2002 A Ride for Judy

"I would like to thank you for your custom." So said the landlord of the Ship and Castle, Portsmouth one Saturday lunchtime when he visited Hayling and dropped in at the Inn on the Beach in which I had a business interest at that time. The Ship and Castle is right next to the Portsmouth Ferry Port and a few years before we had adopted it as an official watering and eating point for departing riders. But I was somewhat surprised to learn that we were the second most valuable group that turns up at the pub in the course of a year, beaten only by a group that made an annual trip to Le Mans.

This year was to be no exception. As we gathered at the Ship and Castle ready to launch The Ride for Judy, riders were soon drinking and eating as they socialised with the new and old cycling friends. Fred Dyer, having missed last year, was back in full force with all five of he and Judy's offspring ready to cross over with the Five-Day Ride! Eventually it was time to go, and we slipped out into the evening drizzle for the two-hundred-yard ride to the port. No recruitment poster for the Paris to Hayling Cycle Ride will ever feature seventy drenched cyclists on the perimeters of Cherbourg Ferry Port at 7:00 am on a very cold July day. Complete with the standard first morning kitbag of hangover, sleep deprivation and a strong dose of second thoughts I pondered the hundred miles ahead.

As it was too late to back out entirely and a little too early to feign some sort of injury and climb into a cosy support van there was nothing for it but to head for the first climb of the day and get on with it. As we progressed miserably through the wind and the rain, we consoled ourselves with the fact that with every pedal our mid-morning stop was just a little nearer. After the grim ride to that point and after a welcome chocolate chaud and croissants, we headed south along the Normandy Beaches as in the previous year and things got even worse. However, here could not have been a greater contrast to the previous year's weather. The gods had clearly decided to even things up. Instead of a hot wind on our backs we had cold driving rain in our faces. Still, we made almost as quick a time as the previous year since nobody was inclined to stop for anything. The next day and the day after I would miss out on the cycling as I needed to travel on to Paris for a business meeting. The last time I had missed a day in the middle of the Ride had been when I was injured in 1998. Well, as I looked out of my hotel room in Caen, I had a distinct feeling of déjà vu or "already seen" as perhaps the French say; it was like the time I was previously absent, a truly miserable day, a salutary reminder that the weather in this northern part of France is in reality no better than our own shabby offering. My two-day break over, I re-joined the Ride in Versailles along with the Two-Day Riders, the Four- and Five-Day Riders having joined up in Evreux the previous day.

As many of you will know we are not the only major cycling event that takes place each summer in France. The other one is called Le Tour de France! Looking back, it seems strange that we had not met up with the Tour before, perhaps they had always felt a little inferior, but for whatever reason they had, until 2002, always given us a wide berth. But that year we met up in Rouen, some of our riders left early from Versailles so that they could reach Rouen mid-afternoon to see that day's Tour finish. This other event seemed quite well-organised; indeed, they were very professional looking. Not for the them a Paris to Hayling T-Shirt, casual shorts over Lycra and faded trainers — the standard kit at that time of yours truly (I had not yet moved to cleated shoes). The Mappei and Telekom teams were at our hotel, and we looked enviously at their support teams. Learning that they steam cleaned each of the cyclists' three (yes three) bikes after each ride, I asked Crocks if he would kindly sort me out with same treatment. He was normally one of the most obliging of support crew members but his answer in this case was a firm no, or rather something a little more earthy than that. However, I do recall one of the Mappei or Telekom mechanics helping with a couple of minor repairs. Podge Stirzaker recalled that a German film crew had him in view and studied him and his Colnago bike briefly before they began to seriously doubt that he had anything to do with the event that they were here to cover! The same film crew switched from filming their "tour" riders to our more interesting motley crew in their final day fancy dress costumes of splendour, which had now become custom for the last day of cycling.

The last day arrived sadly with the grey skies that were so typical of that summer. The "other ride" had seemed to be generally lying low until after we had gone, although we did try and hand out a couple of our route notes to Tour cyclists. But it's lucky they realized the mistake for apart from going in the wrong directions our ride for the day was longer than theirs. We went out of Rouen by a new route and onto the high ground that separates the Seine valley from the Channel coast. With a new route came a new breakfast stop but the selected café proved very disappointing. No attempt had been made to staff up for the sudden influx of Paris to Hayling athletes and consequently many of us cycled on to the next village. When I had enquired as to why this stop had been chosen, it turned out that the owners' apparently extremely attractive daughter had been working the day that the recce crew had called, and they had been very impressed. However, it did not seem that this was reciprocated since today she was nowhere to be seen. So, riders were left to deal with her old father looking as miserable as the weather, we never went back!

A few miles further I was overtaken by ride veterans Pete Horsnell, Normand Howison, and their regular cycling group. Pete of course was practically a Ride founder, having first come in year three and after that had come every year since. It was an interesting reflection of how old the Ride was becoming that when he first took part Pete was the oldest Rider! If he entered for the first time now, he would have been right on the average age! Normally when this team passes me a few pleasantries are exchanged and I then watch as they hasten towards the horizon. Yet this time something strange happened — I found some speed and kept with them for about twenty miles until I left them back in a café and continued "a grand Vitesse" onward to lunch. "Oh, Pete," another rider normally quicker than me exclaimed as I passed them. I had clearly surprised her, and I was surprising myself! Was I on drugs? Had one of the Tour de France team slipped one of their patent concoctions into my Kronenbourg or was it simply that it was so cold that I had the perfect incentive to race for lunch. I remember this well because it hasn't happened very often!

After lunch, with only thirty miles to go, I cycled along the Normandy coast up the last hills and on to the official stop. Sadly, like the year before, this spectacular beach location was covered in a murky blanket of drizzle. Nevertheless, as always, the clapping in of riders as they arrived warmed up even the coldest participants. Not even a rather tedious interview by a Le Havre journalist who looked like the famous detective Columbo complete with scruffy long mac could spoil this.

For the second year running the Quiet Men entertained us on the last night. They played away until we dropped with exhaustion. After a few hours' sleep it was the usual mad rush to the boat. This year we all made it although our chairman nearly didn't. This was becoming a regular occurrence, each year we checked our bike storage to make sure there were no stragglers and that all had departed for the ferry port and each year we would see one single rather old pink bike still there. Yes, pink! Paul always insisted it was magenta but everyone else considered it to be pink. More than once, there were serious discussions about leaving him behind, but we always took pity and chased him up.

In recent years we had had one or two nasty crashes where, if the riders had not been wearing helmets, things would have been much worse so in 2002, we finally decided to make the wearing of helmets compulsory. While there was some reluctance to do this everyone seemed to understand why we had taken that measure and, save for one rider who said he wouldn't come again, all seem to support the change.

Fred's contribution was magnificent, backed by his whole family and many friends, Fred did not just break the Bikes Ride's fund-raising record he smashed it, raising more than £8000. It was only appropriate that Fred led the riders into the finish. Fred's unparalleled accomplishment apart, it was surely the most touching story of The Ride For Judy.

George Spratt had cycled the Ride on several occasions in the past, as had Ernie. Ernie's achievement was even more remarkable in that every year he was the oldest cyclist! George had initially cycled with another friend who then stopped coming. George was a bit of an eccentric with his somewhat unkempt appearance which led us to refer to him as Wurzel. Sadly, in the late '90s, George's sight deteriorated, and Ernie offered to team up with him on a tandem. Anyone who has ever cycled one of these two-people contraptions knows that they take some getting used to. However, George and Ernie only decided to take the tandem two weeks before the Ride! And apart from getting used to the bike they had to deal with the fact that, while George's sight was not very good, the sighted Ernie could not really follow route notes! This fact alone guaranteed that it would be an interesting partnership and one that would not be without its incidents! They were spotted at the bottom of a hill just outside Rouen having a heated argument about which way they should go with one pulling the bike one way and one the other with an observer reporting that it looked like they were trying to pull the bike apart. I think Ernie won the argument, but the poor sighted George turned out be right!

Having persuaded Pascal Pichon to join our jolly cycle ride, Podge then managed to bring in some other Vodafone employees. The first time they cycled under the "Team Sim" banner was in 2002. One year the team also included a cyclist with an artificial leg. He had two different legs, one specifically for cycling and one for ordinary things, putting the latter back on at the end of each days' pedalling. Maryon

McQuade recalls it being handed to her and Support Team partner Georgie Hesketh to take onto the next overnight stop. As she recalls, "For a short period of time as we were loading my car, we had to leave it in the hotel foyer which got a few odd looks." One evening the leg in question was then handed over to Crocks and Mumfy for some reason who managed to mislay it but fortunately it was eventually located, and rider and leg were happy reunited. I am sure that initially the said cyclist was hopping mad, but all was forgiven and of course, in Mumfy and Crock's defence, losing a leg temporarily could happen to any Bike Ride Support Team.

Vodafone's involvement with the Paris to Hayling was key to the development of their cycling club. A couple of years back, when employed at Qlik, I was approached via our Vodafone sales representative to see if the company could sponsor a charity Bike Ride that Vodafone employees were organising. I must admit that it was with some pride that I was able to tell him that the cycling tradition at the company was at least in large part due to its employees participating in the Paris to Hayling.

Sally Griffith had known Judy since 1979. She had also followed the Paris to Hayling ride for some years but didn't think she would be able to do it. But in this special year she thought she would give it a go in Judy's memory. "I turned up on my first practice ride on a mountain bike. It was so hard." Fortunately, her husband Alan took pity on her and bought her a new and more suitable bike. She already knew Meryl, so she teamed up with her and Jenny for some cycling together with another friend of Meryl and Jenny's, Teresa Finlay. "I was only going to do the two-day but got talked into the doing the four-day! It was a great sense of achievement." Sally would go on to do fifteen Paris to Hayling Rides, joined a couple years later by Alan, and they are still entering to this day.

Another member of the Gibbs family saddled up that year, Rick, son of Pauline and sister of Kerry. He had done some cycling in the past but admits that he still found the first day from Paris to Rouen extremely hard. In particular he recalls the nasty hill into St Germain En-Laye just outside Paris. This "acute slope" which featured for many years was only a few miles into the ride and was, as many cyclists discovered, a rather abrupt reminder that the route wasn't going to be entirely flat! Rick would become a Ride addict, taking part in multiple events, enjoying the bonhomie, and greatly adding to it as well. Like his sister he would serve on the committee. He was also involved in many of the "spin off" rides. During that first Paris to Hayling he became one of a select number of riders who got their wheels stuck in a rail or tram line. In all other cases it ended in hospitalisation but in Rick's case he somehow managed to somersault off his bike and land on his feet. However, he had little time to bask in the applause that followed since by that time the barrier needed to be pulled down because of a pending train! Fortunately, he got off the track just in time! A few years after he first joined us he got stung by a wasp! Probably this was not the only occasion that this has happened on the Bike Ride, but in Rick's case the wasp's behaviour was literally below the belt. He had a swelling and an itch where in polite circles you probably don't want such. Quite understandably he wanted to relieve the itch but the girls cycling behind him, however, were initially shocked! They had wondered why Rick was so violently gesticulating in a downward motion with his right hand until later when his medical predicament was explained to all!

Chapter 19
Ventoux Tumbles, Losing Ernie, and Our Bag Men

2003 was another hot ride in what, as I recall, was a pretty hot summer. We changed the format, resulting in reverting to two rides. This meant there was a Five-Day Ride which went out via Cherbourg and a Three-Day Ride which was akin to the former Two-Day format, except that, having crossed the English Channel, cyclists were deposited early morning in Evreux from where they would cycle into Paris with the Five-Day Ride. I hope you are still following. Most entrants understood, eventually. I would have liked to have joined the Five-Day Ride, but my departure was delayed due to the fact that I was attending a wedding. This was on the Sunday when Five Day Riders were travelling across to Cherbourg. I wanted to be able to catch up with the Ride on Day Three as this group arrived in Evreux.

Among the Five-Day Riders setting out for Cherbourg was a nervous first timer Sarah Farmer. She takes up the story, "I was recently out of law school and working through my training contract at a local solicitor. My boss had done the Ride before, wanted to do it again and persuaded me to join in. I entered for the Three-Day Ride as I hadn't cycled since I was a young girl. I also had to go and buy a bike. I went along to the practice rides and was getting prepared for the event when my boss dropped a bombshell; he was going to have to pull out and offered to give me his place on the Five-Day Ride. I felt I ought to say yes, and I did, but I was worried as I had psyched myself up for the shorter ride, and I had heard that the Five Day one was much tougher with at least one-hundred-mile day!"

Sarah did agree to the longer ride. But if she did manage to get accustomed to the idea of doing more miles she was still in for a bit of a shock. On the practice rides she had met Jon Tawse and on the ferry to Cherbourg he introduced her to his cycling mates. Sarah was a bit confused; these were all experienced and apparently competent cyclists and mostly veterans of many Paris to Haylings and yet they were attacking the red wine with a ferocity that made it seem unlikely they would cycle a hundred miles the following day. As Sarah recalls, "They drank all the restaurant's red wine stocks and had to go and buy some more from Duty Free!" The following day, Sarah set off with her new cycling friends. While it's certain stonking hangovers must have delayed them a bit, cycling with this group was still a baptism of fire for the inexperienced Sarah. She struggled but she hung on! "It was tough but every time I asked what I could do to help with the pain, everyone seemed to have the same answer which was… have a beer!"

Sarah did so well that year that it was suggested that she might want to join a cycling club. She had also met Tony Hart that year and it was natural that she should choose Team Axiom, a cycling club which he had founded. Indeed, Tony and she are now married, and Sarah's obvious talent reinforced by Tony's support has seen her develop into a highly competent cyclist. Apart from a host of club cycling activities, other cycling escapades that she has been involved in with Tony have included a Land's End to John O Groats Ride. There is nothing that unusual about that except that not many people do it in six days!

As indicated in the foregoing paragraphs, there was clearly quite a jolly atmosphere on the ferry to Cherbourg. And indeed, some carried on in a similar mode when they arrived in the French port. Meanwhile, back in England attending the wedding, I came out of the venue in late afternoon to take a breather. My phone rang and it was Bike Ride regular P-Rick (see Chapter 11), whose slightly garbled utterance could be roughly translated as follows, "Pete, you were in that bar with us and now we have moved on to the one around the corner, but you seem to have disappeared!" Two things were clear; P-Rick was in Cherbourg and P-Rick was pissed! I simply replied, "Sorry, P-Rick, it's clearly a case of mistaken identity as I am still in the UK!" P-Rick has always liked an argument, but I think that even he realised in his parlous cognitive state that this assertion was probably beyond challenge".

When I caught up with my cycling mates in Evreux it was clear that I had missed quite a party on that Sunday with one or two riders still feeling rather jaded on the Monday morning! From Evreux, while we were heading for Paris, a familiar enough destination, the route had been changed. If Fred has ever plotted a better route than that morning out of Evreux, I cannot recall it — beautiful and (for me this was just great) beautifully flat. As we progressed through this glorious July morning across La Bellest of La Belle France the heat mounted steadily. A nasty hill before lunch was not welcome but lunch itself surely was. The afternoon was still and simmering. Riding in this suffocating atmosphere was as tough as the

Cherbourg to Caen day two years before. As we rode past corn field after corn field without the faintest movement in the crops any shade was welcome. For a time, such was our discomfort that the miles did not seem to be slipping away in their normal fashion. But gradually the stifling, clammy heat changed to the slightly less repressive balmy warmth of a summer's evening and signs indicating the proximity of Paris duly appeared.

In Paris we met up with the group of weather-beaten riders who had cycled from Montpelier in the South of France. We heard their tales of climbing the Mont Ventoux.[3] How long it took to mount and how long to drop down. In the case of one Dave Edmonds the drop had not exactly gone according to plan, and he had crashed over the side of the mountain, wrapping his handlebars around him, breaking several ribs, and altogether finishing up rather worse for wear, though slightly better off than his written-off bike. Fortunately, he made a full recovery. When Dave first signed up one member of the Paris to Hayling committee wondered if we had recruited a rock star! But this was Hayling Dave Edmonds with an "o" rather than the Welsh Dave Edmunds with a "u" who had big hits as a member of Love Sculpture ("Sabre Dance") and as a solo artist ("I Hear You Knocking"). Bike

---

[3] Mont Ventoux is a well-known mountain in the South of France. Geologically it is part of the Alpes but physically separated from all other high peaks. It is famed not just for its steep climbs but also being very windy (indeed it means windy mountain in French). It has been the scene of several Tour de France dramas, most notably that involving British cyclist Tom Simpson who died while ascending it in the 1967 event. Three years later Eddie Merckx found the climb so grueling that he had to be revived with oxygen.

Ride Dave, where at one of the event's few teetotalers never showed any inclination towards the rock and roll lifestyle. He clearly enjoyed his cycling and along with Bruce was a popular regular rider, but he took it a little more seriously than some other riders! Pete Alloway after a long day's riding delayed by one or two wayside stops recalls a conversation with him in a Rouen hotel lift one night around 9 pm.

"Evening Pete," said Dave. "Are you having an early night as well?"

"No Mate," replied Pete. "We are just on our way out!"

The following day the heat wave continued. There was a little piece of teething trouble with exiting Paris via a nevertheless well-received new route and then out to the countryside. Due to the extreme heat, we were very slow and somewhat behind schedule. However, nobody seemed inclined or able to rush things. After lunch, and having gone through Port Mort, I pulled myself up the now familiar hill, spurred on by the shade offered by the trees at the top.

That winter we had received some devastating new, the bar in Muids, La Chaumiere, had closed. It was quite sad cycling through our favourite village without this special watering hole. It was like Washington without the White House, London without Buckingham Palace, Paris without the Eiffel Tower, or indeed Crocks without his hat. We rested by the river, veterans sighing, staring with moist eyes at the now closed bar. Oh, life can be so cruel! And then on to Rouen, late but still very hot.

Shortly before reaching Rouen a worry incident which I had been keeping in touch with all day finally caught up with me. Ernie Bateman, our seventy-five-year-old veteran rider had been missing in action since mid-morning the previous day. Rod Elliot and Maryon McQuade had been in contact with Police and Consular officials but to no avail. We feared the worst. His son had been contacted in the UK, we were about to go to the press in France with details of this “Rosbif Perdu” and had had a photo emailed over. Rod and Maryon met up with Paul and I and we all set off together to retrace the previous day’s route to see if we could discover anything. We visited the café where we had all stopped for breakfast and talked to some of the locals, but nobody could help us. We arrived in Rouen more worried than ever and then the good news we had feared would never come, he had been found north of Paris, miles off route and rather confused. The police took care of him for the night and put him in a local hotel. A Support Team picked him up the following morning. This was a rather extreme example but in the case of the Support Teams it illustrated the breadth of tasks and responsibilities taken on by the people involved in this aspect of the Bike Ride. As to Ernie himself, sadly it seemed he had had a stroke and it was agreed that it would be too dangerous for him to ride with us again. There were a series of issues which led to Ernie getting lost and remaining lost, but key was the fact that Ernie had cycled past the mid-morning check in but later that day, when we followed up on this, we were told by his Paris hotel that he had checked in! Still, with a thoroughness and commitment to learn when things go wrong, we set about examining our procedures to see what we could do differently to make sure there could be no repeat of such confusion in the future.

Mike Harrington made a rash commitment to join the Ride in 2003. A typical Bike Ride “join up scenario” with a few drinks followed by a “Yes, why not!” which, in this case, took place in a pub on the Hamble River, with his fellow nurse

Ammey Wood. Ammey had herself already done several Rides by then. Mike loved the Ride and was impressed, like so many, by the camaraderie and the way that everyone helped everyone else. "It was amazing; if you had a puncture, before you knew it someone would have whipped out a pump and someone else a puncture repair outfit and a whole team would be pitching in to help you. It was a bit like a Formula One tyre change, though perhaps a bit slower." Ammey introduced Mike to her good cycling friends Marc Necus and Greg Ridley who had first cycled in 1999, and they became a team. Marc was at that time managing English's, a well-known Brighton restaurant. He was a leading fundraiser for some years due, I believe, to "mugging" his affluent clientele a few days before his departure. Greg was, for some reason, always known as Skippy and he was a little eccentric; he and Mike bonded well. They used to cycle in odd head gear, Mike recalls, "One year our outfits were particularly noisy. We had woodpecker heads over our helmets and the beaks kept on rattling as we rode. In cycling circles there has been a lot of references in recent years to "incremental gains" but it's difficult to position this avian innovation in that context. If cycling dressed as a woodpecker or indeed a parrot was a good thing then I am sure that Sir Dave Brailsford would have had Bradley doing it, but he didn't and I can't help concluding that the noise and feathers, not to mention the risk of bird flu, resulted in an incremental loss for these two. But they did make people laugh. However, for the all the fun that Mike and Skippy had cycling on the Ride and the amusement that they gave others it was as a baggage team that they will best be remembered.

Baggage transportation has always worked pretty well on our Ride. For years bags were quietly moved by a small team who focused on that task. Various people did a great job but often they were hardly noticed because their role meant they were apart from the cyclists for most of the day. Of course, if the team had lost bags, then they would have perhaps been more apparent, but they didn't. When we used multiple hotels in one location occasionally a bag might be miss-delivered, possibly resulting in a tired cyclist becoming temporarily a tad grumpy but that was quickly sorted and, in any case, often found to be the cyclist's fault for not placing his bag in the right loading pile for that particular hotel. As far as I can remember the only bag that was ever permanently lost was one belonging to Chris, Fred Dyer's son, but that was due to the fact that he placed it in a hotel foyer with those belonging to a group of tourists from Japan and as far as we could work out it departed with them! But Mike and Skippy were innovators who made baggage transportation a real feature of the event! Each day they would have a different fancy dress costume except, as Mike pointed out, for the last day when it was the cyclists' turn. Having your baggage loaded by a couple of nuns was in itself probably enough to make our Bike Ride unique. I also doubt that any similar events involved luggage assistance from Father Christmas and one of his elves, well at least not in July. One year in Paris they were unseasonably dressed in this way and sorting out loading bags in the hotel car park outside the hotel, when a coachload of Chinese tourists passed them. They were clearly fascinated by the Yuletide duo's activities, so the coach was reversed, and they started snapping what I am sure they thought was some quaint French custom.

Humour was never far away with these two. One year Will Stretch, a Ditcham Park master of whom we will hear more shortly, split his overnight bag. This was the smaller of two bags that cyclists were allowed expressly for the purpose of carrying basic stuff when they did the overnight ferry crossing from the UK. Mike and Skippy were asked to buy a new bag for Will, however Will's pupils suggested, without any consultation with him, that it should be a little flamboyant and Mike and Skippy duly obliged. They delivered Will a nice little pink and sparkly bag the following evening! To be fair to Will he accepted it in good humour and indeed, as Mike recalls, that became his overnight bag on future Rides. They introduced a system of fines for various bag-related misdemeanours with the money going to charity and indeed this proved so popular that in the end cyclists were chucking their spare change into the bucket, regardless of whether they had been found guilty of anything. Mike also partnered with other people for baggage duty and in many years, there were two teams doing this work, but I think it fair to say that this special pair set the benchmark for setting about this essential but inherently rather dull task in a fun way. Mike didn't only pick up bags but a wife too! He met Janet in 2006 when she rode on the twentieth Ride. And when he got married his best man was… Skippy!

I was first introduced to Hazel Barnes and Julie Sills in Paris that year as they dined before setting out the following day to cycle from Paris to Rouen. They were looking just a tad nervous about the ninety miles that lay in waiting! They were newcomers to the Ride, as Julie told me it was her solicitor Richard Wooton's idea, the same solicitor for whom Sarah Farmer worked. Julie told me, "He had done it himself and I think he thought I was quite fit, so he suggested that I give it a try. I didn't want to do it on my own, so I asked my friend Hazel to join me. We both rode for the same local deaf children's charity that Richard supported, The Elizabeth

Foundation. Finding out about this wonderful organization and what they did was a great experience in addition to the cycling in France."

Hazel and Julie both used to attend a local gym and they vaguely knew Jenny Daley and Meryl Browne from there and had heard about them doing a Bike Ride. "When we were persuaded to join the Paris to Hayling we realised it was the same ride that they had done so we told them that we had entered and linked up for practice rides." It was the start of some firm friendships. And various others who had already been doing the Ride such as Wendy Rolfe and Sally Griffiths plus some newcomers formed the nucleus of a team that would not only go on to do a number of Paris to Hayling's and C2Cs but also many other rides including several of those organized by Fred and a regular week of Spring riding in Majorca. They had some great fancy dress outfits and are remembered for such impressive turnouts as the Nutcrackers, the Nurses and the Flapper Girls with Meryl being the main driver behind the costumes. Perhaps most notably they were a bunch of French tarts one year, more details of this being revealed later.

One of the newcomers who joined this gang was Mary Makin. She was introduced to the Ride by Stella Burras, who would have been her room share, but, as she tells it, "Stella broke her arm, and I really didn't know anyone. However, I was room sharing with Jenny so soon met some ride regulars. Jenny noticed I had brought a book with me to read in the evenings. Jenny thought this amusing and pointed out that I wouldn't have time to do any reading and she was right." Mary recalls, "I had a Trek hybrid with very small twenty-four-inch wheels. Reg Beacher improved the gearing but even in the highest gear and pedalling as hard as I could, I couldn't keep up! But I enjoyed the Ride although I also found it terrifying at times given the number of miles we had to do." Mary, like so many, got the bug and a better bike and then a few years later an even better one. She went on to do a number of Paris to Haylings and Channel to Channel and other associated rides. She also organised a couple of holidays for cycling friends in the Mediterranean on boats which also transported bikes which could be used when the boat docked.

This expanding friendship circle would regularly go out cycling with Bob Parkinson and under Bob's expert tutelage, Bob's Babes would migrate from nervous rookie pedlars to quite accomplished ones. Hazel and the ladies still cycle regularly with a few male interlopers, sometimes as often as three times a week! Hazels Rides is really a cycling club but one which only exists because of the friendships made when cycling in France. Hazel said the impact on her social life and her friendship circle has been astonishing and listed some of the parties and the fitness classes, and the regular film clubs that have all come about as a result of the friendships she has made. She smiled and, reflecting on her constant social whirl, said that it was almost too much. And as she reminded me, the positive impact on the family didn't just stop with her. Ian, her son, has become a sailor and an archer all because of her Paris to Hayling contacts.

In 2003 we only had a hundred and twenty-eight entrants; this was the lowest for some years, though numbers had been declining since 2000. We had changed routes, adding some variety, and had maintained a tradition of good last night parties. It's difficult to say exactly what was going wrong but perhaps the cycling had got a bit serious and just a little of the fun had disappeared. There had always been one or two people connected with the Ride who wanted it to be seen more as a serious cycling event than a fun one. Maybe at this point this tension was beginning to show. However, things were going to get better and soon.

Chapter 20
Making a Hash of It!

About the same time as I started the Paris to Hayling Cycle Ride, I was invited to take part in something called a "hash". I was holidaying in the Algarve at the time when a friend of mine who lived there, John Kerton, a future Paris to Hayling rider, explained that every week he and some mates used to run around a trail and drink some beers afterwards. John was not really into running, and so I was intrigued by this and duly turned up one night in the Algarve town of Almancil to run with the A2H3 (Almancil Area Hash House Harriers). It was a revelation! A little light jogging through splendid countryside that you would never have seen by car, the odd toothless peasant chasing you off their land, and afterwards lots of Sagres Crystal or Superbock (the local beers). Everyone had a hash name such as "Iffy", "Stinky", "Hairdresser" (he was bald) and "Market Stall". After each run there was the ritual of the "down, down", which involved citing the various indiscretions/omissions/faux pas of the runners and requiring them to take a large drink from a potty or similar! An almost Masonic fervour for ritual (if somewhat tongue-in-cheek!) was emphasised by the bizarre titles of the hash officials, such as "Religious Advisor" and "Grand Master"! I soon discovered that, with variants of the same theme, there were hashes all around the world.

Hashing started back in the 1930s in Malaysia, when a group of expatriates organised a variation of "Paper Chase" or "Hare and Hounds" the old English game. After their runs they used to have a meal at a club which they called "The Hash House" and so they became known as "The Hash House Harriers". World War II put a stop to it but soon afterwards it was revived and from the early '60s began to expand from its South-East Asia base. Today there is an international fraternity (and sorority!) of over one thousand and seven hundred hashing clubs with hashers being welcomed wherever a club exists. It remains very strong in ex-pat communities, which is where many Brits have first become aware of it, but there are well over a hundred clubs in the UK, including several in Hampshire.

I never set out to model the Paris to Hayling on hashing, but there were obvious parallels. In both cases people sometimes roamed aimlessly around the countryside, got lost, and claimed a somewhat tenuous connection with a sporting activity. Furthermore, Hashers described themselves as a drinking club with a running problem and some would say, substitute the word "running" for "cycling" and you had the essence of the Paris to Hayling! P-Rick was a very active member of the Isle of Wight Hash and often said that hashing wasn't a sport, it was an attitude, and one that he saw in so many participants of the Hayling Bike Ride. Apart from P-Rick a few of our members had hashed before. Over twenty years ago several members of the Winchester Hash joined us, and I remember cycling into Paris with one. It turned out that some years before he had been with a group of itinerant hashers who had called in at the Algarve after taking part in the grandly named "Euro Hash" in Spain. Here they had joined in with the local group's five hundredth hash and post-run celebrations. I had been there as well. We recalled a fairly raucous party and a Dutch lady who had taken all her clothes off and also the fact that for better or worse (we couldn't really remember which) our group had got intermingled with a Portuguese wedding party next door!

For some time, there was talk of a Ride hash, but it took the enthusiasm of P-Rick and "Bilbo" Vaughan, a fellow member of the Isle of Wight hash, to make this a reality. Having rejected the idea of a hash on bikes (they do exist!), P-Rick, Bilbo and some friends from the Isle of Wight and Hertfordshire Hashes duly laid our first trail in November 2004.They used the Fountain pub at Rowland Castle as our base. For a first event we had a healthy turnout, fairly evenly split between, to use the correct terms, hashers and harriettes. Chaos was soon with us; we had mislaid the "hares," a couple of the trial setters that we were meant to be following, and thus got completely lost. Despite this, however, a very pleasant hour or so was passed running and/or walking around the countryside, intermittently coinciding with the planned trail, and successfully navigating a field of bulls. Afterwards, "virgin hashers" were initiated into the liquid mysteries of the "down, down." Jenny Daley learnt why experienced hashers had chuckled on learning that she was wearing new shoes, when she was requested to drink out of one of them, in accordance with a strict hashing tradition. We did hold a few more hashes and hoped to hold even more. But due to the potential conflict with riding schedules and the ageing bodies of many of the Paris to Hayling regulars this never happened. It was, however, an interesting coupling of two closely related cultures!

Chapter 21
A Family Tradition and D Day Landings

At the AGM in October 2003, Rick Hutchings stood down after some years as treasurer, though not from the committee. Rick had played a vital role in controlling our finances during a decade of strong growth, and we were fortunate in having a capable successor in Will Barnard who rode as part of the Sussex Brewery Team.

The Hayling 13 started in February 2004; as its name suggests, it was a thirteen-mile ride round Hayling. The only ride that short in which we had been involved to date were those which were cosmetic dressing for a pub crawl. This was, however, a genuine ride aimed at families, with mums and dads cycling at their leisure with their children, hopefully gaining some sponsorship for their favourite cause. It was a great success, with over sixty taking part but, although repeated, did not become a regular event, which I always thought was disappointing.

All Rides have been special for me, but I took a great personal pleasure in the 2004 event, in so far as it was the first Paris to Hayling that my son Chris had done. While I think we took a fifteen-year-old on the Ride in 1987, we had had a ruling in recent years that Riders should be sixteen and above. I had hoped that we might bend the rules in 2005, our twentieth anniversary ride, to allow Chris to take part a few months short of his sixteenth birthday should he so wish. However, in May, we had a request from Laurie Warner, who as well as riding on a couple of occasions had sponsored several Bike Ride vehicles. He wanted to enter his fourteen-year-old son, Scott. Scott had done the Channel to Channel that year and there was absolutely no concern about his cycling ability, so our only reservation was that this would create a precedent in what we wanted to preserve as an adult event. However, after due consideration, the committee decided unanimously that it would allow a limited number of fourteen- and fifteen-year-olds providing they were accompanied by a parent or guardian and that they had demonstrated competence as a cyclist. Given the committee's position on Scott, I asked Chris if he wanted to go as well, and he readily agreed. A few months later, Scott won the McQuade Cup as the "Most Impressive Newcomer", while Chris, a little younger than Scott, could claim to be the youngest person ever to complete the Ride. In making the award to Scott no allowance was made to his age as he really was a good cyclist.

Chris of course had grown up with the Bike Ride; it had punctuated every summer of his life. "I can remember the Bike Ride finishes at various pubs on Hayling always with a BBQ. In those days, the prize giving was always back on Hayling, and Dad used to have me help with this." Each year as the Bike Ride date approached our lounge would be full of boxes ready to be filled with medical supplies and refreshments. This was a big exercise for which Maryon took responsibility for many years. She used to organize our offspring, Chris, and his sister Alice, as part of the assembly line that sorted this out. I guess it was blatant use of child labour, but it worked. Sweets and other goodies were involved, and I think it possible that there was a little stock shrinkage as her juvenile workforce set about its business, but in any case, Chris does clearly remember that they often got their share of any leftovers, mars bars and similar at the end of the Ride.

Chris did his first Paris to Hayling on a mountain bike which I had myself used for a couple of Rides. While it was fitted with smooth tires it did make things more difficult for a young lad who was, by his own admission, at that time a little overweight. "Actually, that first year was a bit of a blur. It was hard, I had to always know how many miles were left until the next stop and then broke it down into five mile stretches." While Chris may have struggled at times, he never looked like he was giving up, and duly completed the event, determined to do it yet again — which he did! More notably, Chris would go on to play a key role in the creation of Team Ditcham, which has been such a major part of many of our Rides, and which is covered in a later chapter.

The numbers were better that year with a hundred and fifty entrants, ninety of which opted for the Five-Day Ride, which again went out via Cherbourg. Sadly, on arriving in Caen, Will Barnard, our new treasurer, learnt of the death of his father and had to return home. It was a hot day, which made the nasty hills between breakfast and the late lunch stop a real killer. However, we pressed on, and we grouped at a bar in Gisolles on the edge of Evreux, where we enjoyed a relaxing drink in the late afternoon sun. We met up with the Three-Dayers in Evreux, though the (French) driver of the lorry carrying their bikes seemed to have trouble finding the town which delayed things somewhat! We had a new lunch stop at a restaurant at the edge of a glider aerodrome at the top of a hill (well I guess it wouldn't be in a valley, would it!). Le Vol A Voile was to become a regular stop for some years. At this point we were "caught up" by three cyclists who had cycled all the way from the coast rather than come by coach, emulating the prior achievement of Tony and Bill. I can't remember the exact details, but essentially, they had done over a hundred miles by around 2:00 p.m. on a hot summer's day (not for me thank you!).

The following day when we cycled to Rouen was enlivened by the fact that the fourteen-strong Nutcrackers team duly donned their tutus before we cycled along the Seine and out of Paris. That winter, Jeannette Koleno from The Café de la Poste in Muids had written to us. She knew we had been accustomed to stopping at the La Chaumière and indeed the previous year one or two had stopped in her small bar in the main street of the village. However, it was so small that most of us hadn't realised that it was even there. Having clearly heard of our fondness for a drink or two, she had offered to stage a reception for us this year. We did not know exactly what to expect and were a bit concerned about the size, but were pleasantly surprised to find tables, chairs and an additional bar set out opposite the Café de la Poste in the grounds of the church! This was the first time that riders had drunk on consecrated ground, but fortunately the church roof did not cave in — well, at least not while we were there.

After our stop in Rouen, we headed for Le Havre where we had a splendid finish at Les Trois Pics café. In the hot weather many took the opportunity to bathe, some with not a lot on, before we returned to the hotels with a disco run by cycling hero Scott Warner. By the look on his face, I think that he would have preferred not to have done this after five days of cycling, but Dad had volunteered him!

2004 was the first time that Hector Forbes-MacCallum joined us. He had spent most of his working life in the navy. He hadn't really cycled since he was a boy but had been persuaded to sign up by the landlord of his local pub in Gosport who had himself done a couple of our Rides. As preparation for the July event Hector also entered the Channel to Channel in May and it was in the courtyard of The Red Lion in Salisbury at the end of Day One of this event that he first met Sue Wilson. They met again on the Paris to Hayling and had their first date a few weeks later and have been together ever since. Like Sue, Hector has not missed any of our events since first joining. As Hector put it, "It's a real challenge but so much fun. When we look at our diaries for the next year the Paris to Hayling dates are critical; everything has to be arranged around that. And doing that is a great tonic, especially with meeting so many old friends, you finish on a real high!" Along with Sue, Hector's participation in the Paris to Hayling hasn't always involved actually riding and he has also helped out over the years with Support including baggage handling. As with so many others, involvement with the Paris to Hayling has kindled a broader interest in cycling and since the fateful day he signed up for our event, Hector, together with Sue, has taken part in cycling events all over Europe and both South and North America.

Richard Willis was another Paris to Hayling newcomer in 2004, but by that time he was already very familiar with our antics. He had first met Meryl Browne in 2001 and he saw her setting off on the 2002 and 2003 events. Richard had joined in some practice rides and then decided to join himself and would subsequently do over ten Rides. He was not a cyclist, but he had kept himself reasonably fit and, unlike many new entrants, did not find it hard. But he was a struck by the social side — indeed, the year that Richard joined was a particularly social period. Some of the practice rides use to last a long time or at least the conclusion in the pub did. As Richard puts it, "I never thought I would need lights when I went out for a daytime ride in June." In that first year Richard was indirectly responsible for keeping two people out of their hotel room and having a rather uncomfortable night's sleep! He takes up the story. "We had come over to Cherbourg on the daytime ferry. That night, having found our hotels, we went out for a meal. I came back to the hotel with Paul Fisher, but our two dinner companions, Rick Hutchings, and Kevin Knight, decided to go for another drink. When Paul and I got back to the hotel we managed to persuade the night porter to supply us with a night cap, and, well, one thing led to another and before long we were drinking a few brandies with him." Meanwhile, Kevin and Rick had continued their night out in Cherbourg. As Rick recalls, "Eventually we had had enough and decided to go back to the hotel, but on our way back we got lost. We knew the hotel was near the coast so I said to Kevin that we should try and follow the sea gulls as they would not be far from the coast!" Rick didn't appear to have any clear recollection of how good this navigational ruse was, but they did eventually stumble and/or stagger back to the hotel, however they hit a slight snag! They could get into the outer foyer of the hotel but to enter into the main part they needed to ring the night bell to beckon the porter. While it appears that they were still capable of ringing the bell it seems that by this time the night porter was unable to hear it because he was busy drinking with Richard and Paul. Unable to get into the main hotel rooms they were forced to sleep in an outside building, hardly ideal preparation for the near hundred-mile adventure that lay before them in a few hours. They did, however, manage to accomplish it!

Richard did his first ride on a standard Halfords bike but then he decided to build his own and remarkably, with no experience, he was soon building several bikes for himself and for others. Richard's interest in cycling grew and he was instrumental in organising the first group of Paris to Hayling cyclists who went to Majorca for some early summer riding in April. This became a regular event! Richard fitted in well on the Bike Ride and was always willing to help less able cyclists and/or those who knew less about bikes. When I interviewed Richard recently his biggest takeaway from the event had nothing directly to do with cycling. "I really treasured the firm friendships made with people whom I probably would not have met otherwise." He had had a very good naval career and had retired as a Commodore, but we found some aspects about this rather amusing. As a metrology specialist he was stationed for a time at a NATO establishment in Lisbon. Lisbon, of course, enjoys rather good and typically sunny climate! We thought it must have been quite easy to forecast the weather there, but he tried to explain that his duties were a little more complicated than that. I am sure he was correct, but we never really listened because to do so would have been to spoil a good story. We were also intrigued by the fact that the only action he saw, was the Cold War! And we were also very envious of his very good pension which had enabled him to retire rather early!

That year Pascal cycled with Bernie Meager, his new partner (now his wife). "When I met Bernie, she had no real interest in cycling, but she came over for the last night in 2003 and loved the atmosphere and so decided to join the Ride the following year. She came on an old mountain bike and struggled. In fact, on the second day she threatened to throw her bike away and it took some persuasion to stop her doing so, however she kept going and made it." Bernie was determined to do it again next year but equally determined that she and Pascal would do it on modern road bikes, which indeed they did!

Bilbo first came on the Ride in 2004. Thereafter we couldn't get rid of him, and he turned up every year after. His surname was not Baggins, but Vaughan and he was not christened Bilbo but rather Malcom. However, Bilbo was a hasher and like all hashers had another name. And since he had a passing resemblance to the Tolkien character, he was duly renamed in hashing fashion. Bilbo came from the Isle of Wight and was recruited by fellow hasher P-Rick. He wasn't a cyclist when he joined but he was pretty fit, which, as he recalls, was fortunate as his first day was the hundred-mile stint from Cherbourg to Caen. "The next day was a few miles under a hundred, but I deliberately added on a few so that I could make it another hundred." There have been few, if any, more popular riders than Bilbo and, possibly due to his tendency to flit between various cycling groups, he has made many friends. He also gained a reputation for his fondness for roadkill. Bilbo explained this as follows, "I grew up in the countryside. We weren't rich and we ate a lot of basic things available in the countryside such as rabbits and pigeons. One day I was cycling on the Ride, and I saw a freshly dead bird by the side of the road, and I picked this up and made up some joke about the fact that it would have made a good meal for me when I was growing up. And I then had a reputation for being something of a quirky gourmet!" When a dead animal was seen on the side of the road the word would often be passed back to Bilbo that there was a snack waiting for him.

I wrote about Sarah Farmer and how, having entered the Bike Ride as a novice, she went on to become a serious cyclist. Rachel Lamont's story was similar. She first pedalled with us in 2004. In common with numbers of others, Rachel was persuaded to sign up at a New Year's Eve party by friends who had done the Ride the previous year. She wasn't really a cyclist. "I had no experience of cycling beyond going to the shops." But she rather enjoyed it and when Paul Beck, a fellow Paris to Hayling rider and a very accomplished cyclist, asked if she would join his team for another charity ride later that year, she agreed. That led to Paul suggesting that she join the Hampshire Road Club of which he was a member. Soon she was doing time trails which she loved, steadily improving her time. In addition to doing more Paris to Hayling Rides, Rachel has cycled competitively in France as well as the UK and cycling has become a big part of her life!

Chapter 22
The Beginning of Our Golden Age

The Bike Ride was on the verge of its most successful period. Kevin Knight had commented that he was particularly lucky to be part of the Bike Ride during its Golden Age, and this was surely the beginning of just such an era. 2005 would prove to be a record year for fund raising but over the next four years we would raise in total over £400,000! Kevin himself was an important part of this; he had first joined the Ride in 1999 and was a regular participant for some years and soon an active committee member. He had put together our first decent web site, proposed the Hayling 13 and helped in many ways with the significant demands of this expanding event. The committee meetings, as he recalls, used to last for hours and strictly speaking this was not really necessary. However, while our chairman Paul Fisher was a fantastic contributor to the Bike Ride, working tirelessly in its interests, he was not the best at chairing meetings as he did tend to waffle. Indeed, some years before when he had decided to stand in the local council elections, it was suggested by a fellow committee member that if he was successful, they would need to introduce all-night sittings in the Council Chambers in nearby Havant. But nobody minded, that things didn't move quickly since it made for a great social event. At that time, we always held the meetings at The Newtown House Hotel on Hayling, where there was every opportunity of numbing Paul's sometimes extended and repetitive prose with a drink or several.

This was the year that the committee decided we should take our contact at P&O out to lunch as a thank you for treating us well in recent years and for giving us a good deal for the coming event. Kevin Knight, Paul Fisher, and I hosted him with a pleasant meal at a restaurant in the Port Solent Marina on the edge of Portsmouth. We were pleased that we were going to be travelling on P&O's newest ferry both ways, however, as our lunch ended, Paul raised the topic of their older ships. "When," he asked, "are you going to throw out the banana boats?" A slightly uncomfortable pause followed. This was not Paul's most diplomatic moment.

This year's Bike Ride proved very popular! Although we had quite a few cancellations, we still took a record two hundred and eleven cyclists. And among those were several new entrants who would be fixtures of the event for years to come. We had a Five-Day Ride starting in Cherbourg, as in the previous year, and a shorter ride with participants again joining in Evreux. However, a few riders decided to join Rick Hutchings in celebrating his fiftieth year by cycling up from Monte Carlo to join the Ride. As with other similar rides that had joined the Paris to Hayling from the south, this was filled with quite a few adventures with two of the group suffering serious injury even before they left the UK! Kevin Knight, who had been training hard, ruptured his Achilles tendon prior to the event but still insisted on going as part of the Support Team even though he was in a plaster cast and on crutches! He needed support himself to get in and out of the support vehicle! Sally Griffiths had broken her collar bone prior to the Ride, which was hardly ideal preparation, so she also had to be part of the Support Team to start with, although, as the break healed, she was able to cycle the last part of the journey. But the incident of the trip was surely down to Jon Tawse, he had been given the responsibility one day of plotting the route, which they did day by day as they headed north. All appeared to be going well and fourteen miles from their destination they decided to relax and stop for a well-deserved drink or three! Pete Alloway, sensing all was not quite right, asked, "Jon, let's have a look at that map." A few minutes later, "Bloody Hell, Tawsey, you had it folded!" It turns out that the map was folded in such a way that had obscured a few miles and that, far from being fourteen miles from their destination, they were nearly seventy! "And it was getting late! Lynne Harris recalls this as being a bit of a shock to say the least. Worse still, an incessant, heavy rain had started to fall but they managed to do the extra miles and reach their destination as planned. Needless to say, Tawsey was not allowed to take on route planning for the rest of the trip.

While we had had some hot days in recent years, this year every day was exceptionally hot! We had the bonus of leaving Paris on 14th July which meant that it was much quieter, and we were treated to another grand reception in Muids. We finished as before, in high spirits in splendid sunshine at Les Trois Pics. The Ride was presented with a new trophy by the restaurant, as well as a generous donation cheque. Here we had the only low point, when three cycles were stolen. In all the years of our event we had lost only one bike, and then in a few minutes, three more!

Spirits were high again that evening when The Crooners, a highly-rated and long-established Hayling Band, entertained us into the early hours. It was particularly fitting that The

Crooners should perform for us on this night since they had played at a fund-raising event the SID team had organised back in 1986. The Crooners played a song which I wrote to commemorate twenty years of the Ride, entitled "My Arse Is Aching" which I guess for many people would sum up the Paris to Hayling experience! We also had a splendid performance from the Can-Can girls. Meryl Browne, Jenny Daley, Sally Griffiths, Hazel Barnes, Julie Sills and Teresa Finlay had been rehearsing for months before their stunning show in Le Havre. This is, of course, an amazingly tiring dance, and to do it not just once but twice (they were forced to do an encore) after a full day's cycling was an impressive feat! It proved immensely popular, and the superb costumes made by Meryl Browne as well as the abundance of high kicks, splits and cartwheels only served to reinforce the authenticity of this popular feature. The dancers were rewarded with champagne, which Paul Fisher and I insisted on sharing. However, contrary to stories at the time, we did not drink this out of the dancer's shoes, or at least I didn't! Quite a few riders made it a special occasion, having arranged to bring evening dress with them.

This was the best year so far for fancy dress; on the last day it seemed that everyone was dressed up. Two clowns on a tandem won first prize but other nominees included some splendidly attired teams including "The French Tarts" (which included the" Can-Can" team), "The Bunny Girls", "The Vicars", "The Tutu Boys" and "The Superheroes". And of course, somewhere out in the Normandy countryside, quietly repossessing some French soil, there was one PC Mumford!

Jenny Daley had taken on the role of Social Secretary/Entertainments Co-ordinator and with the help of Meryl Browne and others she had exceeded everyone's expectations. As well as ensuring that the whole of the last night ran smoothly, she had herself been a Can-Can girl. She also devised "the baton game" whereby each rider had to pass a baton to another nominated rider, the objective being to help riders get to know each other. At some stage both batons were inevitably not passed on, but some fun was had along the way, and at least in part the objective was achieved. Jenny had also been a singer on the backing tape to our version of the Amarillo video, but for technical reasons this did not get shown until our autumn reunion. It was shot on location at the Inn On The Beach on Hayling, and the Cheriton Pots pub, in the South Downs village of the same name which for some years was always the last practice ride we did before crossing the Channel. The soundtrack was added in a makeshift recording studio in Scott Warner's bedroom. While his father Laurie Warner entered full and competently into the spirit of things in the "Peter Kay" role, I think it was accepted that this was technically far more difficult than we had envisaged.

Jenny was duly presented with the "Value Add" trophy for her work that year. We normally awarded the "Proof That You Can" trophy to a new rider who had shown real guts and determination, but in 2005 we awarded it to a veteran who had shown the same. Fred Dyer had been struggling for some time with a crumbling hip. Fred had traditionally been a strong rider but had recently begun to pedal like a baboon who had found himself unexpectedly cast in the role of cyclist rather than a fellow truly at home in the saddle! While his knee would be in line with his bike his hip looked to be hanging over the curb. It was painful to watch him ride, though he had manfully continued throughout that summer. He was scheduled for a hip replacement operation the following winter, and nobody knew how far he would be able to cycle after that with his new ceramic implant. Awarding him this trophy therefore seemed entirely appropriate. However, in 2006, he was to surprise us all with his speedy recovery. It's worth noting his major cycling achievements in that following year included completing all rides organised under the Paris to Hayling umbrella, plus a ride to Newhaven and back, and a long weekend's cycling in France! So, the hip replacement operation seemed to have been a complete success.

Chris McQuade had embarked on a recruitment drive. He had discovered that Will Stretch, a teacher at his school in Ditcham Park, Petersfield, had in the past been a master at Hayling School. Here he had run the cycling club that had introduced Tony Hart, and many other pupils, to cycling. So, Chris persuaded Will to come out of his cycling retirement and enter the Ride, but also to help him recruit a team of fellow pupils. Together they recruited a further six Ditcham Park students, plus three dads. They fully entered the spirit of the event and at the same time were a great advert for their school. They duly won the team prize that year, and Katy Chapple became the first ever winner of the "Young Rider of the Year", something which we then awarded annually. Chris was the only one of the group to do the Five-Day Ride, which meant he had to do the hundred miles on the first day from Cherbourg to Caen on a hot day. While he now had a new bike courtesy of a very generous dad, this was no mean feat for him, and he rightly received a lot of credit from others. Team Ditcham raised money for the Khao Lak Appeal, which had been set up in memory of six British citizens who had died in the 2005 Asian Tsunami, with the aim of helping to restore the village of Khao Lak and thereby giving something back to its inhabitants who, despite losing virtually everything themselves, had helped visitors who were also impacted. It was a cause close to their hearts since one of their fellow pupils had herself struggled in the water for three hours before reaching safety during that tragedy.

Just before we set out on our ride news had come through that London had won the bid for the 2012 Olympics. You may remember that as a close-run thing between our capital and Paris, and the gaffe of French President, Jacques Chirac was commonly thought to have been decisive. He was overheard saying that you couldn't trust people who had such lousy cooking and that, after Finland, it was where you ate the worst. This was seen as likely to have swayed the two Finns on the Olympic committee as well as possibly others with an affinity for London and the UK. Rick Gibbs decided to ride part of the event in a T-Shirt which had emblazoned on the back "London 2012 — Merci Chirac!"

One very notable new cyclist in 2005 was Paul Clutterbuck. He has kindly supplied me with a vivid recollection of his initial involvement in our event, "It wasn't until two years after retirement that I realised that I needed to get physically fit or, at least, that I certainly should be a lot fitter. Rod, a long-time good friend of ours, took me for a pint or three one day. He knew I was looking to raise money for the charity Operation Smile. After about four pints Rod had softened me up and sprang the question. "How about a bike ride?" he said.

"Blimey, Rod, I haven't ridden a bike seriously for nearly forty years!" I gasped.

"Well, I'm doing it. Don't tell me you can't do what I can?" Rod had been pretty much a chain smoker since a teenager and drank in line with my own capabilities. He knew about my missing lung, and he was goading me.

I responded in kind. "Look, if you can do it, you wreck of a human being, then it will be a piece of cake for me. Count me in. What are we talking about, ten miles, twenty…?" I had no idea what I had suddenly committed to.

"This year you have a choice of a three-day or five-day ride. So, it will be either two hundred and fifty or three hundred and eighty miles." He was in the selling groove and had started to assume he had made the sale.

"You'll need a proper road bike and, of course, serious training, which means, mon ami, you'll probably have to do at least two fifty to three hundred miles in preparation to build stamina over the next two months. You'll room share with me, don't worry, and we have a Support Team that ensures we leave in the morning and arrive in the evening, and they will be on standby for any unexpected events. We have route maps and there will be about two hundred riders." He had been talking fast to make sure I couldn't interrupt, however, I burst in at this stage.

"Unexpected events? Room share? Don't we go home at night? Two hundred and fifty miles? Training? What the hell are we talking about Rod?"

"Paris to Hayling Island, in July. We always make sure it's the week the French celebrate Bastille Day, so lots of fun. I'll register you so all you have to do is pay the cost. I'm doing the three-day ride which is only three hundred quid or so. Bloody bargain mate. I'll do it tonight." He had closed the deal in one fell swoop. Fun? This didn't sound anything like fun.

Paul had a lot of fun, so much fun in fact that he completed many more Rides. But he does recall suffering the first year at least and confirms that it was indeed a challenge. "When I got to my hotel in Le Havre, I sat down on the steps and wept... I just could not believe that I had manged to do something like this." And for his chosen charity, Operation Smile, Paul would raise over £30,000! In future years he teamed up with Barrie Dawson and Paul Whayman. Together with a few others they formed a formidable team known as Team C. They joked and sometimes sung their way through France with frequent rehydration stops at wayside cafés. They were an entertaining bunch who sometimes made me feel that Le Tour de France and *Last Of The Summer Wine* had somehow got mixed up.

Another three cyclists all previously unknown to each other also came together that year. Mike Willenbruch had been thinking of doing the Bike Ride for some time, but his wife didn't think he ever would. Finally, in 2005, his connection with the local football club and its need for fundraising gave him a clear purpose for signing up. Mike recalls that he started out his preparation by entering the Hayling 13. "There was still snow on the ground, but I managed it all right, so I felt quite optimistic." However, Mike had overlooked a couple of significant things. The Hayling 13 was only thirteen miles long, the clue being in the name, and it was all on Hayling, which is rather flat. A few weeks later he was on a longer practice ride in the slightly hillier South Downs, and he realised he had more of a challenge on his hands. Here he met up with local GP Colin Turner. Colin had been urged to do the Ride for some years by colleagues and then, after consuming some alcohol at a New Year's Eve party, he had agreed to do it. And then there was Lionel "Jeff" Jeffrey; he had been a keen sportsman all his life but had thought that at sixty-nine his entry would be turned down, but it wasn't! That summer they became firm friends and along with a number of others formed a close group regularly taking part in the practice rides. And indeed, they were so keen to ensure that they were prepared that they added a mid-week ride as well. But it should be stressed that none of these three new cyclists were oblivious to the need to take full advantage of all pub stops.

The three of them were to stick together for more than ten Rides, as well as doing Channel to Channel, and they still cycle regularly together. However, Jeff pointed out to me that he missed the 2012 event at the age of seventy-six because he was in the Olympics. Surely, I said, you mean you were *at* the Olympics. No, he responded, I was *in* them! He could see I was struggling, wondering how on earth this could be but then explained that he was an Edwardian gentleman in a crowd scene during the closing ceremony! A couple of years after the first entry they were joined by an old school friend of Mike's, Andrew Wilson. The friendship they forged between themselves and the friendship they offered others, as we will read in a subsequent chapter, pretty well sums up a key aspect of the event. Colin would also serve on the Bike Ride committee but not entirely by design. "My cycle companions turned up at the AGM and, without any consulting with me, I was nominated, seconded and voted in!"

2005 was also Paul Edward's first ride. His mother was gravely ill with cancer, and he was looking to raise money for the local hospice, The Rowans. He saw an article about the Bike Ride in the local newspaper and thought he would give it a go! He recalls not knowing anyone involved in the event when he first signed up but, then joining up with some of the practice rides which used to be run regularly at that time, that soon changed. Like Richard Willis before him, he was intrigued by these. Paul remembers them being incredibly sociable with a liquid finish at The Ship Inn on Langstone Bridge. "This gave me an indication of what the real event would be like. I found people were very welcoming of new riders, socially it was extraordinary. I was taken under the wing of some great people such as Meryl Browne and Richard Willis. Richard leant a colleague of mine a bike when he decided to do it. It was a good bike, but Richard got pissed on the ferry back and agreed to sell it to him for £60!" Paul recalls the challenge of conserving energy on the overnight ferry to France. "When I first did the Ride Rick Hutchings advised me to avoid the "Ding Dong" crowd. I didn't know who they were. But I soon learnt! After boarding the ferry, I made my way to the bar, as it seemed did most others, and I settled down to drink with some regular riders who were recalling escapades from year's past. Finally, at some late hour, the bar closed, and we all retired to our cabins. And then, after what seemed no time at all… Ding Dong! Brittany Ferries were waking us up at what was probably 5:00 a.m. UK time. Where had the night gone? Not a perfect preparation for the day's cycling. In the first year, apart from drinking too much on the first night, I remember it being really hard but also great fun."

By this time, the Ride was too big to travel back across Hayling ferry and we used to pedal from Portsmouth ferry port and on to Hayling via the mainland, crossing over the bridge at Langstone. Paul felt really emotional coming over Hayling Bridge. "I had this incredible sense of achievement. I had only ridden about ten miles before and now I done the best part of four hundred miles and raised a few thousand pounds for a good cause. For me that seemed quite extraordinary. It was a very emotional moment — I don't mind admitting that I cried."

Paul went on to do seven of our French rides as well as many of the Channel To Channel events. "It's a bug!" Paul was and is fit but he has always taken his time to pedal, preferring to savour the French countryside and its gastronomic delights rather than rushing to the finish. "There were some great restaurants and the organised lunch stop on the airfield just outside Beynes at the top of a steep hill on the Evreux to Paris day was a particular favourite. I remember the first time I visited the place. I was with Pascal Pichon, and we were there eating and drinking red wine for quite a long time before we realised just how far we still needed to cycle, probably nearly thirty miles. I think I put the remainder of my wine in my Camelbak!" He recalls the Dwarfs team with admiration for their dogged determination and then added an interesting perspective! "For me, the Dwarfs were key. For me, they became a measure of pace because they were always at the back. You could go into a bar and linger as long as you wanted to, providing that they were still behind you. But if they appeared you knew you were at the back so you would then move on to make sure that you still had some bar time."

Joy Hayward recalls her joining the Ride that year. "I met Richard Willis and Meryl Browne at my local gym, and they suggested that I might like to get involved in the cycle ride that they did. I wasn't sure it was for me; I had a three-speed shopper bike which I rode the half mile to the gym, and I wasn't really a cyclist. But somehow, they got me out on an early season practice ride to see how I found it. They said it was only nine miles or so, but I think they lied. And in any case, when you had a bike like mine, the hills on the Hants/Sussex border seemed like mountains, but I persevered and did a few more practice rides. Meryl then asked me if I was going to sign up for the Paris Ride. I said I couldn't do it on my old bike, however Meryl sold me her old one and so I couldn't get out of it. And then, being a bit obsessive, I was out there all day every day trying to get the miles in. So, I took the preparation very seriously and spent a lot of time on my new bike. I was coming on nicely, but I was having to get to grips with both cleats and drop-down handlebars for the first time and therefore it wasn't surprising that I came off! I was up the top of Old Winchester Hill and trying to work out whether I should go down the hill on my drops or not. Well, I went to put my feet down while I thought about it except that I couldn't because I was in my cleats!" Her partner Richard Boswell observed her achievement and became interested himself. "I didn't do the Ride in 2005 because I thought it was something Joy really should do on her own. But I did do some practice rides on my old bike." Later that year the first of several autumn rides from Canterbury to Hayling was organised and Richard decided to join in. "It was a steep learning curve as my bike wasn't really up to it. And that is also when I learned about nipple rash! I had unwisely invested in a fluorescent yellow running shirt rather than a cycle jersey. "This wasn't good to wear on a long Bike Ride and it wasn't long before I was soon in real discomfort with nipple rash! Support tried all sorts of ways of alleviating my pain but with no great success. Finally, they fixed me up with what looked like a bra!" I think it's true to say that Richard felt a right tit for trying to cycle in a running shirt and indeed a left one too!

Richard did the main Ride the following year with Joy, and they have been ever present save for one year when family circumstances prevented them from participating and another year when they volunteered to do support. Joy feels that everyone should have a stint at this. "The detail that goes into it is truly amazing. I doubt if any other charity cycle ride is so supportive of its riders"." Joy and Richard, like so many of our cyclists, have used the Paris to Hayling as a springboard to other cycle adventures. They have been regular attendees in Majorca and have done all the Channel-to-Channel rides and other spin offs.

In 2005, Bob Mogg joined, as did his partner Gill Lee and her teenage son Adam Lee. What made this particularly noteworthy was that Gill's father Brian had done the Ride on multiple occasions a few years earlier and this remains the only instance where we have had three generations of entrants from the same family. Gill and her father were spurred on to do the Ride in order to raise money for the MS Society, Multiple Sclerosis being a condition from which Gill's mother sadly suffered. Gill struggled with some of the cycling but didn't give up, and as Bob recently told me, "We remember very fondly the fantastic reception at Le Havre given to Gill. Everybody lined the wall to clap her home, which reduced Gill to tears. Such was the generosity of the Hayling Bike Ride family."

When Bernie Meager asked her boss to approve her holiday leave so that she could take part in the event once again she wasn't expecting her to be so intrigued that she entered herself. Kate Hopeman overcame the minor challenges of having no bike and living in Arizona and duly took part. She rather enjoyed it. Indeed, she recalls the event as being one of her top three all-time favourite holidays! She raised over $12,000 for charity (around £7,000 at the then prevailing exchange rate) and was to return again in 2010 and raise another $10,000! Kate and Bernie had worked together for some years and were friends as well as colleagues so naturally she cycled initially with her and her partner Pascal Pichon. However, at some point they were separated but she wasn't alone for long, soon being "adopted" by another group with whom she made firm friendships over the next few days and has remained in contact with ever since. Kate had not really been a cyclist before, but she soon got the hang of it and indeed won the award that year for the most impressive newcomer! When I chatted to her recently, she told me she now tries to get out on her bike at least two to three times a week. So, in summary Kate joined the Bike Ride, raised a lot of money, had fun, met new friends, and developed a lasting passion for cycling. That sums up the experience of doing the Paris to Hayling, for so many.

John and Pat Clayton, who ran Bishops Stationers on Hayling, were very experienced fundraisers. Pat had started FORT (Friends of Radiotherapy) which raised money for the care of cancer patients in Portsmouth hospitals, and John had been heavily involved in supporting the Chichester Festival Theatre in their fundraising efforts. The Bike Ride supported FORT and we used Bishops for all our printing, so I got to know both Pat and John quite well. I asked John sometime in the spring of 2005 if he could think of something big we could do on Hayling to boost fundraising efforts on our twentieth anniversary year. As a result, he came up with the concept of the '70,000 Mile Appeal', I think seventy thousand being the aggregate miles we saw being covered by all riders. The idea was that we would ask Islanders to sponsor the Ride, at as many £1 miles as possible, to allow us to buy equipment for the local health centre. A wish list of equipment was duly established with local doctors, and a leaflet was delivered to every house on the Island. £50,000 was raised but, due to John Clayton's negotiation skills, over £100,000 of equipment was purchased. The new equipment brought a reduction in waiting times and, according to the doctors, saved lives by allowing local treatment, whereas before a journey to one of the Portsmouth hospitals, might have been required. In all, that year we raised £162,000 for good causes.

The Bike Ride might have been over, but our Social Secretary Jenny Daley wasn't finished yet, since she led the team which organised the Twentieth Anniversary Dinner, which we held in the British Legion in October. Nearly two hundred people — by far the record for our reunion — enjoyed a great evening, with much reminiscing of the Ride's past. David Willets MP was our guest of honour and in a letter which he sent me after the Ride he referred to the Ride as "a great Hayling institution", which I would like to think was a fair reflection on how far we had come in twenty years.

Chapter 23
Some Logistical Challenges and The Pleasure Of "Le Pont de Normandie"

Gerry Woods was a first-time rider in 2006. He had been diagnosed with bladder cancer the previous year and given two pieces of advice by his consultant. The first was "drink as much as possible". When Gerry asked what exactly he should drink he was told "anything you like". The second piece of advice was to get fit. Not surprisingly, given this combination of requirements, entering the Paris to Hayling was for Gerry virtually a necessity. And so, along with some friends, he duly joined us. "We joined in all of the practice rides and successfully completed the 'half' ride. We particularly appreciated the amazing organisation, especially the support crew, the last night party and the emotional return across the Hayling Bridge."

Gerry then took his cycling seriously. "I have since done a number of Paris to Hayling Rides, practice rides, spin-off rides in France and UK as well as the Channel-to-Channel rides. And I have done other rides as well. My average, most years, is around three thousand miles and I have cycled up five Tour de France mountains and nearly up Mont Ventoux (until beaten in the last half kilometre by incredibly strong winds)."

As for the drinking, as Gerry points out, it took much longer to beat cancer than had been anticipated, with him not being given the "all clear" until 2019. "So maybe I didn't drink enough."

I am glad that Gerry wasn't put off after his initial experience of the Paris to Hayling because it was a difficult year and while most of the problems we faced might have been felt most acutely by the organisers, it did make for a Ride which was a bit cumbersome compared to others. P&O had finally pulled out of cross-channel ferries which meant that we had to make a choice of route. We evaluated all available options, something which was complicated by the fact that our chairman Paul Fisher and Brittany Ferries had fallen out, with Paul feeling their prices were too high. Following some heated debate at the committee meeting, we decided to go out using LD Lines. LD was a French transport conglomerate that had taken over the Le Havre-Portsmouth route. But the challenge we faced was that they came back at the wrong time for us to use them for the return leg, which resulted in us choosing to return via Dieppe and Newhaven.

It was all looking a bit messy. There were various logistical challenges, including a lack of cabins on the LD Ferry which we solved by having some cyclists travel out on Saturday night, a day early. Another one was the lack of hotels in Dieppe on Bastille Day, which we overcame, but only just. I think we worked out that, when we secured our last available room, the next nearest one was thirty miles away! Thirdly, we had overlooked the challenge of bringing nearly two hundred cyclists through Brighton on a summer Saturday. This was solved effectively but inelegantly by transporting people by coach (and bikes by lorry) from Newhaven to Littlehampton.

With all these challenges addressed (or so we hoped!) we set off with a surprisingly large party for our annual adventure. I was one of those who went a day early, and therefore spent the following lounging around various bars and cafés before watching the World Cup Final. The French were understandably disappointed in losing to Italy, though apart from Zidane's last-minute strike (at one of the Italian team!), I do not recall a lot of the detail as I was rather tired and emotional from the day's social exertions.

The next day, we took a route from Le Havre to Evreux that we had used in 2001 and 2002 on the Four Day Ride. Early on we had to cross the Seine via the Pont de Normandie. Podge Stirzaker, leading his colleagues in Team Sim, recalls landing in France as follows, "The first day saw us rising at some ungodly hour, when the Ferry arrived in Le Havre. Along with many new cycling buddies, we then had to cycle nearly ninety miles to Evreux. Bearing in mind that we had had little sleep the night before, and that breakfast hadn't really settled, you can imagine the joy as we approached the Pont De Normandie. This bridge brings together all traffic, including cyclists, to cross the River Seine linking Le Havre to Honfleur. Fortunately, cyclists are separated from normal traffic, but, this year, however, road works dictated that we must all share a single lane on the ascent, which was scary."

This was the first year that we had the "pleasure" of cycling over this bridge. It crosses the river Seine in a two-kilometre arch with a span of twenty-three point six metres in width. When it opened in 1959 it was the longest bridge of its kind in the world. Some cyclists have called it challenging and one or two even terrifying. It's very high and the spectacular and panoramic views of the river below are little compensation for the uneasy sensation of traffic whizzing by only a short distance from the bike path! I recently heard a story about a man who had cycled round the world and climbed Everest who, when asked about the most memorable challenges in his adventures, included his pedal over this bridge. We did, however, cross it several more times later when we were to cycle frequently from Le Havre to Caen because it was the most practical way of doing this, but I can't say I ever found it to be fun!

Still, once over this little obstacle, it was a very good ride to Evreux, without the hills of the old route from Caen — and it still included our customary stop at Au Joyeux Normande. We approached our popular lunchtime venue from a different angle this year, which was the excuse of Paul Fisher and I used for getting horribly lost over the last couple of kilometres. There are an awful lot of corn fields in this part of France (and in others, come to think of it), and almost nothing to distinguish one country lane from another, and so it was that Mr. Fisher and I cycled frustratingly in the midday sun for about half an hour before getting back on track and finding Au Joyeux Normande.

For the first time we were visiting Chartres. The inclusion of Chartes, Chichester's beautiful twin city with a spectacular cathedral, was undoubtedly a highlight. On the back of the fact that we were from the Chichester area and had some Chichester riders, we had a civic reception. Paul got the time wrong and turned up late. Beforehand we had been sent a choice of refreshment packages to select and had unwittingly chosen the one without any alcohol! Not surprisingly, few riders were impressed with this, but generally they were impressed by the light show which took place later at the cathedral.

We departed from Chartres for Paris. But as we left there was a bit of an incident at our main hotel Le Châtelet. We had to persuade the hotel to open the electronic gates, to allow the hundred-plus cyclists out of their car park. The hotel had moved to plastic keys and was insisting that they all be returned. While this was environmentally admirable it wasn't normal practice and still isn't and therefore, we had a bit of job in rounding them all up. Kevin Stirzaker takes up the story, "Eventually, forty-five minutes late, we all started to cycle. We had followed the one rider, Fred Dyer, who should have known the way, since he had written the route notes. How foolish we were thinking that he wouldn't get lost. To Fred's credit, however, it was only three miles before he realised his mistake. So, much to the amusement of the locals, a rather large group of cyclists were seen to come to an abrupt halt, say lots of naughty words, turn around and go back to find the correct turning — which was the one with a sign that said cyclists this way!"

The new route between Chartes and Versailles joined our old route at Beynes, just before the location of our popular airfield lunchtime stop Le Vol A Voile. Here we were joined by the riders who had opted for the shorter version of the event before heading on to Paris. The following day we were back on our tried and tested Paris to Rouen route. Everything seemed to go surprisingly smoothly! The only incident that I can recall is Pete Alloway on the final few miles into Rouen complaining of sleep deprivation. Probably the odd glass or two of red wine in the late evening or early morning had not helped on that front. And of course, somehow, he was going to have to get through the final two days which heroically he did.

On the last day we headed out of Rouen, for the first time, in a North Easterly direction towards Dieppe. In the early morning, some riders took a diversion to the village of Quincampoix to visit the grave of Jacques Anquetil. He was one of the greatest cyclists of all time and was the first to win Le Tour de France five times. Much of the route that day was on the Avenue Verte, a converted railway track which ran from Forge Les Eaux to Dieppe. A few thought it was a bit boring and I guess it was, in the sense that there were no lorries to knock you off your bike and no chance of getting lost! I guess you just can't please everybody!

The Avenue Verte started at Forge Les Eaux, which was the town that I'd had an overnight stay in back in 1986 on the first Ride. The first time I was there I had not noticed how charming it was on account of being so tired. This year as we came into the town, we climbed a hill and discovered a café on top of it. If anyone is smart enough to put a bar on top of a hill which features in our Ride, then they can guarantee customers, and this was no exception. This was fancy dress day and I arrived there with the entire "Von Crapp" singers, a take-off of the *Sound of Music* gang. They made a pretty sight, particularly the six-foot-six Jeff Lane dressed as Maria! I was also with the Ditcham Park Cycling Team and then suddenly Ditcham Park's French teacher appeared. By pure coincidence she had happened to be on holiday in the town at the time and had some idea that we were passing through. I am sure that she had already heard all about the fine athletic achievement of the 2005 Ditcham team, and how they were intending to do it again this year. However, as she turned and saw their fellow cyclists, and six-foot-six Jeff Lane in his Maria costume, she must have wondered whether this was suitable company for a bunch of impressionable sixteen-year-olds!

For Jeff this was the first in a series of costumes that rather amused his fellow cyclists and indeed possibly confused some! Earlier that year his cycling group were discussing a fancy-dress theme for the forthcoming ride. The Sound of Music was proposed, and Jeff insisted that if that was the case then he was going to be Maria! Jeff, as I mentioned earlier, was a performer and for him there could be no compromise. "I took this very seriously. When I put on the costume, I really was going to be the goddess, Julie." He got some strange looks as he rode through the French countryside. But Jeff had started something and in subsequent years he would go on to be a fairy, a Maid Marion, and a flapper girl when his team did a Guys and Dolls theme. That was confusing, as he recalls, "Fred joined us dressed as a gangster but for some reason talked the whole day in a German accent!"

We arrived in Dieppe full of trepidation that our attempts to find a bed for everybody would fall apart. Fortunately, they didn't, though it was a close thing. We had also heard rumours that our ship had broken down which might have meant we would all have been sleeping on the quayside! But fortunately, this proved to be something of an exaggeration, and the following morning after a good farewell we duly departed.

As usual we made the Bike Ride awards during the return crossing. Mo Woolcock was a deserving "Proof That You Can" trophy winner. Mo had had a stroke as a child and as result suffered from what is called a "drop foot". This means that for Mo cycling was a special challenge, with one pedal having to be built up specially. However, much to Mo's credit, none of the Support Team were even aware of her disability until after the Ride. Mo's chosen charity was, appropriately, the National

Clinical Function Electrical Stimulation Centre at Woodstock near Salisbury, which provides a range of stimulators to help the mobility of drop foot suffers.

We duly departed from Dieppe and arrived in Newhaven ready for the bike people, bag loading, and transportation to Littlehampton. If there is any charm to Newhaven, I have completely missed it. Indeed, it's so scruffy, and such a contrast with neighbouring Brighton that if I was a Frenchman arriving there, I would quickly form an adverse view of our "Green and Pleasant Land" and take the next ferry home. Before leaving Newhaven in this rather unorthodox manner, we did run into another potentially major hitch, namely a lack of room for all the bikes. We looked at this from all angles, and even our most practical committee member, Pete Alloway, was stumped. However, an idea from Will Lennard solved the problem. On reflection, Will, along with David Willetts, is our only Oxbridge-educated rider. Who knows what other cock-ups we might have avoided over the years with more academic muscle! The stop at Littlehampton in the Arun View worked out very well. We lunched in glorious sunshine on a specially-prepared paella, and then cycled the twenty-five miles to the finish on Langstone Bridge. The only drawback to the end was that we could not manage to all come in together, which meant that some atmosphere was lost, but the overwhelming feedback was that it was another good ride, albeit with a somewhat cack-handed finish.

Kevin Stirzaker reflected, "Such joy. Did I suffer? Of course, I did. Would I do it again? Absolutely!"

Chapter 24
More Spin-Offs and Dodging Ditchling

The Paris to Hayling was involved in other activities from its early years. It had a quiz team which was very successful, winning close to fifty competitions. At one time it was even invited to audition for "Egg Heads", though the offer was declined since we felt little desire to be humiliated on national TV. As I related earlier, we also organised some hashes.

In addition to the Paris to Hayling, we had our established Santa Ride and the Channel to Channel but there were other rides too. A ride to Gorron, Hayling's twin town, was organised over a long week-end and then after several years this was followed by other short French rides. Fred Dyer and Lynne Harris took the lead in the organising which meant they were generally referred to as "Fred's Rides". Some of our cyclists started going to Majorca for some early season training in this favourite haunt for those seeking vertical challenges. For a few years there was a ride organised in September from Canterbury, the CC2CC (Canterbury Cathedral to Chichester Cathedral), in which Fred and Lynne were also key organisers along with others. There were also cycling weekends in the Cotswolds and rides around Hampshire. These weren't charity rides, but simply opportunities for several current and past Paris to Hayling riders, plus quite a few outsiders, to do more cycling and have more of the camaraderie that had developed on the Paris to Hayling. We were evolving from an annual eccentric jaunt from Paris to a very sociable, loosely structured cycling club, though still very eccentric.

I would have liked to have taken part in more of these events myself, but pressure from work limited my opportunities. However, I did do a couple of Fred's Rides. One of these was in Normandy and took me to some places that I had missed despite my many other rides in the region. Another one took cyclists to Amiens in the Somme valley. I did also eventually make a Majorca trip which was delightful but, as I had been warned, not flat. I did also make two CC2CCs. One I remember fondly and set out some recollections. As we left Canterbury and headed for the coast it was easy to see why this part of the country is called the Garden of England. Kent was stunningly resplendent in its late summer foliage. You half expected to meet Pop Larkin from the Darling Buds of May round the next corner of one of the many country lanes we pedalled down that morning. Just before lunch we hit the coast and passed through the lovely little town of Rye, and then on to Winchelsea for lunch. In the afternoon we had a halt in Hastings. Sad Hastings, clearly a town that time had forgotten. It was only twenty miles from Brighton, yet it seemed to be on a different planet. The pub we stopped at rather epitomised the whole town. To put it mildly, it was shabby!

After that, it was on to Eastbourne. I had heard a lot about our hotel from riders who had come the previous year. It certainly fitted in with the image that some have of this being the Costa Geriatric. Most of the hotel guests were clearly rather older than us; there were lots of stair lifts and quite a lot of the seats were covered in polythene. Quite possibly the place we stayed at should have been named the Hotel Incontinental, rather than The Glastonbury!

The following day we had another cracking route. We initially rode along the scenic Cuckoo Trail, part of the Sustrans Cycle Network, before heading along the South Downs until Lancing, where we proceeded along the coast via Worthing and Littlehampton before reaching Chichester. All credit to our route master Fred and his hard-working task force, since although we kept close to the Downs, we had a relatively flat ride. We did at one point pass a sign to Ditching Beacon, famous as one of the highest points in the area and well known as the "Beachers Brook" of the London to Brighton Ride. At that point I upped the pace, trying to get as far away from the sign as possible, but there was no logic to this! Neither hills, however high, let alone signs to hills, can trap you and force you to endure their vertical torture, yet somehow, I felt compelled to get out of the area, pronto. My enjoyment of an excellent route was probably enhanced by the fact that it was the first Cycle Ride that I had ever done where I was not involved in the organisation!

Chapter 25
Braving the Elements and Achieving the One Million

In our £1,000,000 Ride in 2007 all riders were invariably damp, often wet, and frequently downright soaked. Not only that but they had to endure some winter-like temperatures, both in the UK and in France.

While quite a few regulars cycle intermittently through the winter months, for most, cycling begins in the spring. An extraordinary April seemed to confirm that we were in for a scorcher and gave all Bike Ride entrants a chance for some early practice. But little did we know that this record-breaking month was to be better than the next three months combined.

In May, several Channel to Channel entrants decided yet again to cycle down to the start at Weymouth rather than taking the coach. They got drenched! Moreover, as they approached Weymouth from the rather exposed coastline to the east, many nearly got blown off their bikes as the wind rushed through a gap in the headland. While the Saturday's ride from Weymouth to Salisbury was unexpectedly dry, the following day was close to a washout, with many riders heading unashamedly for the nearest train station.

In September of 2006, the issue of choosing the cross-channel ferry for 2007 had resulted in a rather lively committee meeting. Paul was in favour of us repeating the

2006 arrangements going out via Le Havre and back via Dieppe. However, other committee members, including myself, had been uneasy about these in the first place and were even more concerned having gone through with them that summer. By chance in June, three of us had met Graham Smith, a Brittany Ferries executive, in a local pub. Graham, who had always been sympathetic to the Bike Ride cause and had been our "sponsor" within the Brittany organisation, was disappointed that we were not travelling with them that year. He had outlined a proposal which he hoped would get us back in 2007. It looked pretty certain that the following year would be the one when we reached £1,000,000 in funds raised and he promised that he and Brittany would help us to make it special. At the September committee meeting we put Graham's proposal forward and Paul Fisher was a bit upset, accusing us of having gone behind his back, which was a bit of an exaggeration. To defuse the situation, I proposed that we formally put it to a vote, something which we rarely did. The decision to revert to Brittany was unanimous, save for Paul's lone vote against. As Meryl Brown put it not long afterwards, "Paul was digging this hole for himself and no matter what people were saying he just kept on digging!"

Leading up to the Paris to Hayling Ride, several practice rides were virtual write-offs, with only one or two hardy souls braving the elements. Additionally, several other rides took place in conditions in which few really wanted to be on a bike. Indeed, the weather got so bad in June that many cyclists only managed to get in the saddle a couple of times. Still, notwithstanding the bad June, surely, we would see summer eventually. When we reached France in the second week of July, of course the weather would be better, wouldn't it? For this special year we had some exciting plans for a Six Day Ride. We would head back to Versailles but via Alencon and Chartres and those who chose a shorter option would be transported from the Channel to meet us between Chartes and Versailles.

The main ride landed in Caen on a miserable cold Monday in conditions which could only be described as typical January weather! The light rain that welcomed us to France soon turned into a downpour so serious that some of us almost immediately took refuge just a few miles down the road at Pegasus Bridge inside the Café Gondre. We waited, sipping coffee together with Cognac to fend off the hypothermia in the naïve anticipation that the weather would clear up. However, it did not, and we were forced to press on. If anything, the weather got even worse mid-morning before improving a little after lunch, but still the question that everyone was asking was, "Was this really July?"

The following morning, while it didn't rain as continuously as on the first one, when it did, it really poured and indeed it remains one of the wettest mornings that I can remember on our event. The combination of arctic temperatures and monsoon showers was most unattractive, and rather took the shine off La Belle France. As I sat shivering at lunch I really wondered, not for the first time in these twenty-two summers, why on earth I was doing this. After lunch Fred had put in a vicious hill which might have been expected to infuriate us all but since it warmed us up more than somewhat, we really welcomed it. We reached Chartres with little or no more rain. This was a new route, and we only had a vague idea of potential afternoon watering-holes. However, a bar was duly adopted by the cyclists as they came past in the ones, twos and threes, and sometimes larger groups. "Le Patron" was clearly delighted with the extra trade. So, for the second time, we were in this beautiful city with its stunning cathedral. Later that night, as a large group of us watched the light show, a funny thing happened. A face appeared on the side of the cathedral — supposedly Jesus Christ, but as the Sussex Brewery Team pointed out, curiously resembling Paul Fisher!

The following day we were spared the rain as we headed for Versailles. Those who had opted for a shorter version came off the ferry at Caen that morning and were transported to meet us en-route. And it was a pretty good route. Well, at least, it would have been, had I not got a little lost! But it still wasn't summer weather and at lunchtime, while it was not as bitterly cold as the previous day, it was a far cry from recent years when riders practically collapsed from the heat! After twenty-two Rides I had made the change to cleats, and as all who have been through this rite of passage will tell you, it is a "cert" that you will come off a few times. And sure enough, soon after lunch I had the accident I was warned I would have! Well, there I was, cycling up a hill, and the chain came off. I failed to dismount in time, and I crashed to the floor! Fortunately, there was no damage, and I was soon back on the bike to complete the short ride to Versailles. Here, riders lingered in the splendid garden for a few beers, but it was still bloody cold!

As you may have already noted from other stories that I have told, it doesn't matter how you plan things, sometimes they can still go wrong and so it was with one of our overnight resting places. The Le Versailles hotel, even after two personal visits and multiple emails, still managed to cock up the rooming list! There really was no excuse, and it's so frustrating when you have taken every reasonable measure to get it right. But the following morning a more frustrating thing happened when we found that two bikes had been stolen from the Ibis car park, even though they were several floors underground and secure. We have been lucky in this area and lost only six bikes in total since the Ride started, but that was no consolation for the unfortunate cyclists. Luckily, we were able to send them on their way on spare bikes but not before the unavoidable visit to the police station and the filling in of forms and so forth.

Leaving Versailles, the rain was still with us, albeit now only intermittently. And that made me more optimistic, especially since later that day we would be back in Muids and as far as I could recall the sun had always shone on us in Muids. On arrival I fully expected the clouds to clear and to be replaced with a more traditional blue sky. However, I was wrong, and we were treated to a lake full of rain but not before the Café de la Poste had welcomed us with their traditional ecclesiastical bar. I didn't shed a tear as I left Muids, but maybe I should have. It had been an important part of Bike Ride history, and with some thoughts about a radical new route for next year, it was by no means certain we would be going back.

We escaped the rain the following day, and in fact by the time we reached Le Havre it finally felt like summer, and as in previous years we had a pleasant time at Les Trois Pics. On the way, I had a spot of bother and another cleat fall. My second tumble came just before the mid-morning stop at Yvetôt. As a result of this, the hanger that holds the gears to the bike frame snapped. Crocks and Mumfy gave my bike and me a lift to a bike shop in Yvetôt. We found a fascinating establishment where the wall was festooned with pictures of the manager, who had apparently cycled as far afield as Scandinavia and the Sahara. But, alas, this velocopedic Marco Polo did not have the part we needed. Indeed, with only a few hours left until France closed for the 14th of July it seriously looked as if I might indeed be short-changed on the million-pound Ride. I stuck with Crocks and Mumfy all morning, and there was never a dull moment with those two, since, albeit in a very friendly way, they were a continuously bickering couple!

At lunch time I got hold of Pete Alloway's spare bike. This was a De Rosa, which was a few years old now but still a lovely bit of kit. However, the saddle was too high, and try as we might, we couldn't lower it. Still, I said I would try it for the short ride into Le Havre and I managed the eighteen or so miles with relative ease, though it was like cycling and being on the rack at the same time. In Le Havre I then heard the news that the Support Team had pulled off a miraculous feat and found the elusive spare part for my bike at a shop on an industrial estate in Le Havre, minutes before it closed. Formidable!

We thought the weather was now all set for summer, but we were mistaken since the following morning we awoke to a drizzling rain. Two riders managed to avoid the rain for all the wrong reasons. Names have been forgotten now but a couple of young entrants had decided to head out on the town the previous night and, on arriving back at the hotel, found that they could not get in. However, they spied an open-backed Land Rover in the hotel car park containing, for some reason, some duvets. Being desperate for a bit of kip they jumped in the Land Rover, pulled the duvets over themselves, and went to sleep. Fortunately, nobody drove off in the said vehicle and at about 6:00 am they were able to get back into the hotel and crawl into their beds. A couple of hours afterwards, when they should have been waking up, they not surprisingly overslept! But the good news for them was that when they did eventually rise the rain had cleared and the sun was shining. Fit and youthful, they soon caught the rest of us up and were none the worse for their overnight escapade. As you may recall, this was not the first time riders couldn't get into their hotel rooms due to their overnight jaunts. I am not aware of any other instances, but I would not be surprised if there were!

It was a short day riding along the coast to Pegasus Bridge, necessitating another trip over the high Pont de Normandie, before turning inland to Caen and we hoped that this would be a fitting end to our historic ride, and ultimately, we were not disappointed. The weather soon improved and as we gathered for our evening party it was a truly balmy evening. We had arranged an event for our £1,000,000 at the Café Mancel inside the walls of Caen Castle. For an hour or so we sipped Kir Royale in the grounds of William the Conqueror's historic pad (courtesy of the Calvados Tourist Board) before sitting down to a sumptuous meal in the café. This was among the best examples of "mass catering" that I had ever experienced. Graham Smith from Brittany had kindly introduced us to the café's management and also to the people at the tourist board and in so doing had helped us create a truly special evening.

We then had a fantastic few hours of our band The Crooners. They had everyone on their feet and dragged several riders up to perform. Their singer Mark Fordham even got me to sing with him which proves that one or both of us had been drinking. But we were fortunate to have Mark with us at all.

Mark had taken part in our event but, on leaving Le Havre, and despite specific route instructions to the contrary, had decided when crossing over the Pont De Normandie to turn left instead of right and head up the Seine. This would have been ideal had he been gigging that night in Rouen but was totally useless for someone who was performing in Le Havre! A search party was sent out for him and eventually our missing chanteur was appropriately retrieved.

The Crooners' performance was interrupted while most of us went outside and scrambled up the ramparts to watch a firework display over the town. Negotiating our way down the ancient steps, pissed and in the dark, was probably among the most challenging features of our week-long jaunt. When things closed at the Castle a number of us found ourselves in a couple of bars opposite the hotel, where the 14th of July was clearly being celebrated well into the 15th. Miraculously, all the committee, even Paul Fisher, who was notorious for not being a morning person, made it to our committee meeting at 9:00 am where we deliberated on the awards for that year. On the last day we were let off the usual early morning scramble to the ferry as for the first time we were able to use Brittany's fast craft service with a lunchtime departure.

As we got on board and made our way to an area specially reserved for us cyclists, we were assailed by the not unwelcome sight of a large number of open champagne bottles. The bubbly flowed excessively, courtesy of Brittany Ferries, for a very generous slice of the return journey. I couldn't resist asking Paul Fisher, who was furiously quaffing the free fizz, what he thought now about the decision to come to Brittany. He mumbled something which I took to be a grudging approval! The "vets" among us judged it by far the best return we had ever had! Indeed, I became concerned that if we were to delay the presentations any longer, the power of speech might desert me.

The awards were duly given out, comments almost inevitably punctuated by the odd slur. Mumfy got the “Value Add” Award. Surprisingly, for such a consistent chump, he had never won this or its various antecedents before. In this special year, I really saw it as a lifetime idiot’s award for which he should be duly proud, and perhaps certified. It was well appreciated, particularly by those old timers who really knew what his full contribution had been.

One rider whose gritty enthusiasm was praised during the award ceremony was Sue Loveridge. She had first become interested in the Ride when a fellow Hayling beach dog walker, and by this time Ride regular, Sally Griffiths had approached her for sponsorship. However, her teaching commitments had meant that that she couldn’t fit it in. But in 2006, by which time she had gone part time, she took the plunge. She had never done anything like this and found it hard but very enjoyable. And in 2007 she had returned with her son Will and then in 2008 the whole family were to come, which meant entries from husband Pete and daughter Rachel. That was a bit of a shocker because she was actually a very good cyclist! While not unique among first time entrants, it was certainly rare. She was an international rower and as part of her training regularly did some serious cycling. Perhaps for the first time, we were welcoming an elite athlete into our midst! She found the Ride fun but unsurprisingly not particularly challenging!

Sue and Pete got really involved in cycling. They took part in many of the spin-off events including the C2C and most of

Fred's rides. One year they pedalled down to the South of France and another year to Spain. And they also completed Eurovelo 6, which runs all the way from Nantes to Budapest! While they have missed some of the main Rides, due largely to their other cycling commitments, they have returned regularly, loving the social side of it and in return helping to enrich that aspect of our events. Pete and Sue were not especially proficient riders or exceptional fund raisers, but their story is a great example of how cycling in the Paris to Hayling can lead to other things and have an impact on people which lasts way beyond that first summer.

Chapter 26
Team Ditcham

One of the most noteworthy trophy winners in 2007 were the cyclists from Ditcham Park School. For the second time they won the Team Award, which no other team had managed. The recognition yet again reflected the continued and indeed increase commitment that the school was making to the Bike Ride. Following the participation of Chris McQuade and then his friends in 2005, more and more pupils got involved. There have been over a hundred participants from the school as well as many parents. They have now raised over a quarter of a million pounds for various good causes. They have had a further significant statistical impact on the Ride, by dramatically reducing the average rider age! The enthusiasm of the youngsters has been impressive, with diligent practice over the preceding months to ensure successful completion of the Bike Ride, which indeed all have managed. We could have had even more entrants, but often we had to introduce a quota to make sure it remained an adult ride in which they were invited to participate, rather than the other way around!

But the story of Team Ditcham cycling didn't end with our Ride. Indeed, that proved to be only the beginning! The interest generated in cycling at the school has given rise to a thriving cycling club which is believed to be the only one in any Hampshire school, and when I last checked had seventy-five members. Given that the school (excluding a junior section) has less than three hundred pupils, that is extremely impressive. Colours have been awarded for cycling and the school's North Drive has been the setting of not only its own annual hill climb time trial but also the British Schools Hill Climb Time Trial Championships, and the club now has both an "on-road" and "off-road" section.

Several very good cyclists have emerged from its ranks. One in particular, Al Murison, who took part in our ride in 2006 and 2007, joined the Equipe CMI team, and has made a name for himself at a senior level. Other former pupils have also ridden at a high standard, attracting prestigious sponsors. Will Stretch eventually retired from Ditcham (and he only started there after he retired from Hayling School!) but remained involved in cycling activities for some time and took part in many Paris to Hayling's. Will is quick to point out that the growth of Ditcham Park Cycling has been due to strong support from successive head-teachers and other teachers and parents, several of whom have got involved in cycling for the first time.

But it is for his pedalling pupils that Will reserves his greatest praise. He is proud of the fact that many of his senior riders have enthusiastically helped coach younger ones, and indeed have continued doing this even after they have left the school. "I think that the way in which the older pupils have worked with the younger ones, mentoring them and riding alongside them, has helped change the culture of the school, bringing different year groups together in a way that would be difficult to achieve otherwise."

The two parents who eventually took over management of Team Ditcham from Will were Bike Ride veteran Roy Marshall and Ride regular Chris Williams. Recently, Chris made an interesting observation about the pupils. "In entering the Paris to Hayling they have been set a hard but achievable goal and had to work towards it. This is a great life lesson. Those Ditcham pupils that have completed the Bike Ride have had to commit to turning up every Sunday morning for training rides, often irrespective of the weather as the departure date approaches. They have had to dig into themselves as the training routes get harder and longer. Even though they are tired, I have never heard moans or complaints from them; what a fantastic attitude! The setting of goals, believing in yourself and achieving them is such a valuable lesson that can be applied to so many aspects of a young person's life." Furthermore, as Chris and Will both pointed out, taking part in this event ticked many boxes for pupils that entered for the Duke of Edinburgh's award scheme, something that the school has heavily promoted.

Chris emphasised the benefits that parents got from this event as well as the pupils. "The ride has not just influenced the school's pupils but the parents and their friends too. I cannot begin to estimate the number of non-pupil riders the school's participation in the Paris to Hayling has brought into cycling, but it's certainly a good number." Not all of these necessarily participated in the Paris to Hayling but rode on training rides, gained the benefit of exercise, and became supporters of the charity fund raising and cycling in general. This has also led to a set of spin-off ride groups and friendships. It has been a major part of my life for over a decade, and I am eternally grateful for its existence." The unexpected consequences from our Ride have been a continued source of immense satisfaction, and the fact that Chris McQuade and Will Stretch sparked the interest in others, which has led to so many people getting involved in cycling, is obviously a great example of this.

Chapter 27
The Loire Valley and Mayhem in Angers

After every ride we had always requested feedback from riders and no matter how much they had enjoyed it there were always things that could be improved. So, every year we refined our model. While we had often made small changes in the route, a good part of it wouldn't change from one year to the next so that made it easier to get things right. Eventually we thought it was inevitable that we would need a radical change of route if the event was to continue to thrive. When that happened, we wouldn't have the luxury of gradual improvement over twenty years, we would have so much to get right very quickly! But we felt that we would need at least two years to plan such a change.

With this in mind, the initial work on such a change could be said to have started in July 2006. John Adcock and I did a quick "recce" of some possible new towns/routes for the future as well as revisiting Versailles, which we planned to use again in 2007 and indeed did so. On this trip we "discovered" Alençon, Laval and Rennes. Alençon was an interesting place with a very historical core but also a very industrialised western perimeter. It was the latter aspect with its multiple roundabouts which presumably made twinning with Basingstoke a perfect cultural fit! Laval was a real discovery;

a delightful old town perched on the River Mayenne and on the edge of Brittany and Anjou. Rennes, the capital of Brittany, is of course a big city, comparable to Rouen, and like Rouen it was also rather picturesque. Our trip also took in St Malo, a port we felt bound to use if the Bike Ride shifted to the West, and Coutances, a pleasant town in the Cherbourg peninsular, though worryingly surrounded by some challenging hills! We had the idea that these towns would perhaps form the basis of a tour around Western Normandy and Brittany and be a replacement for the traditional Paris route in 2008.

Except for some roughly plotted routes, we had reached no firm conclusions on this when, in August 2007, Meryl Browne and I were having conversation about possibilities for the 2008 ride. She said that Angers in the Loire Valley looked nice but that she supposed this would be too far away. Well, I had always fancied cycling in the Loire Valley but that had been my view as well. It was some way to the south of the new towns that we had been looking at. But if we could organise a six-day event as in 2007, I wondered if we could somehow stretch ourselves to make it down to the Loire and have at least a day cycling along it before making our way back. Meryl and I were soon in France looking at practicalities. We liked what we saw, and when she spied a branch of Galeries Lafayette in Angers, Meryl, as keen on shopping as cycling, was adamant that we would be in the Loire valley in 2008!

Soon, back in the UK, Fred Dyer and fellow committee member Kevin Knight were closely studying routes. This involved hours of looking at maps, but also looking at mapping software. This was probably the first time that we had seriously used this. It wasn't as function-rich then as it has become now, but over the years, we have found this to be very valuable. Using mapping software is no substitute for physical inspection of a route but it perfectly complements that exercise and indeed allows you to design a proto-type before you even leave your home!

Things began to come together. We were fortunately able to use aspects of what John Adcock and I had found on the 2006 Recce. After initial communications with over a hundred hotels in nine towns we settled on a route which took us to Brittany via the Portsmouth — St Malô ferry and then on to Rennes, Laval (via lunch at Hayling town of Gorron), Angers, Tours, Alençon and Caen. Apart from booking thirty-two hotels and arranging the new set of wayside stops for morning, lunch and mid-afternoon breaks, every yard of the new route had to be plotted, checked, rechecked, and documented. This involved many days' work and at some stage most committee members made one or more trips to France. Although we were not going to be cycling in Paris, we decided, given its strength as a brand, to keep the Paris to Hayling name, albeit with a rather convenient subtitle of "Le Tour de Tours".

Everyone on the committee was excited about the new route. Moreover, this enthusiasm was generally communicated in terms of real confidence that the event would be a success. But I am sure I was not the only one to have some level of doubt, given the organisational challenges we faced. One night I woke suddenly worried that I had booked some hotels in Tours for the wrong date. That seemed unlikely since there were numerous checks and balances with others involved, as well as myself, but that did not stop me promptly going downstairs and opening my laptop to make sure that I had not made a blunder!

The first three days of the Ride as we headed from St Malô

down to the Loire probably appeared to the untrained eye to pass largely without incident, although for the organisers there were one or two situations where things were not quite as we wished and which we knew we would change before next year's ride. The one real negative was that we had a pretty nasty accident when two members of the Vodafone team crashed into each other and incurred some pretty nasty facial injuries. Not only were they out of the Ride, but at the time it looked like they would need a long time to recover, which thankfully turned out not to be the case. The accident, as both cyclists freely admitted, was due to horseplay and therefore their own fault. It was a salutary reminder that although a healthy and relatively safe pursuit, cycling can on occasion be dangerous if you don't concentrate. Serious injuries put the Support Team to the test, and this was no exception. One Support Team crew had to be focused on their needs, waiting for the ambulance to arrive, while liaising with the hospital and helping them to make arrangements to return home. I am proud to say that on this occasion, as on others (though fortunately not too many!), our organisation passed this test with flying colours, much to the appreciation of both cyclists involved.

On day four things nearly went horribly wrong as we left Angers. We had a hundred or so confused cyclists at the end of a dirt track, queuing to carry bikes under a bridge along an eighteen-inch-wide ledge overlooking the river. One slip and bike or cyclist, possibly both, would be on their way down to the Atlantic. Surely this couldn't be right? One or two cyclists had taken a wrong turning, and as often happens, those that were in close pursuit (in this case unfortunately the majority of riders) followed them without bothering to look at their route notes. I was myself among this confused group, but together with several other committee members agreed that this seemed unlikely to be the correct way. However, despite a scrutiny of our notes, it wasn't clear what the right route was. I rather uselessly volunteered the information that even though I was the President, it didn't mean that I knew what was going on. "That is obvious," retorted one of many riders, confused that they now found themselves on the Paris to Hayling Cycle-Cross. Tempers were probably on the point of failing and possibly the Ride's famous bonhomie might have been in danger of becoming a little less bon. However, at that moment, regular rider Jeff Lane probably saved the day. "I hear," he exclaimed, "that it's about to get difficult."

When there is a confusing turning, as was obviously the case here, there is normally a support vehicle lurking in the vicinity, or at least the Support Team will have put up some signs but strangely, neither were apparent here. So, I called our Support Team member Rod Elliot, only to discover that unfortunately the team were having their own crisis. Angers' confusing road system meant that most were having trouble finding their own way out of the ancient Anjou capital. Indeed, at least one of the support vehicles was now accidentally on the motorway whizzing towards Paris!

We had had a route crisis of a similar nature before, and indeed in 1988 we had completely lost the route out of Paris, but I thought after two decades that we had probably got beyond that! Rod tried to clarify the route for us over the phone, but we were still confused so we decided on balance to press on alongside the river. Only later, after we had scrambled up the riverbank and joined a real road, did we discover how a very minor route note glitch had led to this confusion. It was a glitch so minor, I should add, that quite a lot of the more sensible riders had figured it out, ignoring the turning we had taken and kept on the right route!

The rest of the day passed without a hitch in July sunshine, ideal for cycling. The magnificent landscape of the Loire and its tributaries, the châteaux and vineyards were all simply breath taking. Most stopped in Saumur, a delightful town between the Loire and Thouet rivers, for their lunch break. The smiling faces and countless comments along the lines of "This is the best day's cycling ever!" said it all. In Tours that evening, virtually every rider seemed to radiate a glow of contentment after this truly memorable day. The following morning, we were again a bit worried. In order to stage the Angers to Tours leg of the Ride, we needed to follow it with a long (ninety-five miles) and potentially hilly ride to Alençon. We wondered if this would prove too much, and if the pleasure of the Loire would be viewed differently after we reached Alençon. At lunchtime, the sweat streaming from most riders suggested that it had been a fairly tough few hours, but in the afternoon, when many had thought things might get even hillier, a cleverly-plotted route by Fred managed to avoid virtually all the hills and in particular some nasty elevations close to Le Mans. All riders were clearly glad to arrive in Alençon, but none seemed inclined to attack the organisers, which we took as a positive.

The next day went quite smoothly as we headed for Caen. Traditionally, on this last day, many wear fancy dress. The Sussex Brewery team looked superb as mime artists and even manged to buy their first round of drinks in complete silence. Assorted fairies, elves and other creatures also contributed strongly to a colourful display and to plenty of strange looks from the French.

The nightmare of a booking disaster briefly looked likely to become a reality when a hotel in Caen told us that they had no record of our reservation. Fortunately, this was an administrative error on the part of the hotel, which was quickly rectified. Soon we were into our traditional last-night bash in Caen Castle, with much of the fun due to the Crooners, who again kindly travelled over specially to play for us free of charge. This proved to be a marvellous conclusion to our week's cycling. The smiling, if somewhat haggard faces the following morning as we again headed back on the Fast Cat from Caen to Portsmouth, left no room for doubt. Although we had taken a risk on a new route and had some issues to sort out, it had been a success.

Andrew Wilson was a first-time entrant in 2008, teaming up with his old school mate Mike Willenbruch and with the cycling friends Mike had made a few years previously, Colin Turner and Lionel "Jeff" Jeffries. They called themselves Team CALM, after the first names. Although, given some of the incidents in which Andrew would later feature, I did wonder at one time if this was a corrupted abbreviation of CALIMITY. Andrew was fifty-eight and, by his own admission, did not look like a cyclist and had not really done anything active for nearly twenty years but he relished the experience. And, like his cycling mates, Andrew would do many more Rides and still cycles most weeks throughout the year. Now in his late sixties, he claims that due to his bike escapades he is fitter now than he has been for years. "I played football when I was forty and was put in goal because I couldn't run, but now I reckon I could run round the pitch." Andrew never told me whether he was referring to a full-size or five-a-side pitch, but I think the point is well made and others have said similar. Liz Marsden, leader of the "The

Dwarfs" and about the same age as Andrew, also recently told me that she was convinced that she was fitter now than she had been twenty-five years ago when she first entered the Paris to Hayling.

On the day of departure from France, Andrew Wilson decided, like a number of riders, to continue wearing the fancy dress outfit that he had worn the previous day. But, having dressed in his quintessentially English costume and with the ferry leaving in a few hours, he realized that he had left his passport back in Rouen. There was no time to retrieve it, so he needed to visit the local police station. I am sure the local gendarmes were somewhat surprised to have a visit from a bicycling Morris dancer. However, that might well have made them all the more eager to give him the necessary emergency paperwork to get out of the country.

We finished 2008 in pretty good shape. The huge investment on recces and the strengthening Euro had hit us financially, but we had some reserves from years when we had made a slight profit and so we were able to absorb this. Moreover, given its success, we planned to keep the same route for 2009 and so recce costs would reduce. As we looked out to 2009, the reputation of British cycling was surely at an all-time high. Not only did we amass a truck-load of medals at the Olympics (a foretaste of 2012!), but also Bradley Wiggins and Mark Cavendish distinguished themselves at the Tour de France in July. Paris to Hayling riders may not have been of the same sporting quality and few had or would obtain medals or garlands for their cycling prowess, but the fact that their efforts once again raised thousands of pounds for charity surely made them cycling heroes too.

Chapter 28
Riding Out the Global Financial Crisis and Cow Trouble

During the winter of 2008/2009 we were presented with several challenges. As the global financial system crashed and sterling plummeted against the Euro, I wondered if we would have a 2009 ride at all. Over 60% of our costs related to expenditure in France, so we were rather vulnerable. Moreover, it was soon clear that many regular riders could simply not afford to come or were just too busy ensuring that their jobs or businesses survived. We also found that some of our 2008 sponsors were not going to be able to help in 2009.

In January, with the real prospect of sterling reaching parity with the Euro, we held a crisis committee meeting. Regrettably, we were forced to make some stringent cuts in our costs; the last-night party would have to be a less elaborate affair than in previous years, and while no comprising would be made regarding safety, the size of the support crew would have to be reduced. Possibly our meeting has some direct impact in the fate of sterling as it slowly began to strengthen, which certainly helped as we paid hotel deposits in the coming months.

I had some interesting feedback that winter when the CEO and Chairman of Qlik returned from a visit to the World Economic Forum in Davos. They had been at a cocktail when they said they heard a Brit close by talking about cycling and referencing the Paris to Hayling Ride. Obviously, I was quite chuffed by this. Could this have led to an entry from the UN Secretary General or a world statesman? We never managed to establish who it was that they heard talking and we never got a resulting high-profile entry, but it made me smile. Barak Obama, we would welcome you. Donald Trump? Well, I have a feeling that entry is lost in the post!

On the weekend of 17th and 18th May we staged our annual Channel to Channel Ride. This popular event was about to celebrate its tenth birthday. Unfortunately, the howling wind and torrential rain on both days made it, in the view of many "vets", one of the toughest rides we had staged. I have probably never felt more uncomfortable on a bike than when pedalling across the Somerset levels, with absolutely nothing to break up the wind and rain coming in furiously from the Bristol Channel and almost no trees to hide under. When we left the Levels it got little better. However, when you are descending a hill, you don't expect the wind to be blowing you back up it, but sometimes it felt like that this year. But, notwithstanding the weather, all seemed to enjoyed the weekend in a masochistic sort of way.

In July we set off on the Paris to Hayling with a hundred and forty-six cyclists, the smallest group for some years. Except for omitting the diversion to Gorron on day two, the Ride kept to the same route as 2008, which meant landing in France at St Malô and then returning to Portsmouth via Caen. It took us three days to reach the Loire Valley via the Brittany capital of Rennes, and Laval before heading off for Angers. Twenty-five miles south of Laval at Château Gontier, we met the coach carrying the three-day riders as we had done in 2008.

A few miles short of Château Gontier, I saw a very strange thing. I had just re-joined the official route, having accidentally taken a detour, and was cycling a short distance behind Magnus MacFarlane when he suddenly fell from his saddle into a bush, and lay there motionless, with just his legs sticking out of the bush towards the road. I drew up alongside him fearing the worst. Magnus cried out, "I cannot move!" leading me to think that this could be serious — maybe a heart attack! Fortunately, he quickly elaborated on his predicament "I cannot move," he said, "because I am surrounded by bloody stinging nettles!" It took some time for a group of us to help Magnus carefully extricate himself from the bush. We searched for a few dock leaves to deal with the stings he had sustained, but miraculously he seemed to have no other injuries. Apparently, his chain had jammed, which is a common reason for Bike Ride falls, as myself and my body know all too well. However, when I saw him the following night he was covered in bruises, leading me to think that he had been a bit more damaged than I thought, but these turned out to be the result of a second fall! Needless to say, "Tumbling Magnus McFarlane" won an award that year for his cycling "prowess".

As we left Angers and followed the River Loire eastward to Tours, we were blessed, as in 2008, with superb weather. This complimented the stunning scenery, with elegant castles lording over spectacular vineyards, and of course the river itself. Perhaps it was even a bit too hot in the afternoon, as my water bottles ran dry, and with our limited Support Team stretched by a few injuries, I was getting rather thirsty. But then I stumbled on another innovation, a support vehicle with a gin and tonic tap. Pete Alloway and Lynne Harris had agreed to do a year on support to bolster a team which we had found it hard to assemble, even though its size was reduced compared to previous years. As seasoned riders, they clearly knew what a fellow cyclist would want on an afternoon such as this!

Unfortunately, the weather deteriorated over the last two days, and riders had to contend with strong winds and heavy rain. On the Tours to Alençon leg I had agreed to drive a vehicle, to allow one of the Support Team to have a day's riding. Given the weather it was a good call! About halfway through the morning one of our riders had a unique accident. Fergus Houghton-Connell, a member of the Ditcham Park Team, encountered a cow crossing the road at the bottom of a descent. I saw a rather mangled bike before I saw Fergus. It did not look good! However, rather surprisingly, Fergus was rather less bent out of shape than the bike, and indeed was almost unscathed, as was the cow, who disappeared into a neighbouring field before we could have words with him. Fergus was transported in a van for the rest of the day but was back on a borrowed bike the following morning. This was a Ride first. No cow had ever disrupted our ride before or equally none has done so since. The bike was completely wrecked, with not one component undamaged. The frame hung on the wall in the bike shed at Ditcham for several years, I guess as a kind of trophy!

Luckily, by the evening of our final day, the rain had stopped, so we could yet again sample the delights of an apéritif in the grounds of Caen Castle before our last night party at that venue. Sadly, there was no band this year and a limited menu compared to previous years, but it still provided a good end to an enjoyable evening with copious celebratory drinks.

Next morning, on board the Brittany Ferries' Fast Cat, we had perhaps the roughest crossing in our history. Indeed, so rough was the weather that for once nobody seemed to want to drink, and we were lucky the ferry had not been cancelled, particularly since we would have had to revert to a Plan B which, as far as I recall, did not exist. But even though we were rolling everywhere, we were still able to present the Bike Ride Awards to great acclaim and we were treated to an "Ode to Tour de Tours Nights" by our "fallen hero", Magnus MacFarlane.

Sarah Jeffries first entered in 2009. "My son Simon did the Ride for the first time in 2008, aged fourteen, with Ditcham. He texted me telling me what a great time he was having, how much I would love cycling in France and that I had to do it the following year. Not likely, I thought! When he returned, he made me get on my bike and took me for a six-mile ride which nearly killed me — I had only cycled to the shops and back a few times in the previous twenty years." Will Stretch then encouraged her to train with Ditcham Park Team, starting with short rides and lots of stops. "Will made it easy and enjoyable." She persuaded he friend Judy Hunt to enter the Paris to Hayling with her. Judy's son Ben had been one of the earlier Ditcham riders back in 2005. "We both loved every minute. The ride from Tours to Alencon was in about forty degrees of heat and Roy Marshall kept telling us there was an ice cream shop in a couple of miles to keep us going! Eventually, about twenty miles later, we found it."

Although Sarah would not give up cycling, she only cycled on the Paris to Hayling once more in 2012. She had planned to cycle again in 2010 but it was proving difficult to assemble a Support Team, so she agreed to help out. Except for 2012, Sarah would henceforth be a key member of the Support Team, but in addition she would join the committee. Sarah was a proven "doer" with great organisational skills, having, for example, been heavily involved in producing a celebrity cookbook to raise money for the Khao Lak Appeal (see Chapter 22) and she brought this quality to our event with some great results in future years.

Lori Poore was another new rider who would go on to be a valuable committee member. She had met Joy Hayward and Richard Boswell at a gym near her Fareham home. "The first year's ride was a tough 5 Days. I had only ever ridden 30 miles before."

But it didn't put Lori off since like many before her she was to find the experience addictive and indeed life changing. The next year she was back and greatly improved as a cyclist and has been involved ever since.

"It's a wonderful event and I particularly like the fact that you can chose your own charity."

Despite the uncertain economic climate, we felt confident that the 2010 Twenty-fifth Anniversary event would be popular. So, by August we were already in deep planning mode, and places were being filled with unprecedented speed. We then had some dreadfully tragic news; Meryl Browne had died from cancer. Even after being diagnosed, she had still done the Ride twice, but sadly she had been too frail to take part in 2009, though she did join us for the last night in Caen.

In recent years nobody had contributed more to the Bike ride than Meryl and it was not surprising that many Paris to Hayling regulars were among those who packed St Marys Church on Hayling for her memorial service. I was asked to say a few words on behalf of the Bike Ride. As a committee member, and indeed latterly deputy chairman, she gave so much to the Bike Ride in so many ways. She was, of course, a key proponent of adopting the Loire Valley route and helped with much of the initial planning for this major change. The Paris to Hayling owed her a very great debt and would remember her fondly. I felt truly honoured to be asked to speak and to reflect on how she had become a huge part of the bike ride. It certainly struck me, not for the first time, just how expansive the effects of this event have become. It seemed only appropriate that the 2010 ride should be dedicated to Meryl.

Chapter 29
When Mary Met Mark

Together with hundreds of strong friendships, this Bike Ride has resulted in at least eighteen marriages or long-term relationships. We never set out to be a marriage bureau, but we seem to have become quite good at it! However, there is one that brings a certain romantic symmetry to the Bike Ride story and which I think worth covering in some detail.

Mary Burras was the twin sister of Louise, the baby whose cot death had led to the original Paris to Hayling ride. She and her other siblings had obviously grown up aware of this annual event and its special connection with her and the family. As previously mentioned, her parents had done the Bike Ride several times and her aunt Barbara and her uncle Chris had also taken part, as had two cousins. In 2009 she and her lifelong friend Charlotte McGrath, whose father Steve was also a Paris to Hayling rider, decided that they would give it a go.

As Mary recalls, "I borrowed my Aunty Barbara's bike and Charlotte and I joined in the official practice rides held on a Sunday from the Ship pub. We were pretty slow. There was one cyclist Jeff well into his seventies who was much faster than us. Disaster struck when we had a puncture. We didn't have spare anything and even if we had we wouldn't have known what to do with it. As we were at the back anyway, all the cyclists had gone on not realising our problem. Fortunately, a passing cyclist unconnected with the Paris to Hayling stopped and fixed the puncture, giving us his own spare tube." When Mary and Charlotte got back to the Ship they told the story to the speedy septuagenarian that they had encountered earlier. He was, in fact, Jeff of Team CALM and he and fellow team members Colin, Andrew and Mike suggested that the girls should stick with them in future. "And we did. We became part of their team and we practiced together that summer often on Wednesdays as well as Sundays. Charlotte and I then went on the shorter Three Day Ride. But on the second day after ten miles, I stopped and cried, aware that I still had over eighty more miles to do. I had done all that training, and my body had seized up!"

Mary had discovered, like many before her and since, that part of the challenge of our ride is that it's repetitive. There may be charity rides who cover more miles in a day (though not many) but doing the distances we do day after day and ignoring the aches and strains gained on previous days adds to the achievement. But anyhow, Mary got through it. "The team stopped, and Colin Turner told me I could really do this and that they would not go on without me. After that and one of Colin's energy bars I was all right!"

Mark had been persuaded to do the Bike Ride by a past rider after a few drinks at a New Year's Eve party. He was reasonably fit and active and found the ride less of a challenge than Mary. Realising that they should have bells on their bikes, Mark and his cycle companion had stopped and bought them in a Decathlon somewhere en-route. "We then decided that if we came across any fit birds with nice bums, we would ring our bells." And thus, it was that Mary received a ring of Mark's bell. Nothing was said, although glances were exchanged. So, I guess you can say there was a slight frizzante! Then after the long day in the saddle they were both in the same hotel in Alencon. As Mary arrived exhausted in her cycling clothes, she encountered Mark already showered and changed, having arrived some time before. Their eyes met and then Mary uttered the magic and indeed unforgettable words, "I don't suppose you have a spare phone charger?" Unfortunately, Mark couldn't oblige, but they introduced themselves. Mark recalls, "I knew the basic history of the Bike Ride and how it started so when Mary told me she was the other twin my jaw dropped"." Mary remembers, "I had just cycled over ninety miles and was in a pretty dreadful state, yet he still seemed interested!"

That night they ate with their separate groups but did spend some time talking between then and the end of the Ride. At the finish on Hayling they were chatting and having a drink. They agreed that they should exchange contact details, but Mark then disappeared. Charlotte, her friend, reported that he had been seen being greeted by a woman and had left. "Did it look like his sister?" asked Mary hopefully. "No" she replied, "Definitely not"." Mary was bereft; she really thought they had clicked. She then met up with her father, so proud of her for having completed this ride that was so special to the family and poured her heart out to him. "There was this man, there was really a thing and then there was this woman." Mike calmed her down and comforted her as best he could but in any event for two weeks she heard nothing!

Mark takes up the story. "I really liked Mary, I wanted to stay in touch, but I was in a relationship. This was coming to an end anyway, but meeting Mary brought that to a final conclusion. But I wanted to properly end that first. When I had done that, I didn't know how to contact her, so I joined Facebook. Having found Mary that way I then messaged her. I told her I was sorry that I didn't say goodbye, that I really wanted to see her again and that I found my time with her enchanting."

They arranged to meet and Mark, being a romantic tree surgeon, gave her a Bonsai Tree, though Mary didn't know how to look after it and it subsequently died! A couple of years later they married and now have two lovely children. You couldn't make this up, could you? The Bike Ride that had started out of something so tragic to the Burras family had now all those years later brought happiness to Louise's sister! Well, dry your eyes now and get ready for the next chapter.

Chapter 30
A Ride for Meryl

It was clear that the 2010 Ride would be something of a watershed. It marked twenty-five years of the Paris to Hayling, and several key committee members had announced their intentions of standing down. I had myself announced that I wished to become a less "hands-on" President.

Bike Ride numbers came in at an unprecedented rate, no doubt largely due to the special anniversary. Financially, we had come out of 2009 far better than expected, although monies raised were significantly reduced. We were able to invest in a larger Support Team for this year and plan a more lavish final-night party. In keeping with it being the Ride for Meryl, it was heart-warming that her four children, Joshua, Kate, Alex, and Oliver, along with her sister Caroline, all signed up for the event. As Oliver commented after Meryl's death, "Straight away, we knew we'd all do the tour this year in her memory. This has been such a defining thing for her; it seemed a natural thing to do."

The 2010 event again went to the Loire valley. For the first time in many years, we had only one ride with everyone cycling all the way from Hayling to Tours and back. This saved the hassle of arranging to transport bikes to France. We had been lucky that for some years Kuhn and Nagel had generously provided us with a lorry for free but arranging this and ensuring that the two ride groups had linked up had always been problematic. As a compromise between the six- and four-day rides of recent years, we settled on a five-day itinerary. This meant that we had two ninety-mile days but, while this and often strong winds made it a tough ride in some respects, it was once again a success. The generally good weather no doubt helped, as of course did the magnificence of the Loire Valley.

The traditional fancy dress on the last day was particularly noteworthy, with more than half the riders dressing up. We had two Robin Hood teams, a Peter Pan group, Andy Pandy, Louby Loo, and many others. Paul Fisher and I joined in as Team 118 118, though sadly my moustache kept on falling off!

In Caen we once again had a great party in the castle. We had had a little glitch a few days before when we found that the band we had originally booked had got the date wrong, but we were saved by local Hayling band Where's Billy. The party went on well into the night or early morning, even though we had to get up at 6:00 am for our ferry. Sadly, we weren't able to catch a lunchtime boat this year due to changes in the timetable. We had not had this early start for a few years and certainly had not missed it! There is always a worry that we won't get everyone to the ferry on time to catch the boat, but as in previous years we managed, just! The last one to rise and depart from his hotel, as his fellow organisers could have anticipated, was none other than Paul Fisher himself.

During our award ceremony on the ferry, Paul announced that he would be standing down as chairman of the Ride at the next AGM. Paul had been chairman since 1994 and had turned a successful event into a highly successful one. The amount of time he had invested in the event had been truly staggering. It was very much his decision, and I think it took everyone by surprise. I suggested to Paul that it would be fitting if he joined me as Co-President, a position which he duly accepted.

Perhaps Paul wanted to make sure he would not be forgotten, but for whatever reason he felt the need to have a spectacular tumble shortly before we left France. Cycle falls are often amusing to look at and this one, outside the famous Pegasus Bridge Café, was no exception. Paul, in his haste to see if Madame Gondrée was in residence, misjudged a kerb at the café's entrance and broke his fall by hitting and indeed demolishing a postcard stand with a widespread scattering of postcards onto the café's patio. It's fortunate that Paul was unhurt since his cycling companions were in no fit state to assist due to being doubled up with laughter. Equally fortunately, perhaps, the postcard stand was undamaged, and I believe all postcards were retrieved. Paul, however, took it in very good spirits, and graciously accepted the "Value Add" trophy during the award ceremony on the boat in recognition of the amusement his tumble had given us. This was not just the fall of the 2010 Ride, but one of the most notable ever.

So, it was over; twenty-five years. We raised in excess of £85,000 that year, which meant that since 1986 we had raised over £1,200,000, and in that time had benefitted about five hundred good causes. What a great formula! You spend a few days in France, see some fantastic countryside, eat, and drink what you want under the pretext that it's fuel for the cycling, and then return having raised money for charity. Clearly, I never imagined, twenty-five summers before, when I did my first solo ride for Cot Death Research, that things would turn out like they had, and they certainly would not have done if that group of friends had not pushed me into doing a second

Ride. So many people had brought us this far. committee members, cyclists, and Support Team members, and I know they all shared in the satisfaction of having contributed toward a successful and sustained event. Above all, it had been Paul Fisher with his constant effort and enthusiasm who had taken up the Paris to Hayling challenge and got us to Year Twenty-five. There were still some more Rides to come and with them some twists and turns, a lot of happiness and fun times but also some sadness.

Chapter 31
Lots of Changes

2011 was the beginning of a new chapter in the Bike Ride. While Paul Fisher stayed on as a committee member, Jon Tawse took over as chairman. Their styles were somewhat different. In contrast to the verbiage used by Paul, Jon was rather more succinct. This meant that meetings were shorter and generally run in a more efficient way, a format which we have adhered to ever since. Jon could also see that the committee had become rather large. At one time it had close to twenty members. Few stood down but new people kept on volunteering and election was automatic. Jon began to rationalize this as well recognizing that there was a small core that were key to the committee's functions, whereas others who may well be able to support the Ride in various ways didn't need to be at the meetings. And in this respect also, the Ride is operating today under Jon's revised approach.

One of the first tasks facing Jon and his committee was working out a new route. The Loire Valley rides had been very popular. However, if there was a shortcoming, it was the long ride out of the Loire from Tours to Alencon. We had had longer days, but it was long enough, and for the last thirty kilometres there was not a single en-route bar! However, the timing of ferries back to England meant that we had to return via Caen and an overnight stop in Alencon was the only practical way of doing it. So, Jon Tawse and his team organised an innovative new ride, which all who took part in seemed to thoroughly enjoy. It was a tour of Normandy and Brittany. The route took in some of the 2010 Ride, heading from St Malo to Rennes and then on to Laval, but rather than then making for the Loire valley, riders headed northeast to Le Mans and then on to Argentan before the last night in Caen.

In 2011 we introduced shorter and longer options on several days. The previous year Jon had seen that some riders finished so late that their meal choices were limited due to the fact that restaurants were booked up. He felt that this change would give some of the slower cyclists the opportunity to get in earlier. There was a bit of nervousness about it with a fear that it might just turn out to be somewhat shambolic with us losing track of which route particular riders were on but in fact it worked out very well. At certain points on selected days riders simply had to make a choice between taking the long route or the short one and the Support Team were then divided according to the volume that chose each of the options. Another first was having two social evenings — not just the last-night party but also one mid-week in Le Mans. In both cases we were entertained by our very own Bike Ride band The Kings of Le Mans which featured, among others, Jon Tawse on bass guitar.

We were cycling between Le Mans and Argentan on July 14th. As normal on this public holiday, there were limited wayside stops at which to get lunch, let alone a drink. However, there were a few boulangeries open en-route in Alencon which we conveniently passed through around lunchtime. But there were no bars open, which greatly disappointed Paul Fisher and I since we wanted a beer. From previous visits we knew there were a couple of bars by the station and after I suggested that they may be open we headed off in that direction, fully confident that with our good knowledge of the town we would be able to re-join the route from there. We had our beers and indeed did re-join the route. But the gods looked favourably on us that day because by re-joining this from a different angle we entirely missed what was reckoned to be the worst hill that had featured on our Ride in years! It was all quite unintentional but also very fortunate. But as we got close to joining the rest of our group, a few miles from the town of Sees, Paul had a puncture. He repaired it and then soon had another one and then another. After the fourth or maybe the fifth I looked at Paul's tube. Being frugal is one thing but this was ridiculous! It couldn't really be described as a tube at all just as series of patches holding a few slivers of rubber together. Paul conceded defeat, I gave him a spare tube and we went on our way puncture free for the rest of the day.

In the autumn, the Paris to Hayling organisation helped another bike ride. Some months earlier I had met with Mark Glen, CEO of Hope HIV. This charity, now renamed as WeSeeHope, supports vulnerable children and adolescents in a number of East and Southern African countries. I suggested that we could apply our expertise and experience in supporting them in their own charity cycle event. Thus, was born their London to Hayling Charity Bike Ride. This was staged for a number of years and raised nearly £150,000 to help some of the World's most needy children. We organised a route, thanks largely to Fred Dyer, supplied Support Teams, offered some general advice on charity bike rides, and also recruited a few cyclists! We linked up with WeSeeHope on the Channel to Channel as well since for some years on the last morning of this event we have invited cyclists who have enjoyed their weekend to throw some money in a collection bucket for this worthy charity. And they have been most generous!

Chapter 32
Something Different: Going Dutch

We thought we had been innovative moving out of Paris to other parts of France but what we did next was a real major step. The idea of going to Holland came from Sarah Jeffries. As has often happened, getting involved with our event had led to other things and in this case it resulted in Sarah and her friend Judy Hunt entering another Bike Ride in Holland. She was very positive about her Dutch experience and suggested we give it a go! I think there was some scepticism at first because it was such a change and of course it would be different. Riding all the way back from Holland was not practical in an acceptable time frame, let alone cycling there and back. And it was realised there would be a need to transport riders to Harwich for the ferry to the Hook of Holland. However, Sarah was very persuasive and the committee, having examined all the practical issues, decided that even though there were some challenges and risks we should do it. Although we referred to it as a Ride in Holland, Holland technically refers to one area of Netherlands, divided into the provinces of North and South Holland, but we also rode for a time in the province of Utrecht.

As in 2011, numbers were down on past years. There was no doubt that some of our more geographically astute regulars had picked up on the fact that Holland wasn't in France and didn't like the idea but other factors, and in particular the economic climate, played a bigger part. In any case, our entry capacity was limited by the overland transport requirements, so we were by no means despondent. Hotels were duly arranged, although it was strange not to be dealing with the familiar Ibis and Mercure chains. Ferries were sorted, there would be a night onboard both ways, and a route was plotted.

Holland is arguably the most cycle-friendly country in the world. Everyone seems to ride a bike and there are reputably more bikes there than people. Cycling is embedded in their culture. One aspect of this fact was brought home to Tony Hart and Sarah Farmer as they set about route planning. Although we had some challenges in figuring out ways in and out of Paris and some other smaller cities, setting a route in France had generally involved identifying country routes which conveniently wound their way through France's rural expanses to our major stops. In Holland it was typically a matter of choosing the right cycle path from a number of options connecting towns in a well-developed network. And of course, in Holland we didn't need to factor in which route would avoid the nasty hills because they all did! Invariably they were real cycle paths and not some miserly piece of marked-off main road as can happen in the UK and also, unlike in the UK, they didn't suddenly end, plunging you back into traffic. Often, they were highly sophisticated with traffic lights to manage the intersection of multiple cycle routes and sometimes even with roundabouts. A consequential difference of choosing this multi-cycle-path landscape was that that the roads were often some way from the route. This slowed down the plotting process as it was necessary to do much of it on a bike and we were a little concerned that it could pose a problem for ride support with vans and cars being separated from the charity pedlars. But we remained optimistic as we set out for Harwich and the start of a new chapter in the Bike Ride's history.

As one rider put it, "A great ride, it's just a pity you didn't organise it in the summer!" Over the years our annual ride has had varying weather from outrageous heat waves to cold and wet. But this was beyond anything previously experienced, with daily torrential rain coupled with arctic-like temperatures. The biggest medical risk in 2012 was hypothermia rather than sun stroke. And then there was the wind, but of course Holland is flat, and the abundance of windmills is a bit of a "give-away", so perhaps this should not have been such a great surprise! But despite all these challenges, it was a great success. The feedback from riders was very positive and I personally enjoyed it!

Generally speaking, we dealt well with the risks and challenges. Riders had to take off their pedals to help with the storage when we loaded the bikes for transportation to Harwich. Taking your right and left pedals off is easy but it's important to put them back on the same cranks! If you don't and mix them up you will damage the threads because there is a right hand and a left hand pedal! It wasn't always the case but the Wright brothers, cycle shop owners as well as aviation pioneers, came up with this concept to get over the fact that the left hand pedal use to loosen after a time. Thanks to Orville and Wilbur, I and other organisers feared that somebody would (pardon the pun) screw up on the pedal front but I was wrong and against all odds every cyclist managed to put them back on the right way with no threads being damaged! Cycling in Holland is different from France. While the latter is quite bike friendly the former is excessively so. Not only is there an abundance of paths everywhere but also when they meet a road, bikes rather than cars have priority. We got some strange looks on occasions when we were waiting at a crossing or junction for a car to pass when they were of course waiting for us. Support, as we anticipated did prove a challenge, but certainly not impossible and as usual the team led by Joe Macey performed superbly. Sadly, we had one pretty serious accident with one rider falling and breaking her hip. There proved to be complications with the injury but fortunately she was back on her bike for the following year.

Our expectations of a flat route were fully justified, although we did refer to a couple of minor inclines as being "Dutch Mountains". Generally speaking, the "biggest" climbs were over the slightly humped bridges that frequently spanned the many canals that we encountered. We did miss the rolling countryside of Northern France, but the Dutch landscape was not without variety. On the first day we spent much of the day riding across sand dunes and at other times we cycled through forest and of course alongside many canals and rivers. Water was never far away and during the course of the Ride we took no less than six ferries. Also, on one occasion, when meeting the Rhine near Rotterdam, we cycled under a river!

The towns we passed through were generally very pretty and well preserved. The definite exception to this was Hook of Holland which was certainly not pretty but then very few ferry ports are. From here we made our entry and exit to Holland. On day one we headed north of here to the Scheveningen pleasant resort which is essentially Hague by the sea. It is, however, as anyone who is reading this aloud will have worked out, a tough word to pronounce and as I understand it a particularly tough one for any non-native Dutch speaker to pronounce correctly. For this reason, during World War II the Dutch used to use it as a test word. If someone was pronouncing it incorrectly then they may be a German spy, the "sch" part in particular being certain in the Dutch view to be delivered by a foreigner in an unintelligible spit spray! From Scheveningen we had perhaps the best riding of the trip with a ride over sand dunes along the North Sea Coastal path to the city of Harlaam.

The following day, coming into Amsterdam was interesting to say the least! We arrived at around 5:00 pm and it was rush hour on the cycle paths. Sharing these with local commuters was quite intimidating and indeed fraught with danger, particularly since many people seemed to be cycling while carrying an umbrella or answering a phone or indeed in some cases, I believe, both. Our night in Amsterdam was good and some of us had the advantage of a guided tour of selected local cafés hosted by rider and former local, Paul Clutterbuck. Paul has written a book "Inside Amsterdam" telling the story of some sixty of the city's historic cafés. (No, not that sort of café! Those featured are "brown cafés", local watering holes.) Paul wrote the book to raise money for Operation Smile, the same charity for which he had entered the Bike Ride. An enjoyable bi-product of his writing was of course that he had to spend quite a bit of time in these establishments as well as quite a few others which didn't make it into the final publication.

There is real history involved with each of these cafés and almost all are still independently owned. We couldn't visit all of them during the course of the evening, though we did our best. Among those we did enter were the In't Apfen and the Wynand Fockink. The former was housed in one of the few remaining wooden buildings in Amsterdam and contained an amazing collection of artifacts. The latter is both a bar and distillery. Paul insisted that no trip to Amsterdam was complete without a gin tasting at this celebrated establishment, and, of course, a predictable snigger as visitors first discover the name! Leaving Amsterdam, the following morning was perhaps the wettest part of that wet ride. I left the hotel with a group of cycling companions but as we did so the heavens opened. The rain was so heavy that within less than a hundred yards we got off our bikes and took shelter. With no café of any sort in sight we had to settle for the entrance to an office block where we waited some minutes before feeling brave enough to continue.

As we pressed on towards Utrecht, the wet and the cold got to everyone. A shivering Ditcham Park pupil had to be wrapped in silver foil blanket to fend off hyperthermia. And Andrew Wilson had a fall. Medical assistance was summoned and indeed an ambulance soon arrived but, from the writing on the side, it appeared that this was a veterinary ambulance! However, the bemused Andrew wasn't complaining since the vet or paramedic who attended him was apparently very attractive. They covered him up with a horse blanket. His fellow cyclists should of course have been concerned for his welfare but not a bit of it. Shouts of "Give him a sugar lump" or indeed a carrot were interspersed with attempts to photograph Andrew's rescuer who was undoubtedly brightening up a very dreary day. He was bundled into the back of the ambulance and taken for further medical examination. At this point Andrew might well have been nervous. Where was he going? To a hospital, hopefully, but maybe the knacker's yard! Fortunately, it was the former and he was soon checked out, informed that all was okay except for some bruising and later that day he re-joined the Ride.

For me, Edam and Delft were particularly attractive. In Edam it occurred to me that we had completed visits to three famous cheese towns in the three countries where I had ridden since 1986. Pont L'Eveque in France. Cheddar in UK and now Edam in Holland. In Delft we were surprised to see the tower of The Oude Kerke leans more than the one in Pisa!

The Dutch people were very friendly and, with their good command of English, asking the way on the rare occasions when riders did get lost was pain free. One day I was with a small group of misplaced pedlars and when we asked for directions he got in his car and called out for us to follow him, soon leading us to the right route. And I believe there were other similarly kind acts. In general, the overnight stops were well received but the Postillion hotels on Wednesday and Thursday night were really outstanding and, in my view, possibly the best hotels we have had in twenty-seven years of this event.

With the move from France, the issue of our name obviously came up again. We were now some way from a Paris to Hayling Ride. Some years previously, recognizing that we might go elsewhere, we had decided to brand the web site as The Hayling Cycle Ride, and this clearly helped when we moved to the Loire Valley, and it did again with our Le Mans ride and Holland venture. Moreover, in these years there has always been a sub-title such as Le Tour de Tours, Le Mans 26 and Hayling to Holland. But the Paris to Hayling brand was by now so strong that it understandably lingered and was often used. But, in any case, what's really in a name because, as I pointed out, Panama Hats are made in Ecuador; Munich's Oktoberfest is largely in September and The Tour of France normally involves other countries as well.

Chapter 33
A Surprising Development

Paul Fisher's contribution to the Bike Ride over many years was truly impressive. While I was always involved to some extent, family and business commitments meant that at times my input was limited. Paul, however, was a constant presence, running the committee meetings, acting as recruiter-in-chief and as the interface to most of the charities and other organisations with whom we dealt. Even when he stepped down as chairman, he still made a big contribution. There were times when Paul's pedantry and tendency to waffle could irritate me, and I am sure equally there were things about me that got on his nerves but generally we had a very good working relationship around the Bike Ride and indeed were close friends. We held similar views on a range of matters and often cycled together.

Given the above, the events that unfolded after the 2013 Bike Ride were particularly upsetting. Shortly after returning home Paul disappeared. His partner Lynne contacted Rod Elliott, who had known him since school days. Together they established that, unbeknown to anyone, including Lynne, he had lost his job the previous year and, to cover his serious financial problems, he had defrauded the Bike Ride. For years he had held one of the organisation's credit cards with our treasurer monitoring usage. However, with nobody in that role following the prior incumbent's resignation, Paul had offered to become treasurer. He had then used the card to cover personal expenses with nobody checking his expenditure. People accepted Paul's monthly financial updates at face value given his long service to the Bike Ride.

It was inevitable that Paul's actions would eventually be found out and some issues in Holland, with the acceptance of the Bike Ride credit card, were an indication of the mounting problem. With Rod and John Adcock's help we understood the full extent of Paul's theft, which was approximately £31000. Through a combination of delaying credit card repayments, the willingness of some ride organisers to wait for reimbursement of expenses and drawing on reserves, we were able to address the immediate financial crisis. Paul had by now returned to face the music. He indicated he was unable to repay the money. While I was and remain convinced that Paul's misuse of Bike Ride funds was limited to the activities of the previous year and borne out of muddled desperation rather than calculated dishonesty it was clearly a serious matter, and we had no option but to take it to the police.

In due course in 2013 Paul was prosecuted and convicted. He was given a two-year suspended jail sentence and three hundred hours of community service. He was also directed to repay the stolen money. I was on holiday at the time of the sentencing, but I was alerted to the fact that he had given a BBC interview outside of the court. As I watched this from Portugal, I couldn't help thinking that it was a shame given all the damage that had been done that Paul had agreed to do this.

A few months later Paul did make a repayment, as directed by the court. This drew a dreadfully sad episode to a close. These events of course happened some years ago and the Bike Ride has moved on. Its ability to survive and indeed thrive after this proved just how robust an institution it had become. Paul decided to stay on Hayling and seems to have rebuilt his life and while it's difficult to forget what he did I don't think any connected with our events continue to bear him any deep ill will regarding actions for which he was duly punished. I have previously not made any public comment about this matter save to say that it would not stop the Bike Ride from continuing. And in the circumstances it would have been tempting to have entirely left this episode out of this book. However, it's the story of the Bike Ride and this was an important if regrettable part of that story. But at the same time, it should not detract from the huge and largely positive legacy that Paul left the Bike Ride and through that, the major impact he had on many people lives.

Paul's crime was a tragedy on many levels. For the Bike Ride, it was a sad episode that to some extent blemished the fantastic achievements since 1986. It was a particularly painful one for all those who had worked closely with Paul and had subsequently to sort out the mess that he had created. And it was a tragedy for Paul. He lost his connection with an event for which I have no doubt that he had a great passion. He had lost most of his close friends, and much of the respect in which he was held by the wider local community.

A few months later Paul did make a repayment, as directed by the court. This drew a dreadfully sad episode to a close. These events of course happened some years ago and the Bike Ride has moved on. Its ability to survive and indeed thrive after this proved just how robust an institution it had become. Paul decided to stay on Hayling and seems to have rebuilt his life and while it's difficult to forget what he did I don't think any connected with our events continue to bear him any deep ill will regarding actions for which he was duly punished. I have previously not made any public comment about this matter save to say that it would not stop the Bike Ride from continuing. And in the circumstances it would have been tempting to have entirely left this episode out of this book. However, it's the story of the Bike Ride and this was an important if regrettable part of that story. But at the same time, it should not detract from the huge and largely positive legacy that Paul left the Bike Ride and through that, the major impact he had on many people lives.

Chapter 34
An Awkward Landing and Ejection from a Nunnery

Inevitably, I had been heavily involved in the crisis management, given my long Bike Ride connections, and I agreed to take over once again as chairman. While dealing with Paul's theft remained the immediate priority, we had also to think about our plans for the following year. Some had thought that this was the end of the Bike Ride. However, the current committee and I we were determined that this would not happen. And through our efforts and the support of others, and in particular Rod Elliott and John Adcock, we made sure that we came through this difficult time. We were particularly encouraged by the attendees at our AGM in October 2012. AGMs for most organisations, including ours, are normally poorly attended but this year we had a massive turnout. While all obviously wanted to know what had happened, they were unanimous in their support of the committee and the Bike Ride. Quite simply, like the committee, they all thought that Paul would never have done this.

Obviously, we were planning for 2013 in difficult circumstances with some uncertainty regarding our financial position. There was some thought of returning to France but that was rejected. A lot of effort had been put into the Holland preparation the year before and it seemed rather to demean the investment by not returning for a second year. We didn't see Holland as a long-term regular venue, but it had been a good Ride and indeed a change. Also, moving back to France would mean either choosing a new route or at least using one that we had not used for some years and either way we would need additional "recess" and hence additional costs, which not be welcome at this time. We settled on a similar Dutch route to 2013. As previously indicated, supporting cyclists on cycle paths which were out of reach of traditional support vehicles had presented us with a challenge in this venture. The Support Team had managed competently the previous year, but it was something we wanted to address. Therefore, in 2013 we introduced two light mopeds or, as the Dutch call them, "snorfiets". These were able to follow us on almost all the paths and most of the ferries and made a real difference.

This was the first year my good friend John Kerton joined the Ride. We had known each other since schooldays when he got to sign my death warrant. Perhaps I should explain! Way back in 1973 we were rehearsing for the school play, Arthur Miller's the Crucible. I played the heroic John Proctor who is hung at the end of this splendid work whilst John played Ezekiel Cheaver, the toadie "yes man" of a court clerk who signs my death warrant. Despite that, we have been friends ever since. We first visited the Algarve together in 1982, which is where he now lives and where I spend as much of my time as possible. John is very active with a local cycling group, and I join in with them on their rides when visiting. However, John is a recent convert to cycling. Back in the winter of 2013 he thought he ought to finally enter the event that his mate had been organising all these years. He had also conveniently been encouraged to get involved with the said local cycling group by some friends in the Algarve.

The beginning of the Ride couldn't have been more different to 2012, with the first two days, from Hook of Holland to Haarlem and then on to Amsterdam, featuring excessive sunshine and heat. While the remainder of our visit was not quite so good the weather was still much better than the previous year! But for me the Ride will be memorable for the wrong reason! On the North Sea crossing, as we approached the Hook of Holland, I arose still half asleep from my top bunk bed rather too casually. I put my foot on the step ladder that would return me to the deck. I either slipped or totally missed the steps. I am not sure which but the result in my case was that I hit the floor with an almighty thump. I didn't fall over but in hindsight it might have proved better to have done so because, unfortunately, my left ankle took all the weight. I felt a brief but very painful sensation just above the said body part. I hobbled to breakfast but hoped that all would be okay and that I would soon be successfully riding away. When I mounted my bike, it was a little uncomfortable, but I did manage to cycle out of the port and onto the start of the day's route. I felt some further intermittent pain during the day, but I was managing to cope. One of the cyclists was a doctor and he checked out my injury that evening. Although my lower leg and ankle were swollen, he felt that I probably hadn't done any major damage and if I felt okay to cycle then I would probably be safe to do so!

As the week continued, I adjusted to cycling with the injury quite well. When I got home, I thought I would just check it out with my sports physio. He did a couple of quick tests and then issued the very precise instruction, "Get down to A&E now! You have ruptured your Achilles tendon!" Many asked me how I managed to cycle all week in that state with what is a notoriously painful and debilitating injury. I think in that context it's important to emphasise once again that Holland is rather flat. Had it been France I would have been in trouble on the first hill. Secondly, it is quite likely that the initial damage was not that bad and indeed that my tendon wasn't truly ruptured at the time but just torn. But if so, this had been made worse by continuing with the cycling! In any event, that put an end to my pedalling for some months. And this period of lay off was made worse by the fact that I subsequently suffered a blood clot, potentially a far worse injury than the ruptured Achilles tendon. However, with good treatment from a local surgeon and from my physio I made a good recovery, though an occasional ache in my left calf is a reminder of my unfortunate experience on our second Dutch ride.

Another incident that year, less injurious but just as strange, was when Rod Elliott, Paul Clutterbuck and I were thrown out of a nunnery. I have previously written that possibly no charity cyclists had ever drunk a bar dry before us and equally I think it highly unlikely that any have ever been ejected from such holy premises. It was all so innocent really. Mr Clutterbuck was repeating his excellent evening tour of Amsterdam that had been so successful in 2012 when we stumbled across a nunnery ("Beguinage"), as you do! It looked like you could just wander in and look around the pleasant garden, so we did! But immediately on entering we were promptly told to leave!

While feedback from this year's Bike Ride was positive, I don't think there was much doubt in the minds of Bike Ride regulars. Holland had been a pleasant interlude but now it was time to head home to France. Had I any doubt about that, the last few miles travelling along a windswept cycle path from Delft to the Hook of Holland reminded me of one thing I wouldn't miss about this generally very agreeable country and that was the wind! Although not as bad as in 2012, we had our fair share this year also and it seemed a disproportionate amount of it blowing in our faces! Wind might be great for windmills but when they have to press against it for mile after mile it's decidedly unpopular with cyclists.

Chapter 35
Back to Our "Routes"

So now we started planning for a return to Paris, going "back to its routes (sic)"! We had hoped to stay at the Hotel Mercure in La Defense, which we had used so often before. But even a year ahead they were already booked. We tried a few more in the same area but to no avail. I was concerned. In any other year, the answer would have been to go to France and sort it out "in situe". But I was now incapacitated by my ruptured Achilles tendon and nobody else close to this aspect of Bike Ride planning was available. However, I finally found a hotel online, namely the Ibis on Avenue de Cliche. This looked fine and was in a central position close to Montmartre. That would be a good location for any with the energy to do some sightseeing. It was a couple more miles into Paris than we really wanted but we thought that would be quite manageable.

Hotels in the other places we planned to stay were generally booked with relative ease, it being possible to use the same ones as the last time we had cycled this way. However, there was ever so slight a problem using La Biche in Evreux since it had disappeared! I recalled the words of one of the Hayling Fire Brigade team who had joined us ten years before. They had felt that La Biche would never have got a fire certificate in the UK. Presumably, it had had the French equivalent but that was somewhat irrelevant now because it had been completely destroyed by fire! Perhaps, given the historic nature of the building, it wasn't that surprising that the blaze had been covered in the nationally circulated Le Parisian newspaper. This reported that over eighty firefighters had been deployed in fighting the fire. However, alternative hotels were located on the other side of town, which we subsequently felt gave us a different and I believe even more favourable perspective on this small city.

As soon as my left leg was sufficiently robust, I planned a short trip to Paris, combining business with a quick view of our chosen hotel. It wasn't a bad hotel and indeed it was by far the largest and most luxurious Ibis I had ever seen but everything around it was under reconstruction. That included some changes to the roads which, in any case, were often blocked or interrupted due to the work on adjacent buildings. It also looked likely that most of the current work would still be in process the following summer! This could be problematic! However, a significant deposit had been paid and we had no way of changing hotels now even if we could find something suitable, which seemed unlikely since that is why we had finished up here in the first place!

A couple of months later I was back in Paris again and planned to stay at the hotel. I took at taxi at the airport. "The hotel is at 163b Avenue de Clichy. There are a lot of demolished buildings next to it. The area looks a bit like Beirut!" Or at least that is what I said in my halting French. The taxi driver merely answered, "Have you been to Beirut?" Despite twenty-five years of globetrotting in business the answer was that I hadn't. To this, the driver replied, "I am Lebanese."

"Oh, shit!" I thought, not my most diplomatic statement.

The rest of the journey to the Hotel Ibis passed without any words exchanged and I could not wait to pay him off, feeling obliged to atone for my faux pas by giving a generous tip.

A full "recce" was carried out in late January to reconfirm everything at the hotels and to check way-side stops. We were shocked by the change in some of the villages. In seven years, the economic climate, and the general trend in France as much as in the UK seemed to have led to the closure of many small rural businesses. Bars, boulangeries and patisseries we remembered from previous years were no longer there. And even places that claimed to still be open were often closed due to extended lunch breaks, delayed opening, early closing or possibly a combination of all three! Rural Normandy, it seemed, was largely closed! However, at least some of our old stops were fortunately still there. We were delighted to renew our friendship with Le Montcient on the edge of the village of the same name, Le Vol a Voile, a great lunch stop, at the airfield in Beynes, and Café La Poste in our beloved Muids. They all remembered us fondly and were happy that we were returning. We were a bit startled when we visited Le Montcient, who not only remembered us, but had quite a thick file marked Paris to Hayling. What had we done? We had only ever stopped there for a brief mid-morning coffee and possibly a croissant. As far as we could recall there had been no bad behaviour, it being far too early in the day for that. And if there had been, presumably, they wouldn't have been pleased to have us back. But that didn't stop us speculating as to what the file contained! We also met with new proprietors of Au Joyeux Normande who were pleased to do business with us. On the positive side, "Le Patron" seemed to get the "joyeux" bit better than his predecessor! With these, plus a few more cafés that we checked, we felt we were in reasonably good shape regarding way-side stops.

We also looked again at the challenges around reaching and leaving the Ibis in Paris and made little progress. However, Tony and Sarah Hart were due out shortly to do a route specific recce and we were hoping that this would fix this. But perhaps not surprisingly, Tony and Sarah also struggled with this issue. Indeed, I believe they spent nearly a day on this part of the route and no doubt at times cursed me for having booked it. Finally, however, it seemed we had what we believed would be an okay route into and out of Paris, arranging for it to join our former route from La Defense as soon as practical. So now, after some sweat, we were all set for our return to France. And there would be more sweat to come because 2014 would prove to be a very hot year.

Before we set off for France, we of course had our annual Channel to Channel Ride. In recent years, with the exception of the odd day or two, we had seen some really bad weather on this event. And we had certainly not had a whole weekend that was as good as 2014 turned out to be. When Fred Dyer and I checked the route a few weeks before the event we were more focused on bad weather since, following a dreadful winter, parts of our possible route were still under water. But in May there was not a drop of rain on either day as we went for the third year from Bristol through to Salisbury on the Saturday and then on to Hayling. In some past years, the weather has caused people to rush to their destination, with lingering at a way-side stop being the last thing on their minds. But this year, it was so different! We left a clutch of happy landlords across three counties!

And the good weather continued for the Paris to Hayling,

which was probably the hottest we had experienced. We believe that temperatures on the open road were close to forty centigrade at one time. The return to France certainly did prove popular. The weather showed off the spectacular countryside to good effect, even if did make some of the longer days (two were over ninety miles) and the occasional tough hill even more challenging. Riders were delighted to revisit Au Joyeux Normand in Grandchain for our lunch on the first day. Despite the change of ownership, the quality of the fair proffered was as before and it was again a highlight of the Bike Ride.

The following day while we prepared to leave Evreux, Jerry Way, a Ride regular, reported feeling unwell. Fortunately, our cycling GP Colin Turner realised from his symptoms that this could be serious and had him go to hospital. Jerry had had a heart attack. It was by no means clear that he had had it on our Ride, and it could have pre-dated it by several days. But either way, it was a concern and dangerous for Jerry, who was in a French hospital for over week before being able to return home. Fortunately, however, he did make a good and quick recovery and was back in his bike within a couple of months.

Reaching the Hotel Ibis in Paris did indeed prove a problem with a good deal of cursing from tired cyclists who had got totally lost. But the departure the following morning was surprisingly trouble free. That day we headed to Rouen and en-route there was also a nostalgic return to Muids where we received the traditional warm welcome from our friend Jeanette Koleno at the Café De La Poste. In this delightful village many chose to refresh themselves with a quick dip in the Seine. This was perhaps the hottest point of the hottest day of that Ride. Conscious of the fact that we still had twenty-four miles to cycle in some quite uncomfortable conditions, I did not drink very much but I felt very reluctant to get on my bike on the clammy Normandy afternoon. I rode the next few miles with the same small group with whom I spent most of the Ride. This included long-time Paris to Hayling rider Pete Alloway. It was a measure of the unusual temperatures that as we passed through the village of Pitres he suggested we all stop for an Orangina! Indeed, I think we had two! For Pete, with a reputation for zealous drinking of red wine and beer this was a very surprising proposal! Over the next couple of days there were more Oranginas, though after those first two I think they were laced with vodka.

We officially ended the Ride at the Pegasus Bridge Café, the scene of so many previous finishes. Party night in Caen was a great success, with Chichester-based Ska band Bigtopp, fresh from their success at the Isle of Wight Festival, providing the superb entertainment. Two of the band were ex-Paris to Hayling riders and most were ex-Ditcham Park School pupils.

In the autumn of 2014, I organized and led a small charity ride from Lisbon to the Algarve for the charity Medair and repeated it the following year. This had nothing to do with the Paris to Hayling as such, but I am sure that if it hadn't been for my experiences on the Paris to Hayling I would never have had the confidence to do this, so yet another unexpected consequence.

Chapter 36
Farewell to Bob

In April, just before the cycling season got under way, we had received the tragic news that Bob Parkinson had died after suffering from cancer for some time. Long-time Bike Ride participant Bob was good friends with many riders and undoubtedly enriched their experience of cycling with us. Like a lot of our riders, Bob forged many friendships which subsequently extended beyond our own events. He spent many hours cycling with a group of ladies who styled themselves "Bob's Babes" and I think the fact that many of them have become very proficient riders may be due in no small part to Bob's support and encouragement. Jenny Daly summed up the feelings of many when she commented, "A sad day for us today; a very good friend Bob Parkinson passed away after suffering with cancer. We have lots of very good memories with Bob that we will cherish and never forget. Bless you Bob, we will always think of you when we are on our bikes."

The farewell to Bob was a wonderful humanist service presided over by our own Jeff Lane and attended by many cyclists. It was emotional to see the coffin carried in with his cycling helmet on top and even more so to hear that he had been cremated wearing his Paris to Hayling cycle jersey. But there were then a couple of other events to commemorate Bob. First, we held a memorial ride in early October over one of his favourite routes in the New Forest. It was a splendid day with a great turn-out and the fine weather we had come to expect that summer! "Bob's Ride" has now become an annual event. There was also a fund-raising event at Hayling Island Sailing Club for the Rowans Hospice where Bob had spent some of his final days. It featured the tribute band Not the Rolling Stones which was very apt since in the past Bob had organised two charity events with them at the same location for Help For Heroes. I was asked to make a short speech. Just as at Meryl's funeral, I felt honoured to be asked and to know that the Ride had made such an impact on someone's life. I have done a lot of public speaking both in my private and business life and often it is unscripted, but in the case of something important or sensitive I will tend to write it down first and then learn by heart. This is what I did in this case, and I repeat it here because I would like to think it says a lot about Bob.

"Ladies and Gentlemen,

I have been asked by some of his friends to say a few words about Bob Parkinson, who of course is very much in our thoughts tonight.

Like many here I came to know Bob through the Paris to Hayling Cycle Ride. Bob was clearly a very good cyclist and although he definitely liked a drink, I don't recall Support having to drag him out of a bar and tell him to get back on his bike, so on those two counts we really didn't have much in common. But what we did share was an affection for an event which, with its various spin-offs, has long since transformed from being merely an eccentric pedal through Normandy into effectively an extremely sociable cycling club. A sociable cycling club to which so many people have made valuable contributions, including, very notably, Bob Parkinson. It clearly meant a lot to Bob, and the fact that he was cremated in his Paris to Hayling shirt obviously underlines that. Bob was never on the Bike Ride committee, Bob didn't feature in lots of Bike Ride photographs, Bob rarely, if ever, won a Bike Ride award. But Bob's exceptional contribution to the Ride was to selflessly transfer his love of cycling to others and help make good cyclists out of many who, when they first entered the Paris to Hayling Ride, may well have found the whole thing a bit of a challenge. His willingness to share his time and expertise strengthened the Paris to Hayling itself and encouraged many to come back year after year but at the same time it went way beyond it and many of you in this room used to go cycling with Bob more or less every week or indeed sometimes twice a week.

Now I am sure Bob would not want us to be morbid tonight. Indeed, before he pedalled off to that eternal pub stop in the sky, he left some money so that we could have this fun evening. And in fact, he had organised two events here previously to raise cash for Help For Heroes, a charity which Bob as an ex-servicemen himself felt particularly strongly about. Both of these things say so much about Bob, and local cyclist and novelist HG Wells could have been thinking of him when he wrote the following, "Whenever I see an adult on a bicycle I have hope for the human race." Now actually, over the past thirty years, I have come across a few people who are clear proof that that sentiment is sometimes flawed and indeed I can see one or two examples here tonight, but with respect to Bob surely it did apply, since I believe he was, in the views of all who knew him, a fine member of the human race. Ladies and Gentlemen, please raise your glasses to Bob Parkinson."

Chapter 37
Team C Get Delayed and Party Time!

We have always liked landmark rides on the Paris to Hayling. The tenth anniversary had been a big one, the twentieth and twenty-fifth, likewise, as indeed was the million-pound ride. The thirtieth would be no exception, especially as it might also be the Ride when we topped the £1.5m in total funds raised. We knew that many past riders would come back for this one, sharing one last celebration of an event which they had enjoyed through multiple summers. And, of course, it was going to be an excuse for a party, but along with that we had a few minor technicalities to sort out, such as fixing the route and recruiting riders.

We had moved back to Paris in 2014 as a dress rehearsal for the 2015 event. But we felt that with the traffic and the likely numbers we were asking for trouble if we were to stay in the centre of the city again. Versailles seem to be the obvious choice and it was one we had used before, albeit some years previously. It was a truly special location, close enough to the French capital to be considered "Paris" but far enough out to make both arriving and departing somewhat easier than Paris itself. While using Versailles obviously meant changes to some of the 2015 route, it did mean we could use most of it, which made our route planning relatively straightforward.

Serious preparation began as always soon after the previous ride with a blast of emails to hotels enquiring about capacity. We opened for registration in autumn 2014 and were immediately overwhelmed with interest. Even with provision for two hundred and fifty places (easily a record number) we had very soon to create a waiting list. And, in addition to those who wanted to ride to and from Paris or merely from Paris, we also wanted to accommodate some past Ride "vets" who, although not able or inclined to do an extensive ride, wanted to join us for the final part. So, we also offered a special package allowing a limited number of invitees to take the overnight ferry to Le Havre, which, as in 2014, would be our penultimate overnight stop, and then to cycle the following day to Caen. Here they would celebrate with the rest of the riders at our last-night party.

As always happens, we had several dropouts and we finished up with a group of two hundred and thirteen "two way" cyclists plus an additional thirteen joining us in Versailles via Eurostar to ride back to Hayling. But in addition, we had a group of twenty-eight "vets" meeting us in Le Havre. This was our largest group; we had to manage bookings at twenty-four hotels as well as dealing with increased complexity in other matters.

Over the following months the various activities needed for a successful Ride came together. The size of the group and the need to meet with all hotels necessitated several recces, even though we had no need to plan major route changes. On the first of these trips, we found that one of our lunchtime stops had gone bust and then, only weeks before the Ride, we had news that another had gone the same way. This was the Joyeux Normand, possibly the best lunch stop we had ever had. It was perhaps the saddest news Bike Ride planners had received since we heard of the demise of La Chaumiere, our original bar stop, in Muids. This presented a real challenge since we knew that there were so few lunch alternatives in this rural part of Normandie. An entirely new, lunch-friendly route would be needed and quickly! However, within a few hours it was on the way to being fixed. Fred Dyer and I worked out a new route using a combination of mapping software and traditional maps and Fred was able to validate it on a route check which he carried out, shortly afterwards.

But remembering our priorities, and indeed our reputation, we had also got into the details of the last-night party quite early in the planning process. The committee's hearts wanted to hold what we hoped to be a monumental bash, at the Café Mancel in Caen Castle, the location of many previous happy soirees. Our heads, however, knew that it could not really cater for the likely numbers. We therefore subsequently settled on the Hotel Mercure Port de Plaisance, which had the added convenience of being, along with the adjacent Ibis, the place where the largest proportion of riders would be staying. Many years ago, it had also hosted a successful Tenth Anniversary party.

In the build-up to the Ride, we tried hard for increased publicity, and I worked with Paul Clutterbuck and a committee member Martine Walling on a mail shot which we sent to every suitable media outlet. We were also aided in this activity by Sally Simmonds. Sally was a Meridian TV reporter who had signed up for the Ride in a private capacity but was happy to get us some exposure on Meridian as well as coaching us with regards to other outlets. We certainly had more coverage than we had had for many years and the highlight was indeed

Sally's own interview with myself and several riders a few days prior to our departure. For this interview Sally had persuaded me to have my original bike restored. This had been hanging up in my garden shed for years in several bits, but it proved relatively easy to get this done up. But it really was from another age; hand-made in the UK by Dawes with ten gears and with the levers in the frame! This was a real piece of cycling nostalgia!

I had always made it clear that 2015 would be the last Paris to Hayling that I organised. I had not lost my enthusiasm for the event and indeed planned to continue cycling but there were other things I wanted to do in my life which might not have left the time required to lead the effort necessary to stage a Ride of this sort. Moreover, there were times when the responsibility did get to me. For example, while it had never happened, I did have worries that sooner or later I would book a hotel for the wrong date! There were a couple of features about my stepping down but with misleading headlines such as "Final Ride for Bike Ride Founder" it felt like I was reading my obituary.

On Sunday 12th July, we gathered at the Ship and Castle pub next to the ferry port in Portsmouth, full of anticipation for our latest adventure. The new riders often looked a little nervous, perhaps concerned about the distances but possibly also worried about how well things would be organised. Would they get lost, would their luggage get delivered to the right place and indeed would they always have a hotel bed? Veteran riders were of course more at ease. Old friendships were renewed, stories of various stunts across northern France and indeed also Holland were retold and of course efforts were made by these recidivist pedallers to put new participants at ease.

I was pleased that I was joined on this trip by three of my oldest friends, all of whom I had known for over forty years. John Kerton had joined me on the second Holland ride and Roger Charles had cycled on several occasions since 1989. He had thus become a member of a fairly exclusive club, namely riders who cycled with us in four different decades. In addition, Johan Coorg joined in for the first time as a motorcycle support rider.

As riders signed in for the event they were asked as usual to give details of the likely sponsorship for that year. It was clear that with stated pledges and factoring an element of Gift Aid, participants would raise in excess of £85,000. With money raised previously and with some surplus due to a profit on the past two Rides, this meant that we would reach £1.5 million in funds raised since 1986. Fantastic news!

In a week of generally good weather, things didn't start that well the following morning as riders headed off from the overnight ferry on a rather damp morning for the ninety-mile ride to Evreux. After a few miles of flat cycling to the picture postcard village of Beuvron En Auge, we were soon climbing some thigh-clenching hills through the splendidly named and temptation abundant "route de cidre". However, I believe that all resisted stopping at one of the many cider farms, conscious, no doubt, that there were quite a few miles still to pedal. As we headed on to lunch in Bernay we were covering Fred's new route which I was pleased to note was well received.

By mid-afternoon, the weather was much brighter, though still with some cloud, and that would be the same for the following day when, after our night in Evreux, we headed for Versailles. It was the 14th of July, Bastille Day, and above us as we cycled through the cornfields, we could see what seemed to be the French equivalent of the Red Arrows performing some impressive acrobatics. Someone quipped, looking at the five planes above, that he was surprised that the French Air Force was that big. I naturally emphasised that this fly past had been organised specifically for Paris to Hayling Riders. In accordance with the normal plans for 14th July it was very much a case of 'do the best you can for lunch' given the limited number of establishments that would be open. As far as I can recall, we all managed and indeed most seemed to assemble in the same village crowding the same spot of grass outside an open boulangerie who must have thought it was Christmas rather than Le Quatorze as we grabbed every bit of bread that they had. However, Team C's experience was a little different.

They were at the back, which was typical! Sometime after midday, conscious that by 1:00 pm almost everything would be closed, they were getting desperate for food. Cycling through a small village, Le Mesnil Simon, they saw what at first appeared, judging by a fluttering of flags, to be a restaurant. However, on closer investigation it turned out to be a gathering of two hundred or so villagers about to celebrate France's special day in a converted barn. Various village notables were there, including the mayor, who invited them to join him and the masses in return for a payment of €15 a head. As Paul recollects, "It was to be an all-you-can-eat-and-drink five-course Bastille Day binge. We settled into the middle of the villagers. Although water was needed, only large glasses of red and rosé wine were given out." They started to make friends, swapping smatterings of French and English. There was a session from a singer who, while apparently trying his best to mimic classic French chanteurs such as Charles

Aznavour and Sacha Distel, was, according to Paul, "more in the style of an Irish pub singer after fourteen pints of Guinness". Then the Mayor spoke and finished by welcoming the English guests. Team leader Barrie Dawson went to the front, hugged, and kissed the mayor and decided he would give a speech. Paul remembers it well. "To describe Barrie's address to the teeming mass in the barn as like Henry V's speech before the Battle of Agincourt would be an exaggeration, but not much of one. After each sentence that he delivered, he kissed the wife of the mayor. As he finished, the villagers spontaneously rose as one to sing "God Save The Queen". Barrie immediately led the whole barn in a rousing rendition of "La Marseillaise". It was time to leave." Apparently, they were invited to stay the night and Paul admits it was tempting but there was the small matter of a charity cycle ride to complete so they got back on their bikes, eventually arriving somewhat late in Versailles.

Riders loved finishing in the park at Versailles, where most stopped for a well-deserved drink or two. While it was far from my first visit I was still struck as always by just how impressive this location is. The gardens with their neatly manicured lawns, extensive flower beds and abundant sculptures together with acres of adjacent woodland are truly exceptional, and of course the Chateau provides a splendid back drop.

The next day we had a long ride to Rouen. Having cycled through the Forêt de Marly in the early morning we soon crossed to the north bank of the Seine at Meulin where we joined the previous year's route from Paris. Much of the subsequent route to Rouen had been the same for many years (irrespective of whether we have started from Paris or

Versailles), and I have always had a sentimental attachment to it. After a coffee break at Le Montcient, our regular stop, we climbed through the picturesque Vexin Natural Park along the Routes des Cretes to reach some splendid views of the Seine before a spectacular downhill to Giverny past Monet's Gardens and then on to Vernon where most riders stopped for lunch. Previously, we had organised a lunch stop just beyond the town but that had gone bankrupt. But here, unlike the challenge we had faced with the demise of Au Joyeux Normand at Grandchaine, there were plenty of options for riders to make alternative arrangements. Many bought foods for a picnic and stretched out on the picturesque riverbank next to this charming town's notable sixteenth century mill, painted over the years by hundreds of artists. Others selected from a variety of cafés and restaurants in a town which, although heavily bombarded during World War II, still has many streets that look like they have come straight out of the Middle Ages. However, for me the highlight of this day and, indeed one of the big features of the week, was the return visit later that afternoon to Muids. It's always been memorable, and this year was no exception. The Bar De La Poste greeted us with an accordion player, bunting, an official photographer and, last but certainly not least, a good supply of local cider. Many riders lingered quite a while here, some as always bathing in the Seine, and by the end of our visit Jeanette, the proprietor of Bar De La Poste, was even dancing with some of our jolly cyclists.

Approaching Rouen, we swept down the steep Bonsecours Hill but of course, as always, that was a reminder of the fact that we would have a corresponding need to climb out of this historic city the following morning. And after perhaps too little time in the splendid Normandy capital with its famous cathedral, an abundance of fascinating buildings and great restaurants, that is indeed what we had to do! In fact, we had twenty-five miles of intermittent climbing as we headed out of Rouen and into the hills that lie to the north. As we hauled ourselves up incline after incline Deputy Chairman Pete Alloway and I were in true grumpy-old-man mode, moaning about these inconvenient slopes. We wondered why on earth we were still doing this at our ages. However, after a mid-morning coffee at Yvetot, all was different as we set off for our lunch stop at the Relais St Sauveur in Ecrainville, just over twenty miles away. The terrain changed to the gently rolling from the uncomfortably lumpy and cyclists had a warm wind on their backs. Many I spoke to, agreed with me, that it was a wonderful vignette from the week, only slightly marred by the fact that on arrival at the lunch stop we discovered we were all covered in small flies inadvertently swatted along the way. This was our one organised lunch stop of the week. We had used this some years before and it had been as excellent then as it was now. We were welcomed by a piper. However, we hadn't booked him and neither had the restaurant. He just turned up to play! The bizarre thing was that he had done the same thing last time we were there, seven years ago. He had obviously been awaiting our return! In Le Havre we finished in the afternoon sunshine at a newly found beachside bar, many taking the opportunity for a refreshing swim in "La Manche".

The following morning, augmented by the extra cyclists and an additional baggage team that had arrived especially for the last day, we set out from Le Havre to Caen. Today was fancy dress day and we had some great outfits. A couple of clowns won first prize, though as someone perceptively commented, there were many to choose from on this Bike Ride. Among other very impressive outfits was a Satnav and a Support Team member splendidly dressed as the Queen. Mike and Stella Burras had suitably assembled a team wearing a T-shirt design similar to the Cot Death Research one I had worn on that first ride; I found this quite moving. Pascal Pichon's Snow White was intriguing but any chance he had of being really convincing was somewhat marred by the fact that when he appeared for a photo call, he proceeded to smoke a cigar. This, as I recall, wasn't in the fairy tale I read or indeed in any of the pantomimes or films. Even less convincing, but highly amusing, was Johan Coorg, our new motorbike rider, who was dressed as a nun. Easy Rider meets Mother Theresa, an intriguing combination!

As in previous years we were all a bit nervous crossing the Pont De Normandie. The last few miles onto the bridge were along a cycle path which led right up to it. I noticed how neglected the path was and indeed sorely in need of repair. This got me thinking. Perhaps no one else other than Paris to Hayling cyclists were daft enough to cycle over this high bridge and therefore the path was of no general use because it didn't lead anywhere else. After a pleasant interlude in Honfleur we set off for the final miles to Pegasus Bridge. In 2014 as we headed in the same direction, we had taken an inland route which was possibly the most direct way but missed important ingredients of any top-class cycle route, namely bars and restaurants! So, this year we took we took the coastal road via the "Cote de Fleurie" towns of Trouville, Deauville St Villiers, and Dives before passing over Pegasus Bridge to our traditional finish at Café Gondree. Riding over

Pegasus Bridge is always special and even more so on this notable year, and the cheer of your fellow riders as you arrive in front of the famous café is such special memory for all participants and a great illustration of the Bike Ride's great camaraderie. The weather sadly was not playing the game. For the first time since early Monday morning, we now had rain, but it could not dampen the spirits of the assembling riders who were generally happy to linger a while to welcome subsequent arrivals. Here it was good to meet up with the legendary Mumfy who had arrived from Portsmouth a few hours earlier, complete with the equally distinguished Crocks. Paul was perhaps predictably dressed in his famous policeman's uniform and was, as in past Rides, enthusiastically directing the traffic! Andrew Wilson, as you may recall, had previously, had a casual relationship with his passport. In line with that, this year, as he rode back to Caen from Pegasus Bridge in the wet, it got soaked! Fortunately, the following day this mass of paper machet was able to get him out of the country but Andrew was up to the passport office the following Monday for a new passport.

That evening a memorable party followed at the Mercure starting with a drinks' reception featuring past photographs, cycle jerseys, shirts and one other notable memento, namely my original bike. One of our riders, Johnny Griffiths, a professional musician and in particular a highly competent saxophone player, had assembled a fantastic band which included his fiancée and fellow rider Chloe Swaby, an amazing vocalist, and Adam Alloway who had participated in the week's cycling as well. And, as in the Twentieth Year, we had a performance by "Can-Can" dancers, which was tremendously popular. They had worked hard to bring us this entertainment. Indeed, I felt rather guilty since, following a brief, half-hearted request at a committee meeting, Sally Griffiths had gone away and put together a troupe who had then seriously practiced and made costumes and then, after at least one day's cycling, though a whole week in some cases, had provided great entertainment. Sometime just after midnight when the official entertainment had finished, I decided to ride my old bike around the venue. Somehow, I managed to avoid falling off!

Hangovers and a few hours' sleep later, we were boarding the ferry for home. The thirty years and £1.5m was beginning to sink in. It was all getting a bit emotional. Thirty years, that was half my life! And £1.5 million was a sum that just would not have even been dreamt of in 1986 or even in 1987, the year of the first "mass Ride"! While I am used to speaking in public, I knew I would find presiding over our awards session a bit of a challenge and I was right! My fellow committee members had unanimously nominated a non-existent rider for one of our awards, the Meryl Browne Trophy. The fact that I had not heard of the apparent winner did not surprise me with so many entrants. This trophy is generally given to a rider that has overcome a challenge or challenges to complete the event. I duly announced the award winner only to find out when deputy chairman Pete Alloway appeared in stage, that it was a hoax and the name fictitious. They had decided that I should receive the award myself. I was speechless. And indeed, someone referred to that as a unique Bike Ride moment in itself! I also felt very honoured, though I guess over the years I have indeed overcome one or two challenges, both as an organiser and as a rider. I am sure that Meryl, herself a massive contributor to the Ride's success, would have found it all very amusing. We had a moving speech from Barrie Dawson following a special award for his magnificent fund raising these past fifteen years. "There is a special reason why I am so passionate about the Bike Ride. Fifteen years ago, I registered for the Ride, but in the summer, I was diagnosed with inoperable cancer and basically told to go away and die. But sod that, I thought, I am not going to go away and die. I want to make the Ride next year. I did make the Ride the next year and I loved it so much that I wanted to carry on and do it again and again and again. And I really want to say sincerely that one of the reasons I beat cancer was because of the Ride. It stimulated me to get on my bike the next year and the next year and the next year. So, Ride, thank you so bloody much!"

Lumps had appeared in all throats by this time. Fred Dyer presented the Support Trophy, which is in memory of his wife and great Paris to Hayling team member Judy. He fairly pointed out the huge combination of all in support under the amazing leadership of Jo Macey who had by then been in charge of support for more than a decade and was year after year a key factor in the Bike Ride's success. But his presentation of this award to the lead baggage team of Mike Harrington and Skippy was very popular. Mike had been key to this essential component of the Bike Ride for some years and, particularly since he teamed up with Skippy, had brought immense humour to what might seem such a mundane task. Mike even got himself sponsored and raised over £2500 for St Wilfred's Hospice. A few other awards followed according to the normal Ride format. I was particularly pleased to be able to mention Sarah Jeffries' winning of the Presidents Cup, which went to a committee member who was judged by me to have made a special contribution. And she really had met these criteria. Not only did she follow up from me on hotel bookings, correcting several of my “cock ups” and moving on to the challenging job of allocating specific rooms to riders, but in addition she took the lead role in planning our party. Upon docking we were carefully marshalled towards the final few miles and an excellent organised finish at The Olive Leaf. At Langstone Technology Park, just before we crossed from the mainland to Hayling Island, I had exchanged my current bike for the original Dawes. This was the first time I had ridden the bike on the road since the late 1980s and yes, it did feel strange!

I am sure that on Sunday morning, the day after the Ride, many involved felt, like me, rather deflated. After months of preparation, the big one was all over! We have regularly asked ourselves if this was the best Ride ever. And I think 2015 could well claim to have been just that! We had cyclists who invaded a Bastille Day celebration, we had en-route fun in Muids, we had a baggage team who got themselves sponsored, we had a fabulous last-night party with great musicians and dancing girls. In addition, of course, we had a record number of riders and raised a lot of money! And all this was put together by an entirely voluntary organisation. Not a bad achievement, I guess.

For me, personally, it took a few days to recover physically, but probably longer to deal with the emotional side. I felt very privileged to have been at the centre of something so special. I thought of all who had contributed to it, going right back to the beginning with the pioneering riders on heavy bikes with limited gearing but great determination. But I also thought of the current committee who had all played such a role in this year’s success. And I thought of my wife Maryon and my children Chris and Alice and the fact that none of them had known a year of family life when mid-summer was not dominated by Paris to Hayling preparation; their support and understanding had been critical. I had made so many good friends through the Ride and I knew that experience was not unique. Indeed, I had lost count of the number of people who had told me that the Ride had changed their lives. That was a legacy in which all involved could take credit.

Chapter 38
The Other Cyclist

Blimey! It must be from the taxman! That is what I thought when in late November 2015 I nervously received a letter from Her Majesty's Government. I quickly opened it to clarify and therein were the words which gave me one of the biggest and most pleasant surprises of my life. I was to be recommended to Her Majesty to receive an MBE! I was asked to confirm that I would accept the award and keep quiet about it until it was officially announced online in the Gazette at 10 pm on 30th December. The first request was easy, the second somewhat more of a challenge. However, thought of a possible stay in the Tower of London or worse did limit me to telling only very close family and friends.

At the advised time on 30th it was duly announced and immediately the media, who had had twelve hours advance notice, published details. And my daughter proudly posted the news on Facebook. The congratulatory calls, email messages and texts started immediately. I was touched and indeed overwhelmed by these. I discovered that a couple of years previously Rod Elliott had orchestrated a campaign whereby Paris to Hayling cyclists and others from various aspects of my past life had written in nominating me for an honour. Many of them had regularly looked at the twice annual awards lists to see if I had been duly recognised but thought that by now my chances had gone.

While the award was given to me for my charity work with the Bike Ride, it also clearly fitted well with my role at Qlik since at that time I was head of the company's global CSR activities. Better still, and to the delight of my employer, the picture of me that had been picked up by the media was the one taken of me on the last day of the Thirtieth Ride wearing a cycling jersey emblazoned with their logo. Lars Bjork, Qlik's CEO, and other employees added their congratulations to those received from friends. In early January 2016, a company "kick off" was broadcast to all staff. Lars, in closing the session, followed a series of company awards by saying that there was another award he wanted to mention but that it had not been given by the company, but rather by the Queen of England. More Qlik stuff was to follow. I had already been booked to present at three Qlik sales team meetings in San Antonio (USA), Singapore and Rome and now I was asked to ride onto the stage on my bike in my lycra. Lars would introduce me and ask me a few questions around what an MBE was, and I would explain, making a joke or two about the anachronistic tie with the British Empire, and I would then give a talk about CSR activities to the assembled sales team. In the USA, on the first leg of this world tour, I was given a rough and heavy steed to ride on stage which was understandable as it was, after all, a stunt and not a proper bike event. However, I realised that on the next leg in Singapore I could sort this out for myself since I had a good friend who was the local Cannondale distributor! He duly obliged and leant me a $12000 Cannondale mountain bike known as a "lefty" due to the fact that the "fork" only has a left side blade which meant of course that it wasn't a fork at all! I rode this magnificent bike through the streets of Singapore to our conference venue. My journey included an accidental detour onto the Marina Coastal Expressway which was really an urban motorway. Around the world it is generally and understandably strictly forbidden to pedal on such roads. So, in Singapore, where they even arrest litter touts, I felt sure that the police would take a very dim view of my accidental diversion but fortunately I was not apprehended. As I travelled around these three events, it was interesting to note that people often thought that receiving an MBE was a bigger thing than we know it to be. Some people seriously asked me if I should be called "Sir" and indeed I must confess that I didn't always try that hard to put them right.

A couple of months later I was duly informed that I would be needed at the Palace on Friday 13th May to receive my award. Maryon and I had sadly decided to separate by this time, but there was no doubt in my mind that she should be there given the big part she had played in the Bike Ride's success and of course I wanted my children there as well. There were new clothes for all the family and we all looked forward to the great day. When we arrived, we were duly divided into award recipients and guests. Recipients were taken off for a briefing and informed that Prince William would be officiating that day. We mingled for some time beforehand and were told exactly how and what we were to do as we approached the prince for our awards. I spotted a vaguely familiar figure across the room. Only vaguely familiar because I had not seen him in a suit before. It was Chris Froome. I was not missing this opportunity! I quickly approached him, and we were soon in conversation about our respective rides and also about riding in Africa. He had grown up in Kenya and I had cycled in nearby Malawi. While you would hardly expect him to have looked fat, he looked so very thin! Indeed, he look a little feeble! Was this really someone who had already won the Tour De France twice? In real life he looked like he might struggle to bike it to the local shop! But as one of my cycling friends pointed out afterwards, you would hardly expect anyone who succeeded in such a gruelling event to be anything else than excessively svelte.

We duly queued for our gongs and Chris Froome went some minutes before me. While I was in the line a lady usherette checked to make sure that we were in the right order. This was obviously important. Prince William would have a few words to say about us but if, for example, I was mixed up with someone who had won the award for flower arranging, it would have made for two very odd conversations. "Peter McQuade?" she called out and I confirmed that I was he, "Ah, yes," she said, "you are the other cyclist." Interesting, I thought, that would mean Chris Froome and then me. It seemed rude to contradict and so I didn't, reflecting instead on the unanticipated and rather underserved honour of being associated with such a great cyclist!

I was naturally personally delighted to receive the award, but I also saw it as a great honour for the Bike Ride itself and for the large number of people who had contributed to it over the years. By chance, many of these were assembled in Bristol on the night of my investiture ready for our annual Channel to Channel Ride, which was starting from the city the following day. I booked a private room in a good Italian restaurant, and it was a great way to celebrate with them and to say thank you to a special bunch of people.

Epilogue

So that was it! Well, not quite. There had been some talk of the Bike Ride finishing in 2015. And indeed, at some point I may have even talked of personally calling it a day, but neither happened. I wanted to stand down as chairman and Jon Tawse took over again for a couple of years before I moved back into the role again for my fourth spell. I was reluctant to do this but the committee that we then had in place persuaded me that they could make sure my duties were not too onerous and that I need not even attend all the meetings. They duly delivered on this and have proved to be highly efficient.

Keith Stringer who has cycled in many of our Rides has proved to be a superb treasurer. Lori Poore has been unbelievably diligent in handling entries and other admin matters. Sarah Jefferies has managed the difficult job of hotel bookings plus taking the lead on social gatherings. Jo Macey has contributed her years of experience of support and related logistics and worked with Sarah on recces and route plotting. Roger Borton has been the final member of this team, carefully documenting actions needed and in general leaving me with little to do but turn up at occasional meetings and drink a glass or two of wine! At times I have pleasantly felt almost superfluous.

We repeated the 2011 Le Mans ride in 2016 and then followed that with a somewhat vertical Brittany-focused trip in 2017. But, although tough, it was good to get to see some places that we had never visited before in what is a unique region of France. In 2018 we were back to the tried and tested model of Versailles, largely repeating the 2015 route. And in 2019 we returned to Chartres, though using a different route to that chosen previously. In 2021 as I finish this book, we are dealing with the necessity of cancelling this year's ride as well as the one in 2020 because of the Corona virus, but hopefully we will be back in 2022 with a ride to Versailles.

The ride numbers in recent years have been significantly less than those in peak years. This is due to a combination of things including there being so many long-distance charity rides now and the fact that many of our "regular clientele" have decided that they no longer wish to cycle the very long days that Paris to Hayling entails. However, we are still attracting a good number of new riders and getting impressive feedback.

The C2C, although also cancelled in 2020, was revived in 2021 and continues to thrive. Indeed it celebrated its twentieth birthday in 2019. Most C2C riders are past Paris to Hayling cyclists and this, of course, is just one example of a wider impact of the Bike Ride. Various social riding groups continue to meet as a result of contacts made during those French adventures and in general it has created a strong network of friendships that I am sure will endure.

As far as I am aware, the Paris to Hayling is the second oldest charity Bike Ride in the UK. The London to Brighton is older by four years but that, of course, is a single-day event. So that makes our event the longest multi-day event in the UK. Given the fact that the UK is one of the few countries in the world that has supported this type of charity event, that could well make the Paris to Hayling the world's oldest long-distance charity cycling event. I don't know how long the Bike Ride will continue but I have feeling it will last a few more years yet and, who knows, I may have to issue an updated version of this book to coincide with our fiftieth anniversary. This year, for the first time, we were going to take e-bikes on, so that should keep some of our Bike Ride regulars in the saddle for a few more years.

As I look back on the Rides completed, I feel some pride and satisfaction in having been involved in an event that has touched so many people's lives in so many ways. But I also feel very lucky to have been involved with a large number of special people who have themselves made a massive contribution. That's made it such fun and it's that fun that has sustained the Paris to Hayling and allowed us to achieve so much in many different ways. But I think it right that the final words of this book should be those of Stella Burras, mother of Louise, whose death led to this event. "It's satisfying that something so good has come out of such a tragic event."

For any reader who would like more information on the Paris to Hayling Charity Cycle Ride this can be found at www.haylingcycleride.org.uk